Revolutionary
1783–1815

George Rudé was born in 1910 and educated at Shrewsbury School and Trinity College, Cambridge. Between 1939 and 1959 he taught at various schools in England: Stowe School, St Paul's School, Sir Walter St John's School and Holloway School; before taking up the post of senior lecturer in History at the University of Adelaide in 1960. He was Professor of History at that University from 1964 until 1967, and was then Professor of History at Flinders University in Australia from 1968 for two years. Since 1970 Professor Rudé has been Professor of History at Concordia University, Montreal. He is a Fellow of several international historical societies and his published works include *The Crowd in the French Revolution* (1959), *Captain Swing* (1969), *Hanoverian London 1714–1808* (1971), *Debate on Europe 1815–1850* (1972), and *Europe in the 18th Century* (1972). He has also been a frequent contributor to historical reviews, and has also edited historical collections.

Fontana History of Europe
General Editor: J. H. Plumb

G. A. Holmes
Europe: Hierarchy and Revolt 1320–1450

J. R. Hale
Renaissance Europe 1480–1520

G. R. Elton
Reformation Europe 1517–1559

J. H. Elliott
Europe Divided 1559–1598

Geoffrey Parker
Europe in Crisis 1598–1648

John Stoye
Europe Unfolding 1648–1688

David Ogg
Europe of the Ancien Régime 1715–1783

Olwen Hufton
Europe: Privilege and Protest 1730–1789

George Rudé
Revolutionary Europe 1783–1815

Jacques Droz
Europe between Revolutions 1815–1848

J. A. S. Grenville
Europe Reshaped 1848–1878

Norman Stone
Europe Transformed 1878–1919

Elizabeth Wiskemann
Europe of the Dictators 1919–1945

IN PREPARATION

R. C. Smail
Crusading Europe 1000–1250

Ragnhild M. Hatton
Europe 1680–1730

George Rudé

Revolutionary Europe
1783–1815

Fontana Press

First published in 1964 by Fontana Paperbacks,
8 Grafton Street, London W1X 3LA
Twentieth impression, in Fontana Press, March 1985
Twenty-first impression June 1986

Fontana Press is an imprint of
Fontana Paperbacks, part of
the Collins Publishing Group

Copyright © George Rudé 1964

Made and printed in Great Britain by
William Collins Sons & Co. Ltd, Glasgow

Conditions of Sale
This book is sold subject to the condition
that it shall not, by way of trade or otherwise,
be lent, re-sold, hired out or otherwise circulated
without the publisher's prior consent in any form of
binding or cover other than that in which it is
published and without a similar condition
including this condition being imposed
on the subsequent purchaser

CONTENTS

Preface

This book attempts to present a picture of France and Europe before, during and immediately after the French Revolution. The literature in this field is immense and is rapidly becoming more so. During the past fifteen months, at least half-a-dozen major studies relating to the Revolution, in both its French and European contexts, have been published in France, the United States and England; and no doubt several more are on the stocks. Which is merely another way of saying that the Revolution remains an ever-open field of enquiry, and a short book like this can hope to do little more than present its many unsolved problems to wider groups of readers and whet their appetites for more discussion.

Of these problems, none has perhaps, in recent years, been so warmly debated as the significance of the French Revolution in its European (or world) context. How far was the revolution in Europe a projection of the French, and how far was it the product of its own internal development? It is a knotty question that allows of varying interpretations. It is one, however, that has been sharply posed only in the last ten years, and here, at least, the literature is still comparatively meagre. All the more credit is, therefore, due to Professor Palmer (late of Princeton) and Professor Godechot of Toulouse for opening up the question; and even those of us who cannot accept their view of a "Western" or "Atlantic" Revolution will applaud their pioneering efforts.

In writing a volume of this kind it is impossible to pay due regard to all who, in one form or another, have contributed to its making. Like many others working in this field, I should like to pick out for special mention the name of the late Georges Lefebvre, who has not only inspired all who have attempted to treat the Revolution "from below" but whose works include the best general comprehensive treatment of both the French Revolution and Napoleon. To him, more than to any other, all recent studies on the Revolution, the Consulate and Empire and their repercussions across France's borders owe a debt. In addition, I wish to thank Mr. Richard Ollard of William Collins for his patience, good humour and vigilance in steering my manuscript towards the press; and Mr. William A. Cowan, Librarian of the Barr Smith Library, University of Adelaide, for consenting to read the proofs. Finally, my thanks are due to the University of Adelaide and, in particular, to my colleague, Professor Hugh Stretton, for making it possible for teaching historians to write books.

GEORGE RUDÉ

Adelaide,
1 October 1963

PART ONE

Europe on the Eve of the French Revolution

Chapter I

THE SOCIAL PATTERN

Europe, on the eve of the French Revolution, presented a picture of deep and varying contrasts—the contrast between the developed West and the undeveloped East; between the expansion of trade, industry and population and the relative stagnation of agriculture; and between the wide dissemination of news and ideas and the tenacious conservatism of social relations and political institutions.

For a great part of Europe the eighteenth century was one of growing commercial prosperity. The great maritime powers, owing to their geographical situation and their possession of colonies, inevitably took the lion's share of international trade. Nearly nine-tenths of the gold and silver mined in Latin America was passed on by the original owners, Spain and Portugal, to England, France and the United Provinces, whose great trading companies plied their wares in Asia, Africa and the Americas. England's merchant fleet expanded from 3,300 ships with a tonnage of 260,000 in 1702 to 9,400 ships with a tonnage of 695,000 in 1776; by 1800, her carrying capacity had risen to perhaps five or six times what it had been a century before. France, Britain's greatest trading rival, increased her trade with other European countries nearly fourfold between 1716 and 1788, and the value of her combined exports for the same period rose from 120 million to 500 million livres. Arthur Young, during his travels in France on the eve of the Revolution, was struck by the evident signs of prosperity of the great Atlantic port of Bordeaux, which he considered superior to that of Liverpool, whose slave-traders were reputed to earn profits of £300,000 a year. The prosperity of both ports is a reminder of the growing import-ance of the colonial trade: by 1789, the value of trade with America amounted to one-third of the value of all Britain's commercial operations and to only a little less in the case of France. Meanwhile, the United Provinces, though still a sub-stantial trading power, was falling behind in the race with her two greater and more powerful rivals: already in 1739, it was rumoured that twice as many ships unloaded their cargoes in London as in Amsterdam. The Dutch, however, still held their own over the English and French in banking and inter-national financial operations. In 1777, they owned forty per cent of Britain's National Debt. "The bill on Amsterdam," writes a modern historian, "was to the eighteenth century what the bill on London was to become to the nineteenth cen-tury."[1]

Compared with these giants, the merchant fleets of other European countries appeared insignificant; yet Sweden had, in 1787, an expanding fleet of 1,200 merchantmen and Prussia nearly a thousand. Russia had, since Peter I's time, rapidly extended her foreign trade, had opened her Baltic ports ever wider to the West, and had become Europe's greatest supplier of iron: by the 1790's she was shipping almost 26,000 metric tons a year from her Ural deposits to Britain. Meanwhile, Venice, once a proud trading city, was sinking into decline; and the Ottoman Empire continued to treat commerce as an activity quite unsuited to a great military nation.

Europe's internal economy was still relatively untouched by the expansion of her overseas commerce. Internal trade re-mained backward and limited, bogged down by poor com-munications and (in countries such as France) by a prolifera-tion of restrictive tariffs and tolls levied by governments and

[1] C. H. Wilson in *The New Cambridge Modern History*, VII (1957), 44.

privileged landowners. In most countries, agriculture remained rooted in the traditions of the past and was often quite unable to meet the needs of an expanding population: in Sicily, once the granary of southern Europe, the famine of 1763-64 took 30,000 lives; and, in 1770, 150,000 people were reported to have died of hunger in Saxony and 80,000 in Bohemia. Conditions might vary greatly within the same country: the primitive *latifundia* of Andalusia contrasted sharply with the relatively prosperous and independent holdings of the Basque provinces, Catalonia and parts of Aragon. In France, the lush pastures of Normandy stood out in sharp relief against the barren soils of Brittany and the persistent poverty of the *métayers* of the Cévennes and Limousin. In eastern Europe generally, the rich potentialities of the soil had been little explored and the cultivation remained primitive and traditional. Only in parts of western Europe had decisive steps been taken to revolutionize techniques and to apply scientific methods to crop-rotation and cultivation, and thus lay the basis for the large-scale farming of the future. This " revolution " had started in the Netherlands in the mid-seventeenth century and had, soon after, attracted the attention and spurred the energies of visiting French and English agronomists and noblemen. In France, the new methods had been promoted in certain provinces by the combined efforts of enterprising aristocrats, the school of Physiocrats, or " economists ", and the government itself which, in 1761, set up a Department of Agriculture. In England, they had, by the 1780's, been adopted in many counties following the experiments of Townshend, Tull and Bakewell and the propaganda of Arthur Young. Yet nowhere was agriculture as advanced as in the Austrian Netherlands where, in 1802, productivity was still reported to be thirty per cent higher than in England.

Industry continued, in almost every country, to play an increasingly important part in national economic life. In France, on the eve of revolution, the Van Robais textile mills at Abbeville employed 12,000 workers and the Anzin mining company 4,000, while there were some fifty " manufactories" in Paris employing between 100 and 800 work-people within their walls. In Russia, Catherine II promoted and extended the production of iron, which had already made sensational headway under Peter; and, by 1793, the sailcloth industry of Kaluga employed nearly 9,000 workers. In rural Bohemia, 200,000 workers, mainly women, were engaged in the spinning of flax; and even the tiny canton of Glarus in Switzerland counted over 30,000 spinners. But the great bulk of this industrial activity was carried on along old-fashioned and traditional lines. The modern factory and industrial capitalism had barely made their appearance. The prevailing mode of production was that of the domestic system, operated in rural cottages, under the remote supervision of merchants and merchant-manufacturers, by countless peasant families. In towns, the predominant unit of production was still the small workshop, deriving from medieval times and subject to the restrictive regulations of the guild. The large manufactory, where it existed, was an extension of the dom-estic system, whereby workpeople were concentrated in greater numbers and under the closer supervision of the State or pri-vate employer. The great enterprises of eastern Europe and the textile industry of Bohemia were manned by the con-scripted labour of serfs, or of criminals, vagrants, foundlings and soldiers, and even such great undertakings as the Van Robais textile mills and the royal State "factories" in France were a kind of industrial Bastille in which the workers were subject to a quasi-military discipline. Only in England had there been, by 1783, any substantial progress towards the large-scale introduction of labour-saving machinery and an indus-trial "revolution". But, even here, the modern factory system was still in its infancy; the rapidly expanding cotton industry was still largely driven by water-power; and, by 1780, Watt's steam engine had only begun to be applied to spinning and mining. Even so, Britain had a clear lead over her industrial competitors which was to stand her in good stead in the next round of wars with France. Yet she, too, was still largely an agricultural country in which nearly half the population drew their livelihood from agrarian pursuits; and, in stressing the point in 1770, Arthur Young added the estimate that £66 million of England's national income was derived from the soil as against a mere £37 million from commerce and industry.

In the wake of economic development followed the spread of ideas, which were gradually creating an informed " public opinion " and undermining traditional modes of thought and loyalties over large parts of Europe. The first monthly journal had been founded at The Hague in 1686 and the earliest English daily newspaper in 1702. In France, there was no daily paper before the *Journal de Paris* began to appear in 1777. But, in the last decades before the Revolution, the growth of the periodical press in the West was phenomenal. English parliamentary proceedings were reported at length in the press after 1771; and, by 1782, eighteen newspapers were being published in London. In France, there were thirty-five papers and periodicals of all kinds in 1779 and 169 in 1789. The number of periodicals printed in Germany, though they were often short-lived owing to censorship and repression, was even greater. Even in Spain, the *Gaceta de Madrid* and the *Espiritu de los majores Diarios* served as channels for disseminating the ideas of the new " philosophy ". For, meanwhile, the writings of the Enlightenment—the tracts and treatises of Montesquieu and Rousseau; the Encyclopedia of D'Alembert and Diderot; Raynal's *History* and Voltaire's political satires and letters—had begun, in numerous guises and translations, to circulate outwards from Paris and the Netherlands to find a new and increasingly curious reading public in Rome, Madrid, Brussels, Berlin, Vienna and St. Petersburg. The American Revolution and its aftermath produced a fresh crop of tracts and commentaries that extended still further the boundaries of enlightened and educated " public opinion ".[2]

Economic development and the spread of new ideas would both, in the context of war and revolution, profoundly modify

---

[2] See R. R. Palmer, *The Age of the Democratic Revolution*, Vol. 1, *The Challenge* (Princeton, 1959), pp. 242-4.

prevailing attitudes and relations between classes; but, as yet, European society remained essentially hierarchic and "aristocratic". In almost every country an aristocracy of birth, wealth or legal status lorded it over their fellow-men as governors and magistrates, as feudal *seigneurs,* as monopolists of fiscal privilege and of high office in army, Church and State, or merely in their display of material prosperity, ostentatious living, cultural attainments and foreign travel. "In all states of Europe", wrote the Abbé Raynal in 1770, "there are a sort of men who assume from their infancy a pre-eminence independent of their moral character." While this broad generalisation held true even for the most advanced monarchies and Republics of the West, there were, of course, considerable differences in the wealth, status and power enjoyed and exercised by the landed classes and aristocracy both between and within the various countries of Europe. In Spain, grandees like the Dukes of Osuna, Alba and Medina Coeli, owners of vast *señorios* in Andalusia and Catalonia, or the great *títulos de Castilla* were of a very different social status and importance from the humbler *caballeros* and, still more, from the great mass of impoverished rural gentry, or *hidalgos,* who formed by far the greater part of a nobility that, by now, accounted for nearly one in twenty of the population. Similar differences could be found in France, where the 4,000 or so Court aristocrats, owners of great estates and incumbents of bishoprics and high army posts, looked contemptuously on the far greater number of rural *hobereaux,* who, bereft of capital and vigorous outlets for their energies, had often little more to cling to than memories of past grandeur, their names, titles and cherished fiscal immunities. In Poland, too, the small country gentry, who formed the bulk of the million-strong *szlachta,* might claim all the legal privileges of nobility, lord it over what peasants they possessed, exercise their right to wear distinctive clothing and to occupy reserved seats in church; but their poverty placed them often in ignominious dependence on the dozen or so really great magnates who effectively ruled the country—the Radziwills, Czartoryskis or Potockis.

Similarly, in Hungary, owners of great estates like the Ester-hazys and Palffys and, in Russia, the Cherkasskiis, Galitzines and Dolgoroukis claimed a social pre-eminence, in fact if not always in name, over a horde of proud, though poor and semi-literate, rural gentry. In Venice, there were distinctions of a rather different order between the impoverished ancient families, or *Barnabòtti*, and the jumped-up men of wealth who had, more recently, acquired titles of nobility by having their names inscribed in the Golden Book. In England alone, there was a clear verbal and legal distinction made between the country squires and gentry (the traditional Knights of the Shire) and the 200-odd landed magnates, who held high Cabinet office, sat in the Lords, owned boroughs and manipulated elections to the House of Commons.

Britain, too, was distinctive (a distinction shared only with the United Provinces) in that her aristocracy enjoyed no more than the barest remnants of older legal privileges and immunities. A nobleman might still claim the right to be tried by his "peers"; but, otherwise, peer and commoner were equal before the law and had, legally, equal access to public office and an equal right to hold property in land, commerce or manufacture. All but the eldest sons of peers were classed as commoners. There was a growing tendency for wealth alone, and the power and prestige that wealth could bring, to determine social classification. Elsewhere, the aristocracy enjoyed important legal privileges—rights of jurisdiction and immunity from varying types of taxation. In France, the *noblesse* formed less of a closed caste than in many states of central and eastern Europe, as it was not registered as a corporate body and was not debarred from all professions and trades. Besides, access to the nobility still remained open to wealthy commoners—though to shrinking numbers—by the purchase of hereditary offices. Thus, since the seventeenth century, a new and wealthy administrative nobility, the *noblesse de robe*, had grown up to challenge the social status and pretensions of the old-established *noblesse d'épée* (nobility of the sword): by this time, it provided most of the Secretaries of

State and Intendants and, even more important, it dominated the *Parlements*—the great hereditary legal corporations that, in times of weak or divided government and idle or incompetent rulers, were able to exercise considerable political authority. Such authority was denied to all but very few of the older nobility but, as owners of estates, they still exercised many of the privileges of the old feudal lords of the manor : rights of local justice and village surveillance; rights of monopoly, such as the exclusive right to hunt and to maintain a mill, an oven or a wine-press (*banalités*); and, above all, to exact a wide range of feudal dues, rents and services from their peasants. In addition, the French nobility as a whole enjoyed a considerable degree of exemption from direct taxation. They were virtually immune from payment of the principal and most onerous of these taxes, the *taille* (levied on both estimated income and on land); and, in large measure, too, they evaded payment of their proper share of the *vingtième* and *capitation*, introduced, to supplement the *taille*, at the end of Louis XIV's reign, taxes to which both nobles and commoners were nominally subject. The clergy, whose upper ranks belonged almost without exception to the *noblesse*, enjoyed even greater privileges : in addition to the income derived, as land-owners, from rents and feudal dues, they drew tithe (which might amount to one-twelfth of the yield of land) and discharged their obligations to the Exchequer by the payment of a relatively small percentage of their income in the form of a *don gratuit*, or " voluntary gift ".

Outside western Europe, the exemptions and privileges of aristocracy tended to be more clear-cut and the gulf separating nobles from commoners to be more sharply defined. In Poland, the *szlachta* retained until 1768 powers of life and death over their serfs; in Hungary, none but nobles could own land and, since 1741, they had enjoyed complete immunity from paying taxes. In Sweden, the great titled magnates formed a closed caste : by the Constitution of 1720 the King's right to enlarge their ranks by ennobling commoners had been strictly curtailed. No such restrictions were imposed on the autocratic rulers of Prussia and Russia who, in the course of a century, had largely re-cast and re-defined the functions and privileges of their aristocracies. In Prussia, under Frederick William I and Frederick II, the nobility had been transformed into a class of hereditary State servants, obliged to serve the monarch by holding office in the army or the administration; as compensation, they were given extended powers of jurisdiction and economic control over their tenants and peasants. In Russia, Peter the Great had gone even further and devised a strict Table of Ranks, the higher grades in which were reserved for the landowning class who, in return for a stated period of compulsory service to the Tsar, were granted a highly privileged hereditary status and increased authority over their serfs. The system had, however, been whittled down under his successors. In 1762, Peter III had freed the greater nobles from the legal obligation to serve the State and, under Catherine's Charter of Nobility (1785), the Russian *dvoryanstvo* became, in name at least, something more closely akin to the French type of *noblesse*.

In some countries, the social pre-eminence of the aristocracy was matched by the authority and responsibility they exercised in the nation's political life; in others, this was far from being the case. On the one hand, there were countries like Prussia, where State service by the aristocracy was not only enforced but had come to be considered an honour; or Russia, where the tradition of State service, though it was no longer compulsory, lingered on; on the other, there were states like France, Spain, the Two Sicilies, Denmark and many of the smaller Germanic principalities, in which the aristocracy, while retaining their privileges and dancing attendance at Court, had ceased to play any effective part in political affairs. In Hungary, the greater nobles filled the highest offices in Church and administration and dominated the national assembly; and even the poorer members of the gentry, whose representatives sat in the lower chamber of the assembly, administered justice and raised taxes in their districts. The Polish and Swedish aristocracy had, for a large part of the century, enjoyed a "golden age". The

Polish nobles controlled the diets and the government's policies, besides appointing tax-collectors and running local government. In Sweden, the noble heads of families had, for fifty
years, held the whip-hand in the diets and the secret committee
of the four estates, and had occupied every seat in the Royal
Council. In both countries, there had been a re-assertion of
royal authority in 1772; but, in Poland, the diets continued to
form a sort of "democracy" of nobles and country gentlemen
and, in Sweden, it was not until 1809 that public office became
open to members of the non-privileged estates.

In such matters, the position of the British landowning
classes was closer to that of the Swedish than to that of any
other continental aristocracy. They certainly enjoyed no legal
or prescriptive right to monopolize high office and their victory
over monarchy in 1689 had been far less thorough than that of
the Swedes in 1720. But, while sharing power with the
Crown, they continued to exercise a remarkable degree of
effective influence in government, in both Houses of Parliament and in local administration. The House of Lords still
retained, in its own right as a legislative and judicial body, a
degree of authority that was almost equal to that of the
Commons; in addition, it could immeasurably supplement these
powers by its near-monopoly of Cabinet posts, its family con-
nexions and its ownership of "pocket" and "rotten" boroughs. As Lords Lieutenant of the counties and justices of
the peace, landowners and gentry enjoyed virtually complete
authority in local government. It is true that both royal and
radical influence "without doors" had been at work since
1760 to swing the balance in favour of the monarchic or
popular element in the Constitution—we shall hear more of
this in the next chapter; and the younger Pitt's return in the
general election of 1784 must be seen, to some extent at least,
as a defeat for "aristocracy". Yet the general picture remained little changed: in 1783, Pitt was still the only member
in his own Cabinet who did not have a seat in the Lords; and
it was not until after the Reform Act of 1832 that the Eng-

lish aristocracy began to lose its overwhelming ascendancy in both government and Parliament.

The growth of towns and trade would, sooner or later, disrupt this "aristocratic" society and whittle away its defences. But, as yet, the growing class of merchants and bankers, enriched by trade and financial operations, tended to become absorbed by it, or at least to come to terms with it, rather than to offer any resolute challenge. This might happen in a variety of ways—either by marrying their daughters to sons of the nobility, by the purchase of office or estates, by the acquisition of titles and distinctions, or by creating their own exclusive patriciates in municipal government, guilds or administration. In eastern Europe, where towns were still few and merchants formed an insignificant minority, this process had not gone far; yet, even here, a merchant prince like Nikita Demidov, founder of a great dynasty of iron-masters, could bask in the Tsar's favour; and Hungarian merchants, such as the Henchels and Hallers, were able to acquire title-deeds of nobility. The great trading cities of Germany—Hamburg, Leipzig and Frankfurt-am-Main—and Bern and Zürich in Switzerland had long-established native patriciates of merchants, which, with growing prosperity, had become more proudly exclusive and more jealous of their social distinctions and inherited privileges. In Prussia, the rising middle class found scope for their energies and social pretensions as royal servants in a rapidly expanding and privileged State bureaucracy. In the United Provinces, a wealthy patriciate of merchants governed the great cities of Holland, dominated its provincial estates, and sent representatives to the Estates General to sit alongside those of an older, but poorer, aristocracy of the land.

In France and England, the social impact of these classes had assumed different forms. The costly ventures of Louis XIV had provided a fertile breeding-ground for French contractors, merchants and financiers. It had been royal policy to draw into the service of the State the sons of men enriched by trade and finance. Colbert, the greatest of Louis' ministers, was the son of a merchant-draper of Rheims; and Saint-Simon, an aristocratic critic, contemptuously dismissed the period as "*un règne de vile bourgeoisie*". Monsieur Jourdain, in Molière's *Le bourgeois gentilhomme,* had married his daughter to a marquis; this was one way of climbing into aristocratic society. Later, great financiers and bankers, like the four Pâris brothers and Samuel Bernard, might even, as bankers to the Court or founders of commercial empires, afford to "live nobly" on their own account and to snap their fingers at the common run of courtiers. In the eighteenth century, rich bourgeois built mansions and bought estates and, by setting up as lords of the manor, enjoyed the full exercise of seigneurial rights attaching to their properties; and Jaurès claimed that the feverish re-building of Paris, which was so marked a feature of the last quarter of a century before the Revolution, was due rather to bourgeois than to aristocratic enterprise. A select few became Farmers-General and made great fortunes by "farming" the royal taxes and administering the infernal customs. More commonly, rich bourgeois had been inclined to invest their money by the purchase, for themselves or their heirs, of one of the numerous offices that might fall vacant, or be newly created, in the judiciary, the central administration, or the government of a chartered town. Thus the State might meet its debts and the wealthy merchant class satisfy its social ambitions by acquiring titles and privileges as members of the *noblesse de robe,* or of its provincial cousin, the *noblesse de cloche.* As long as the State remained solvent enough to pay the interest on its loans and such channels of social advancement remained open to them, the French mercantile and financial classes could be relied upon to be among the stoutest defenders of the Throne and of the aristocratic society on which it rested. We shall see in a later chapter what happened when these avenues began to be closed.

In England, these classes had acquired a greater measure of social status and authority in their own right. Enriched by the commercial and colonial expansion and wars of the Common-

wealth and Restoration, they had been the allies of aristocracy
and gentry in carrying through the "glorious revolution" of
1688. They had founded the Bank of England to identify
their own interest more closely with that of the Crown and
had been the most loyal supporters of war against Louis XIV.
Nowhere was aristocratic society so readily accessible to them;
nowhere was the aristocracy itself so closely linked with the
merchant class : merchants sat in the Commons, alongside the
gentry, as Knights of the Shire; dukes and marquises married
their sons to daughters and grand-daughters of London merchants and bankers; and the big landowners themselves were
deeply engaged in trade and invested their capital in docks,
mines and real estate. Defoe spoke no more than the truth
when he wrote in 1726 that "our merchants are princes,
greater and richer, and more powerful than some sovereign
Princes", and contrasted the "immense wealth" of men enriched "behind the counter" with the declining fortunes of
the gentry and many "ancient families". Walpole could
count on the firm support of the great London merchants, sated
with trade and honours, in "letting sleeping dogs lie" in the
1720's and thirties; and even after London turned, a few
years later, to opposition to government, the great bankers and
directors of insurance offices and overseas trading companies
continued to support the policies of Court and administration.
Here, then, as in France, the "moneyed interest" remained,
for the greater part of the century, staunch supporters of the
régime. It was only the rise of a new class of "interloping"
merchants, and others of the "middling sort", eager to challenge the supremacy of their older, more prosperous and privileged rivals, that brought a substantial part of the merchant
interest into conflict with the King and Parliament : of this
more will be said in the next chapter.

England, again, was peculiar in that she alone, having embarked on an industrial "revolution", was creating a new and
independent class of private manufacturers, who were beginning to grow rich on the proceeds of industrial, rather than
largely mercantile, capital. In Russia and Bohemia, large-scale

manufacture was generally the province of the State, or of landowners disposing of the labour of serfs, far more than of the middle-class *entrepreneur*. In the United Provinces, while trade still flourished, manufacture tended to decline or to stagnate. In France, manufacture was conducted either in large State enterprises, such as the Royal "manufactories" of the Gobelins and Savonnerie, by master craftsmen in small workshops, or by merchant-manufacturers directing the domestic labour of peasant weavers and spinners in cottage industry. Such private dynasties as were being created by the De Wendels in iron and the Van Robais in textiles were quite exceptional. In England alone, a distinct class of industrial *entrepreneurs* was arising in the wake of the technical innovations introduced by the Darbys, Hargreaves, Cort, Arkwright and Watt. Where Gregory King had, in his survey of 1696, made no provision for manufacturers, Colquhoun, in 1803, noted no fewer than 25,000 "manufacturers employing capital in all branches, wool, cotton . . ." Though the machine-driven factory was slow to make its appearance, the industrial north was already emerging in the neighbourhood of rivers and canals and leaving its mark on social development. Its leaders, new men sprung from farming and commercial stock, were rapidly amassing fortunes and finding a place in society—men like Samuel Whitbread, the brewer; Jedediah Strutt, the hosier; John Wilkinson, the iron-master; and Josiah Wedgwood, the potter. It took time, of course, for such men, despite their wealth, to be accepted on anything like equal terms by "aristocratic" society; and James Watt could write in 1787 that "our landed gentlemen reckon us poor mechanics no better than slaves who cultivate their vineyards". It took time, too, before such men began to realize fully their own potentialities as a new social force: by the 1780's, they had hardly begun to play any distinguishable part in national politics; and the particular claims of Manchester and Birmingham, which played so large a part in determining the actions of governments in the next century, had yet to be voiced.

As land was the predominant source of wealth, so the peasant was still the typical producer and toiler of the age. Peasant families accounted for 75 per cent of the population of Prussia and Poland, for 80 per cent of that of France, and maybe for nine in ten of that of Russia. Strictly speaking, there was no such thing as a clearly defined and cohesive peasant class, as the peasant's economic and social status and degree of personal freedom varied widely from one part of Europe to another. In England, the medieval village had long since been transformed by the impact of trade, civil war, sales of land, enclosure and industrial "revolution". The yeomen —the surviving remnants of the former peasantry—were a declining class; and the village had, in many counties, already acquired its modern social pattern of landlord—tenant farmer —agricultural labourer. In Ireland and the Scottish Highlands, however, fewer social changes had taken place and older forms still lingered on. Outside the British Isles, serfdom no longer existed in a growing number of countries of western Europe, having been abolished, by law or by changing customs, in the Low Countries, Spain, Switzerland, Norway, Sweden and the greater parts of France, western Germany and Italy; yet, in southern Italy and the Spanish provinces of Castile and Andalusia, where vast *latifundia* were left uncultivated by stay-away landlords, such freedom was only a partial boon and the material conditions of the peasantry were universally wretched and deplorable. In France, perhaps one in four of the peasants owned their land outright—some as relatively prosperous *laboureurs,* others (as Arthur Young found) "poor and miserable, much arising from the minute divisions of their little farms among all the children". One half or more were poor share-croppers, or *métayers,* who owned no capital and shared their produce on a fifty-fifty basis with their landlords; a quarter perhaps were landless labourers or rented tiny plots. Fewer than one in twenty—in parts of the Franche-Comté and Nivernais—were serfs, though not fully tied to the land or deprived of royal justice. But, though his legal disabilities were less oppressive than in many other states, the French peasant bore a heavy burden of taxation : he paid tithe to the

Church; *taille, vingtième, capitation* and *gabelle* (salt tax) to
the State; and to the *seigneur* of his parish, whether lay or
ecclesiastical, he paid a varying toll of obligations, services
and payments ranging from the *corvée* (exacted in cash or
kind) and the *cens* (feudal rent in cash) to the *champart* (rent
in kind) and *lods et ventes* (a charge on the transfer of property); or he might, if not owning his land outright, have to
pay for the use of his lord's mill, wine-press and bakery. The
incidence of such burdens varied greatly, like the status of the
peasant, in the different regions of the country; but, in years of
bad harvests and depression, they proved, as we shall see, to be
universally vexatious and intolerable.

In central and eastern Europe, and in some countries of the
West, the peasant was still a serf bound, as in medieval times,
to the soil and largely unprotected by the law against the
exactions of his lord. In Denmark, earlier attempts to abolish
serfdom had come to nothing (they would be resumed, with
more success, in 1788) and, owing to extensive sales of Crown
lands to speculators, the condition of the peasants had actually
grown worse. In Germany, outside western regions and the
solitary southern state of Baden (where it was abolished in
1783), serfdom also persisted. In Brandenburg, Saxony and
East Prussia, far from being a declining force, it was spreading and becoming intensified as landlords, lured by profits
from the export trade, regimented their peasants to increase
the output of grain; in East Prussia, the peasant worked three
days a week—or even five or six—for his master. As the
Prussian army and bureaucracy extended their operations under
Frederick William I and Frederick the Great, the State-serving
nobility, as we have seen, were allowed to tighten their control, both economic and judicial, over their peasants. In
Russia, too, as the government increased its demands, either in
the form of taxation or of service to the State, on the rural
gentry and aristocracy, whole new populations of hitherto free
producers had been subjected to serfdom. The formerly free
peasants of the Ukraine, wrote a visiting English scholar in
1784, "have lately undergone a deplorable change and have

been reduced, by an edict of the present Empress, to the condition of her other subjects". In Poland and Hungary, and in other parts of the Habsburg dominions, the peasant continued to suffer from traditional vexations and injustice at the hands of his landlord, but in Russia alone was the legal position of the serf becoming markedly changed for the worse. Here alone, he could be sold with his landlord's estate like a chattel, or let out for hire, or (by an edict of 1760) exiled to Siberia by his master when he proved lazy or rebellious. In sharp contrast were Joseph II's attempts to abolish serfdom within the Austrian Empire by his *Unterthanspatent* of 1781, though we shall see that his efforts proved to be largely still-born.

By and large, as we have noted, the growth of industry had left its mark more deeply on rural than on urban life and had developed a rural, rather than an urban, working class, or proletariat; the prevalence of domestic industry, in particular, had converted many thousands of European peasant families into part-time weavers and spinners supplying both the home and export market. But, everywhere, even in eastern Europe, towns had grown apace and city populations were expanding, often spreading beyond old medieval walls into new suburbs, in response to the increasing calls of trade, industry and administration. London, Europe's largest city, had, by the 1780's, a population of some 850,000, Paris of 650,000, Amsterdam and Vienna of 200,000, Madrid of 150,000 and both Venice and Milan of 130,000; other cities, though smaller, might be expanding more rapidly. In these, the ruling groups of aristocracy, gentry, patricians, merchants and "principal inhabitants" formed, of course, a relatively small minority; and the great bulk of the citizens were a mixed population of small tradesmen, master craftsmen, journeymen, apprentices, porters, labourers, domestic servants and city poor—those, in short, whom contemporary Englishmen termed "the lower orders" or "the Mob", Frenchmen the *menu peuple,* and Italians the *populo minuto* or *populino*. Among them the wage-earners had their own distinctive interests as "servants" and producers; but the degree to which this was so varied from one country to another. In London, there was little left of the old traditions of the medieval workshop and servants and masters, even in handicrafts and small-scale manufacture, were already clearly divided; though, even here, master tradesmen had authority to prevent their journeymen from " going abroad " in times of disorder. This division, however, was not yet so sharp or distinct elsewhere. Thus, in Paris, the journeyman in many trades was still closely tied to the workshop, often sleeping in his master's house, eating at his table and, even, on occasion, marrying his daughter (or his widow) and inheriting his shop. Yet such cases were becoming rare and, as the old guild-system declined and became the exclusive preserve of the wealthier merchants and master craftsmen, the journeyman found himself reduced to the status of a permanent daily worker with nothing but the slenderest chance of ever becoming a master.

For the journeyman, therefore, as for other wage-earners, the level of wages was becoming in itself a matter of increasing concern. But " combinations " of workpeople were severely repressed and such workers' organizations as those formed by London tailors and hatters and French printers, building and paper workers were still rare and short-lived and could, as yet, achieve only occasional success. In consequence, an increase in wages tended to be swallowed up by the rising cost of bread. In France, grain prices rose by 60 per cent between 1730 and 1789, whilst wages increased by little over 22 per cent; and, in London, while wages remained almost stable, the price of bread would in lean years (and these became increasingly frequent during the latter half of the century) rise from a norm of 1¼d. or 1½d. to 2d., or even 3d., a pound. Meanwhile, small tradesmen and workshop masters, and independent craftsmen, also felt the pinch of rising food prices, that continually threatened to destroy their livelihood. Thus, though the issue of wages might divide them, shopkeepers, small employers and wage-earners would, as consumers, be inclined to see their overriding economic interest as one and, in times of shortage, to unite in common action against wholesalers, merchants and city authorities. Again, in moments of political tension affecting the common people as a whole, journeymen would tend to be influenced by and follow the lead of their masters. It is for reasons such as these that we shall find emerging in Paris, in the course of the Revolution, a combination of social forces, peculiar to those times but not to ours, to which was attached the common label of *sans-culottes*.

It is not, then, to the larger cities that we should look for the emergence of a distinct working class or for the prototype of the industrial worker of the future. For these we should look rather to the mines of Saxony and Dauphiné, to the old clothing towns of the Netherlands, to the great State manufactories and arsenals of both East and West, or to such centres of the French textile industry as Lyons, Rouen, Lille, Elbeuf and Abbeville. Here, although mechanization was in its earliest infancy, something like a factory discipline and an employer-worker relationship looking forward to those of the next century were beginning to appear. In England's industrial midlands and north, where the new mechanical devices were being rapidly introduced, this process had gone considerably further than elsewhere; and it was not long before the great new factory towns of Manchester, Leeds, Sheffield and Birmingham would produce a fully-fledged industrial proletariat, whose manner of dress and living, speech, economic interests and social attitudes would mark them off sharply from those of their employers. But, outside Britain, such relations existed as yet only in embryo, and they formed no significant part of the social pattern of Europe on the eve of the French Revolution.

Chapter II

GOVERNMENTS AND THE CONFLICTS
WITHIN STATES

Albert Sorel wrote of the political institutions of the Old
Régime in Europe: "Every form of government existed . . .
and all were considered equally legitimate". On the face of it,
it seems true enough. Though the prevailing form of government was absolute monarchy, in which the royal authority
towered over that of the other estates, there were great differences in the way it was exercised, and there were several
states in which the monarchy, far from being absolute, had
been limited by the encroachment of aristocracy or Parliament, or had even been superseded by republican forms.
There were, for example, evident differences between the operation of hereditary absolute monarchy in France, Spain,
Sweden, Prussia and the Austrian Empire; Britain alone had a
"limited", or parliamentary, monarchy; Poland's monarchy
was in practice what the Austrian was in theory—elective; the
autocracy of Russia was of a different order from the absolute
monarchies of France or Spain and the oriental despotism of
Turkey; and the Republics of Switzerland, Genoa and Venice
were very differently constituted from the near-monarchical
Republic of the United Provinces. Yet, with all these differences, all European governments, on the eve of the French
Revolution, were either "monarchic" or "aristocratic":
they all had in common that they severely restricted what political writers called the "democratic" element in the Constitution.

Nor is this surprising, as government was bound to reflect,
within fairly narrow limits, the prevailing aristocratic and
hierarchic society that has been described in the last chapter.
Though the claims of aristocracy were everywhere being in-

creasingly felt, this is not to suggest that the tendency in all countries was towards an " aristocratic " form of government : " monarchic " forms, which balanced competing claims, might suit such a society better. Of course, where aristocracy was weak or only recently rising to social ascendancy, the degree of authority exercised by the monarch would tend to be the greater. In its extreme form, this could be seen in the Ottoman Empire, where the nobility enjoyed only such temporary status as was conferred on its members by the Sultan; and where the Sultan, in consequence, provided he could control the army and the priests, might exercise, in practice as well as in theory, that " prodigious and unlimited authority " described by an English visitor in the early years of the century. In Russia, a somewhat similar situation had existed under Peter I. The Tsar's autocracy had been the more complete because the aristocracy had been weak and divided, had accumulated little hereditary landed wealth, and enjoyed only limited authority over their peasants. We have seen that Peter deliberately raised their social status and extended their privileges in return for binding them to the service of the State. Yet the Tsar's autocracy remained; and, even under Catherine, an English traveller wrote that " the sovereign of the Russian Empire is absolute and despotic in the utmost latitude of these words and master of the lives and properties of all his subjects who, though they are the first nobility . . . may nevertheless for the most trifling offence be seized upon and sent to Siberia ". Yet, by now, this was an exaggeration, as Peter III had already abolished compulsory State service by the greater nobility and, under Catherine, they were being drawn into partnership with the autocracy and would soon be guaranteed their rights and privileges by charter.

In Prussia, too, the absolute monarchy still retained the vigour of its creators. The first King, Frederick I, had admittedly spent lavishly on the arts, wooed the aristocracy and allowed himself to be ruled by his ministers. But his successor, Frederick William I, the so-called " Sergeant-King ", had reversed the process: he had reasserted the royal authority, drastically pruned expenditure on "luxuries", begun to build up an efficient civil service, and left his son a well-stocked Treasury and one of the strongest armies in Europe. Frederick II had turned this legacy to good effect by extending his dominions and further enlarging the scope and authority of his bureaucracy; but, to do this, he had, as we saw, found it necessary to follow the example of Peter the Great and bind the land-owning classes to State service in army and administration in return for extensive legal and social privileges. Thus, the despotism of Frederick William I had been tempered by his son, though its full effects were not to be realized until the time of his successors.

In France, the monarchy was, in theory, as absolute as in Prussia and most other German states. Louis XIV had built up at Versailles a formidable concentration of authority: the old nobility had been stripped of political power and danced decorative attendance at Court; and from the Crown alone stemmed government, justice and promotion to high office in Church and State. Yet, even under the *Roi Soleil*, there remained the residual authority of *Parlements* and provincial estates, and the purchase of hereditary offices assured their holders of a limited measure of independence of the Crown. Under his successors, the royal authority retained its forms, yet its substance had become greatly changed. During the Regency of the Duke of Orleans, there had been a deliberate devolution of authority and, for a short while, *Parlements* and nobility had enjoyed a greater measure of freedom and political independence. Louis XV had, on the death of Cardinal Fleury (1743), returned to his great-grandfather's system; but it soon became evident that it was in name rather than in fact. The King, more devoted to the hunt and the pleasures of the Court than to affairs of state, allowed government to drift and its direction to be disputed by rival factions, in which Secretaries of State, pretenders to office, Princes of the Blood and royal mistresses (such as the versatile Madame de Pompadour) each had a part to play. The Marquis d'Argenson, having fallen from office in 1747, wrote of the Council at this time as

" a republic . . . of heads of factions, each thinking only of his own concern, one of finance, another of the navy, another of the army, and each achieving his own ends according to his greater or lesser facility in the art of persuasion ". Even allowing for the exaggeration of a disgruntled ex-minister, it was reasonably fair comment. And, even when able ministers like Choiseul and Maupeou momentarily restored the credit of the government, other more abiding ills (many arising from Louis XIV's own system) persisted and became magnified. The bureaucracy of hereditary office-holders, as it grew ever larger and more independent, tended to become a buffer, rather than a link, between government and people. And as government lost its authority, or was brought into contempt, the claims of aristocracy and privilege became more insistent. We shall see that even the best-intentioned of reforming ministers were unable to stand up to them or overcome them.

In Spain and the Austrian Empire, the absolute monarchy was, again, of a different order. In both countries, though far more vigorous than that of France, it had never been able to assume sole and unchallenged authority. This was due less to the claims of factious privileged groups at the centre than to those of whole provinces that had never been fully assimilated. In Spain, the Succession War of 1702-13 had seen a determined attempt by Catalonia and Aragon to throw off the rule of Castile; the provincial estates (*Cortes*) of Castile and Navarre continued to meet; and the Basque provinces even enjoyed the particular privilege of not being taxed without their consent. In the Austrian dominions, the problem was more complex. The Empire sprawled southwards to Milan and northwards to the Netherlands and was composed of a patchwork of provinces, whose political traditions, social structure, language and economic development all varied widely and tended both to divide them from one another and from the Court of Vienna. In such circumstances, a certain devolution of authority was bound to persist, and the centralizing efforts of the Emperor were continually challenged by the provincial estates of the Netherlands, the patrician magistracy of Milan, and the diets of Bohemia and Hungary. The internal history of the Empire in the latter half of the century is, in fact, largely one of determined attempts by its rulers to impose their authority more firmly on Hungary and their other, outlying, dominions. We shall see how Joseph II overreached himself, and nearly lost his throne in the attempt.

Unique among the state-systems of Europe was that of Poland. It was a monarchy but an elective one; and the King, as the price of election, had to accept the *pacta conventa* (or traditional " liberties ") presented to him by the magnates. Nominally a monarchy, practically a sort of republic or " democracy " of nobles, Poland was, in fact, governed by the large land-owning families, who controlled the diets, in which a unanimity of votes (the *liberum veto*) was required for any law to be enacted. Meanwhile, the executive authority was further weakened by its division between King and Senate and by the meagreness of its revenues and the absence of a standing army. The combined result of this system was to paralyse both government and legislature and to leave Poland exposed to the predatory ambitions of its increasingly powerful neighbours, Prussia and Russia. The eventual outcome was a series of partitions of Poland between these countries and Austria which, starting in 1772, effectively wiped her off the map for years to come.

Unique, too, in its own way was the " limited " monarchy of Britain. Formally, it was closer to that of Sweden than to that of France, Prussia or Spain; but, in practice, it was poles apart from them all. The essential difference, of course, lay in the more advanced social and economic development of the country that we noted in the last chapter. Englishmen prided themselves on their " mixed " or " balanced " Constitution. " And herein," wrote Sir William Blackstone in 1765, " consists the excellence of the English government, that all parts of it form a mutual check upon each other. In the legislative, the people are a check upon the nobility, the nobility a check upon the people, by the mutual privilege of rejecting what the other has resolved; while the King is a check upon both, which preserves the executive power from encroachments." It was these checks and balances that delighted Montesquieu, and both he and Blackstone were fully justified in noting the considerable powers that the limited monarchy still left in the hands of the King. He still retained the power to select his own ministers and, though he no longer exercised his prerogative right to refuse to sanction Bills passed to him by the Houses of Parliament, he had ample means for influencing legislation and the outcome of elections, and for promoting the policies of his choice. It was George II's virtual abandonment of these powers during the latter part of his reign that excited the determination of his grandson, George III, to restore the royal authority. Yet Blackstone, being a constitutional lawyer, exaggerated the role of the "people" within this system. To him the "people" were the Commons, elected on an extremely limited and anomalous franchise; and the Commons, as we saw in the last chapter, were largely the preserve of the gentry, where they were not controlled and manipulated by the large land-owning families; and as these and the gentry also controlled the counties as Lords Lieutenant and justices of the peace, the "mixture" was not quite what the lawyers proclaimed. It was, in fact, the landed classes, with a sprinkling of wealthy merchants, that provided the effective check on the royal authority. We shall see, however, that "the people", in a broader sense than that intended by Blackstone, had something to say about this in the 1760's and years following.

Finally, there were the Republics, in which monarchy had been superseded by the authority of noble families or of merchant patriciates. By far the wealthiest and most powerful of these was that of the United Provinces; but here the monarchical form had not been fully abandoned. The legislative power was vested in their High Mightinesses the Estates General, who were composed of the deputies, both burgher and noble, of the seven provinces; and each of the large towns (there were several in the single province of Holland) was governed, in turn, by members of local ruling families, called regents.

Here the wealthy merchant class, rather than the older landed
nobility, was predominant; yet the remnants of monarchy survived in the person of the Stadholder, whose office was hereditary in the House of Orange. The Stadholder was com-
mander-in-chief of the armed forces as well as formal head of
the administration; and, in years of public emergency or when
the great merchants of Amsterdam were unable to hold him in
check, might wield an authority that eclipsed that of his rival
to executive power, the Grand Pensionary of Holland. No
such dualism existed in other smaller Republics. In Venice,
only hereditary nobles qualified for public office; and, in 1796,
the last year of its long history as a Republic, some 1,200 of
a population of 130,000 had the right—the right of all citizen-
nobles—to attend the meetings of the Great Council. Switzerland was a federation of cantons, among which, in rural areas,
there was an element of democracy; but the most prosperous
of them—the city-states of Bern and Basel—were governed by
a merchant aristocracy; while the affiliated city of Geneva,
home of Calvin and Rousseau, was ruled by a small privileged
group of "citizens", who jealously upheld their exclusive
rights against the insistent claims of the smaller merchants and
artisans.

It was inevitable that in countries where power was so distributed—in uneasy balance between monarchy and aristocracy, or in the exclusive control of aristocratic groups or oli-
garchies—tensions should arise and demands be voiced for an
extension of authority by some and a share in government by
others. The great question was: should the way to reform be
sought by enlarging the authority of an "enlightened"
monarch at the expense of the estates; should aristocratic or
other "intermediate bodies" be strengthened as a check on
the power of the Crown; or should the power of both be
balanced, or eclipsed, by vesting greater responsibility in the
hands of the people themselves? In short, should the remedy
for existing ills be found by strengthening the "monarchic",
the "aristocratic", or the "popular" element in the constitution? The answers given naturally varied from country to

country and from class to class; they could all, in one form or another and whether offered by rulers or subjects, be justified in terms of "natural law"; and they were no doubt influenced, to a greater or a lesser extent, by the widely disseminated ideas of the political writers of the Enlightenment. But how great this influence was, and how great that of any particular writer, is highly problematical. That the total impact of their ideas was considerable seems hardly open to doubt. Voltaire's political, satirical, and anti-clerical pieces poured out in translation from the 1730's to his death in 1778, and beyond. The Abbé Raynal's *Philosophical History,* published in 1770, went through fifty-five editions in five or six languages in thirty years. Montesquieu's *De l'Esprit des Lois,* first published in 1748, appeared in half-a-dozen French editions in three years, had seen ten English editions by 1773, appeared in Dutch in 1771, in Italian in 1777, in German in 1789, in Russian in 1801; and, according to one report, in Hungary in Latin in 1751. The other great work of the revolution in political ideas, Rousseau's *Social Contract,* appeared in thirteen French-language editions in 1762 and 1763; and, by 1764, had been published in three English editions, one German and one Russian. In the long run, we may assume that Montesquieu's influence proved to be conservative and "aristocratic" rather than "monarchic" or social-revolutionary; that Voltaire's precepts were more congenial to reforming monarchs and ministers than to their rebellious subjects; and that among Rousseau's political ideas, whatever his personal intentions, none had a more explosive and enduring influence than his conception of the sovereignty of the people. Yet this no more makes Montesquieu the consistent prophet of aristocratic conservatism than it makes Voltaire that of "enlightened" despotism or Rousseau of "democratic" or popular revolution. Montesquieu was quoted as an oracle, for quite contrary purposes, by Polish monarchists and French *parlementaires.* D'Antraigues, the later propagandist of monarchist intervention against the French Revolution, drew his political philosophy in equal doses from Montesquieu and Rousseau.

Voltaire, who corresponded on terms of near-intimacy with Catherine and Frederick the Great, came to support the claims of both "burghers" and "natives" against the patricians of Geneva. Rousseau had quite a different message for the French revolutionaries of 1789 from that which he had for Corsican patriots, French aristocrats or Polish noblemen; and, unlike Voltaire, he would have nothing to do with the underprivileged "natives" of Geneva when they sought his aid. In fact, had Rousseau lived, he might well have condemned the Parisian *sans-culottes* of 1793 for the use they made of his teachings as forthrightly as Luther had, 270 years before, condemned the rebellious German peasants. This merely underlines the truth that it is not so much ideas in themselves that are important in history, or even the intentions of their authors, as the political and social context in which they circulate and the uses to which they are put by those who read and absorb them.

Among those who were familiar with the new ideas, or even corresponded with their authors, were the group of monarchs and rulers of the latter half of the century who are generally known as "enlightened despots". This Enlightened Despotism (or "Repentance of Monarchy", as Lord Acton called it) may be termed "enlightened" in so far as its promoters had dipped into the works of the *philosophes,* tried to rule according to "philosophical" principles, or merely gave some evidence of having the welfare of the State or of their subjects at heart. But, essentially, they were rulers who set out to modernize the administration and to strengthen the monarchy, often at the expense of the Church or aristocracy or of other "intermediate bodies". Strangely enough, those monarchs to whom the label "enlightened" has most insistently been attached—Frederick the Great and Catherine of Russia—were, in some respects, least worthy of the name. Frederick ruled Prussia with a firm hand, supervised in person the work of his bureaucracy, introduced judicial and educational reforms and promoted State industries; but these were nearly all developments mapped out for him by his father,

Frederick William I; and the only important respect in which he departed from his father's practice was to staff his administration with men of noble birth and to allow the aristocracy a social importance and a share in government that they had not known before. Catherine's role in Russia was similar: she talked of agrarian reform, abolished torture, practised religious toleration, secularized Church lands, set up new local authorities and strengthened the machinery of central government—measures that had all been anticipated by her predecessors; but her most significant and enduring innovation was to draw the privileged landowning classes into closer partnership with the autocracy. Other rulers attempted more far-reaching measures. The Marquis of Pombal, virtual ruler of Portugal under Joseph I, set the fashion in expelling the Jesuits (1759), cowed and browbeat the nobility, abolished slavery and passed laws against anti-semitism, and against the colour-bar in the colonies. Gustavus III, who ascended the Swedish throne in 1771, carried out a *coup d'état*, supported by the citizens of Stockholm, which abruptly brought to an end the long "Era of Freedom", during which the nobility in Sweden had, for fifty years, ruled the roost almost as completely as that of Poland. His new constitution restored the authority of the Crown, shared the legislative power between King and diet, abolished extraordinary courts and judicial torture, and allowed a limited measure of freedom to the press. Most drastic of all, however, were the reforms attempted by the Emperor Joseph II of Austria. In some respects, he merely followed in the footsteps of his mother, the redoubtable Maria Theresa. Her government had already taken firm measures to end the provincial separatism of Bohemia by annulling its charters and by suspending and reducing the powers of its diet. The Hungarian diet was forbidden to meet for twenty-five years; torture was abolished in Austria-Bohemia; monasteries were dissolved; and, by an Act of 1755, all the Austrian dominions, with the exception of Hungary, were brought into a single tariff union. But Joseph, who had ruled jointly with his mother for her last fifteen years, was far more thorough and, alone of the "enlightened despots", attempted to carry through a consistent and comprehensive policy, combining radical social measures with the assertion of the power of the Crown over every imaginable subordinate authority, whether Church, nobility, provincial estates or chartered towns. In pursuit of the former aim, he completed the abolition of torture, abolished personal serfdom (though not labour service) by his *Unterthanspatent* of 1781, limited the lord's right to punish his peasants, and did away with the *corvée*. In his dealings with the Catholic Church, he anticipated much of the work of the French revolutionaries of 1789: he dissolved a further 700 monastic houses and used their funds to promote education and poor relief; he abolished the Inquisition; he freely tolerated Protestants and extended the civil rights of Jews; he silenced the clerical opposition and permitted public criticism of the Church; he made marriage a civil contract; he undermined the authority of the Pope in his dominions; compelled the bishops to take an oath of allegiance to the Emperor; and turned the clergy into salaried servants of the State. In his war with the nobility, he withdrew their right to claim tax-exemption in the various provinces, drastically weakened their authority over their peasants, and used his political police to suppress their protests. He was equally ruthless in dealing with provincialism: he imposed the German language on his Hungarian and Bohemian dominions, suppressed the local authorities in Milan and Lombardy, and restricted the operations of the ancient guilds and town assemblies of the Netherlands.

But "enlightened despotism", in so far as it was "enlightened", was almost universally a failure. It succeeded best where the object was limited administrative reform rather than drastic social experiment. Frederick II made no profession of such intentions and Catherine, for all her early talk of lightening the burdens of her peasantry, gave up all thought of social reform after Pugachev's rebellion of the 1770's. Gustavus III succeeded in tipping the balance significantly in favour of monarchy in Sweden; but reforming ministers like

Pombal in Portugal and Struensee in Denmark saw most of their work undone when they fell from office. In France, the well-meaning efforts of Maupeou and Turgot to reform the taxes came to nothing. Above all, the experience of Joseph II, who was more determined than any other to build for the future and break with the past, illustrates how narrow were the limits within which a reforming " despot " might successfully operate. For lack of an educated native middle class, Joseph had to depend for the execution of his plans on a small group of enlightened officials at Vienna; but their devotion and the support of a powerful machinery of State—not to mention the goodwill of many peasant families—were quite insufficient to break the resistance of the outraged Church, nobility, provincial estates and chartered towns, whom his reforms and his high-handed methods had alienated and antagonized. The result was that the Netherlands revolted and Hungary almost seceded from the Empire. To save his dominions from disintegration, Joseph and his successor, Leopold II, were compelled to make concessions that virtually destroyed his handiwork. Yet one important legacy remained : " Josephism ", while anathema to the established Church and the privileged classes, had roused a " great hope " among the enserfed and downtrodden peasantry and the lesser bourgeois and craftsmen of the cities; and many of the " Josephians " of the 1780's were to become the " Jacobins " of the nineties.

Perhaps an even more striking feature of the times than the achievements of "enlightened" monarchy was the very tangible reality of the " feudal " or " aristocratic " reaction. This might take the form of a collusive deal between monarchy and nobility; it might take that of a gradual and peaceful extension of the influence of aristocracy in society and administration; or, again, it might take the form of a more deliberate attempt by the privileged orders to regain lost ground or to redress the balance in their favour. We have seen examples of the first in Russia and Prussia; examples of the second can be found in England, France and Sweden. In England, a seat in Parliament could, since the time of Queen Anne, be held only by those owning considerable property in land; peerages tended to be conferred only on members of the landed class; and the justices of the peace were becoming an increasingly exclusive caste. Whereas only one-third of Sweden's army officers were nobles in 1719, two-thirds of them were so in 1760. In France, Louis XIV's practice of promoting bourgeois, or *roturiers* (commoners), to high office in army, Church and State had been gradually abandoned by his successors; in 1789, not one bishop and not one Intendant was a former commoner; all but three of the King's ministers since 1718 had been noble; several of the *Parlements* were now refusing to admit commoners to their ranks; and an *ordonnance* of 1781 made it almost impossible henceforth for a bourgeois, or even an *anobli* of recent vintage, to qualify as an officer-candidate in the army unless actually rising from the ranks. In France, too, the landowners, whether noble or bourgeois, had recently begun to look more closely into their archives in order to seek out and revive old manorial rights, long since fallen into disuse, or to invent new ones. Thus the peasants suffered more than ever from the exactions of their *seigneurs*.

More spectacular were the open collisions between aristocracy and monarchy, often fought out in the name of "traditional liberties" or accompanied by appeals to "natural law" or to the precepts of Montesquieu or Rousseau. There was an element of such an aristocratic resurgence in the parliamentary opposition to George III in England: its leaders were Whig peers and disgruntled ex-ministers like the Dukes of Newcastle, Devonshire and Portland and the Marquis of Rockingham. It continued to play a big part, too, even after 1772, in the politics of Poland and Sweden; but it was perhaps particularly striking in France and the Austrian Netherlands (or Belgium). In France, it was the hereditary magistrates of the *Parlements*, rather than the clergy or the older aristocracy of the sword, that set the pace. After the death of Louis XIV, the *Parlements* had resurrected the ancient custom of publishing their remonstrances, or protests, against those governmental actions and decrees of which they disapproved. From the middle of the century, the government, perpetually in financial difficulties, had made a number of efforts to reform the fiscal system and to compel, or to cajole, the privileged classes to make some token surrender of their immunities. In 1751, the Controller General, Machault, failed to impose a new *vingtième*, or one-twentieth tax on incomes, against the combined opposition of the *Parlements*, the clergy and their supporters at Court. Similar proposals in 1763 provoked a similar response : this time, the *Parlement* of Paris borrowed from the " philosophical " language of the day in accusing the ministers of offending against " the Sovereign, the law and the Nation "; once more, the *Parlements* won the contest, and the offending Minister, Bertin, was dismissed from office. In 1770-71, the Chancellor, Maupeou, took the offensive : having trapped the Paris *Parlement* into committing open defiance, he exiled the magistrates, abolished their offices without compensation, and set up new courts in the place of the old; while Terray, the Controller General, proceeded to reform the taxes. It was a highly successful experiment while it lasted; but the mounting outcry was such that Louis XVI, on his accession in 1774, felt compelled to dismiss Maupeou and Terray and to reinstate the magistrates in office. Terray's successor, Turgot, was a Physiocrat, a close friend of the *philosophes,* and even more determined than Machault or Maupeou to carry out reforms. The almost inevitable happened : his attempts to abolish the guilds and the *corvée* and to reform the taxes provoked such a storm of disapproval from the *Parlements* and other interested parties that Louis, for the sake of peace, withdrew his support. With Turgot's departure went the last serious chance (admittedly still a slender one) of reforming the old institutions of France before the Revolution. Of particular interest in all this is that the *Parlements,* though mainly concerned to defend privilege and uphold traditional immunities, were led, in the course of these disputes, to adopt a language that was calculated to arouse a response among other social classes, whose interests and aspirations were very different from their own. This, as we shall see, was to prove a factor of some importance in the years to come.

In Belgium, the innovations of Joseph II stirred up something like a national revolution; and, like the aristocratic prelude to revolution in France in the same year, it was led by the privileged classes and was concerned to restore the old rather than to re-build the State on new foundations. Yet, in resisting Joseph, the Belgian aristocrats and patricians, like their fellows in other countries, based their arguments not only on historical precedent, but on the writings of the *philosophes* and the experience of the Americans. In the Belgian provinces, all three estates—representing the clergy, the nobility and the guildsmen of the ancient cities—had cherished privileges and "liberties". The nobility and clergy enjoyed more exalted privileges than the humbler Third Estate; but they, too, having become virtually a hereditary caste, clung as tenaciously as the higher "orders" to their old traditions. So when, in 1787, Joseph reorganized the whole administrative and judicial system of Belgium, abolished manorial courts, estate assemblies and town councils, and relaxed the trading monopolies of the guilds, he met with the combined opposition and rebellion of all three estates. Led by the largely patrician "Estates party" of the lawyer Van der Noot, the Belgians drove out the Austrians in 1789 and proclaimed a United States of Belgium, closely modelled on the American Articles of Confederation. Meanwhile, a democratic party, formed from middle-class elements, had come into being under another lawyer, J. F. Vonck, and played some part in the revolution. The "Vonckists" advanced moderate proposals for constitutional reform; and, once the Austrians had been expelled, they were blackened by their rivals as desiring to destroy the Church and to subvert the ancient liberties of the land; they were arrested in hundreds and driven into exile, many to France. It is significant that they were able to return only with the aid of the Austrians, who regained control in December 1790.[1] We shall hear more of these Belgian democrats in the context of the revolution in France.

In other countries, too, the "middling" people were beginning to assert themselves and to press their claims against monarchy or aristocracy. In the city-state of Geneva in Switzerland, a small-scale revolution of a strictly "bourgeois" kind took place in 1768. The Burghers, who made up the second of the three categories into which the inhabitants of the city were divided, had long resented the domination of the Two Hundred, who monopolized office in the governing Small Council and claimed the right to block, or veto, their representations to the General Council, or legislative body. That year, after arming and organizing popular support, the Burghers won a large part of their demands; but when the third category of citizens, the Natives, who were excluded from most occupations above the level of artisan and enjoyed no political rights, voiced their own grievances a short while after, they were suppressed by the combined action of patricians and Burghers. The gains of 1768, however, were short-lived: in 1782, the French government (patrons of revolution in America but not in Switzerland) intervened on behalf of the privileged Two Hundred and helped to restore the old aristocratic constitution of the city.[1]

In England, too, there had been, in the seventeen-sixties and seventies, a radical revival that challenged both the royal and aristocratic control of Parliament. When John Wilkes, the middle-class radical, was, after his return from exile in 1768, not only elected to Parliament but carried his right to sit against the combined opposition of George III and the Commons' majority, this marked a signal victory for both the freeholders of Middlesex who elected him and for middle-class political opinion in general. It also gave a new edge to the radical movement that had, for the past dozen years, been developing in the City of London in favour of shorter parlia-

[1] For the foregoing, see R. R. Palmer, *The Age of the Democratic Revolution*, I, 341-57.

ments and "a more equal representation of the people". Up to a point, this radical challenge ran in harness with the aristocratic opposition in Parliament, represented by men like Rockingham and Burke, who had their own reasons for wishing to curb the "influence" of the Crown. But the partnership was short-lived, as the opposition Whigs, while eager to carry a limited measure of "economical" reform, were quite unwilling to support demands for shorter parliaments, to abolish "rotten" boroughs or substantially to enlarge the electorate. So when the reform movement revived in 1779, Christopher Wyvill and his Yorkshire and London "associators", the advocates of radical reform, were quite unable to come to terms with the Whig opposition and ended up, in the 1784 election, by supporting the new Tory (and King's) party of the younger Pitt against Charles James Fox and his new partner, Lord North. The degree to which the former allies had by now fallen out is illustrated by Wyvill's comment on the result: a victory for the Fox-North coalition, he wrote to a friend, would "have changed our limited Monarchy into a mere Aristocratical Republic".[2] The association of the "middling" interest with Pitt proved to be a set-back for reform; but the movement revived, as we shall see in a later chapter, under the impact of the revolutionary events in France.

It seems evident that, in England, both radicals and opposition Whigs were stirred by events in America: both groups espoused the cause of American "liberties"; merchants in London, Bristol and Liverpool resented the interruption or loss of valuable colonial trade; and Nonconformists were inclined to sympathize with their Calvinist brethren in New England. In other parts of Europe, too, opinion, both middle-class and aristocratic, was roused by the outcome of the American Revolution, the first great breach in the old colonial system. This certainly appears from the mass of writings that the Americans evoked in Europe: Professor Palmer has

[2] Cited by N. C. Phillips, *Yorkshire and English National Politics 1783-1784* (Christchurch, N.Z., 1961), p. 60.

listed twenty-six books on America that appeared in three or four European languages between 1760 and 1790; and the space devoted to the New World in the rapidly expanding press of a dozen countries is more impressive still. The democratic and egalitarian—and even republican—passions that this discussion aroused would have their harvest, in terms of the active participation in revolutionary movements by writers, university professors and teachers, in the next decade; but, for the present, even in countries where this intellectual ferment was most in evidence—in Germany, Italy and France itself—middle-class political activity was largely confined to discussion, pamphleteering, and writing for the press. This was not true, of course, of England; nor was it so of Belgium and Poland; nor again, of Ireland, where the Volunteers and the national movement behind Henry Grattan compelled Westminster, in 1782, to release the Dublin Parliament from its 300-years bondage and restore its legislative independence. The other notable exception was the United Provinces, where something like a middle-class revolution, though an abortive one, broke out in the Patriot movement of the 1780's. The influence of the Americans had already been strong in the Provinces in 1778, when the city of Amsterdam made a secret treaty with the United States and floated a loan on their behalf; and, in 1780, in spite of the opposition of the Orange party (the pro-English party of the Stadholder, William V), the Dutch went to war on the side of the Americans and the French. The Patriot party, which emerged from these events, was a largely middle-class party; and, having democratic tendencies, it challenged simultaneously the authority of the House of Orange and that of the regent families that controlled the great cities. This double challenge proved to be a source both of strength and of weakness: it won the Patriots popular support, but it made it easier for its monarchic and "aristocratic" enemies, normally at loggerheads, to unite against them. The French now threatened to intervene on behalf of the Patriots and the English on behalf of the Orangists. The English were well advised by their minister at The Hague, Sir James Harris, and persuaded their Prussian allies to send in 20,000 troops; and the French, being divided and faced with bankruptcy, abandoned the Patriots who were left to their fate.[8] But the Patriots had another weakness which would have disqualified them from leading a "democratic" revolution to a successful conclusion. It was the one picked out by the American, John Adams, who knew the Dutch well and was certainly no democrat, when he wrote of them that they had been "too inattentive to the sense of the common people of their own country" and had depended too much on the French.

Inattention to "the sense of the common people" was, in fact, to prove the Achilles' heel of more than one incipient "democratic" revolution in Europe on the eve of the great events in France. None of the political thinkers, however advanced their views seemed to the aristocratic society of their day, had shown any clearly marked sympathy for the "lower orders" or "fourth estate". Yet, irrespective of middle-class or "enlightened" opinion, they aired their grievances with existing society after their own fashion. Peasants, driven to desperate remedies by seigneurial oppression or economic hardship, rioted or rebelled or engaged in violent insurrection. In Russia, seventy-three peasant risings have been recorded for the years 1762-69 alone, and the widespread rural disorders that marked the early years of Catherine culminated in the great insurrection led by the Cossack partisan, Pugachev, which was not finally suppressed until 1775. In the same year, there was a rising in Bohemia, when 15,000 peasants invested Prague; others followed in Transylvania in 1784, in Moravia in 1786, and in Austria in 1789—the last provoked by Joseph II's agrarian reforms. In France, under Richelieu and Louis XIV, peasant rebellion had been almost endemic; but, in the eighteenth century, with growing agrarian prosperity and the passing of the great famines, rural *jacqueries* and

---

[8] A contributory factor was that the French Court was alarmed at the prospect of giving support to a "pure democracy" (J. Egret, *La Pré-Révolution française, 1787-1788* (Paris, 1962), p. 70).

rebellions had become scarce. Peasant outbreaks, like those in market towns, were now mainly provoked by rising food prices in years of shortage. A hundred or more of these have been recorded in the French provinces between 1715 and 1785, some taking the form of forcing millers, merchants and bakers to reduce the price of grain, flour and bread (*taxation populaire*). The last great outbreak of the kind before the Revolution occurred in May 1775, in the second year of Turgot's ministry. Being a Physiocrat, Turgot had begun to introduce free trade in grain and flour. These measures coincided with a bad harvest; and the result was panic-buying in the main cereal regions supplying Paris, followed by a series of corn-riots over an area of 3,000 square miles with Paris at its centre. For a fortnight the riots spread, propagated by hardship, anger and rumour, from village to village and market to market, until Turgot got the better of them by a combination of judicial repression, military force and synchronized homilies from the village pulpit. In England, rural disturbances might be directed against turnpikes, enclosures, work-houses, smuggling and militia Acts, or against Methodists' and Dissenters' chapels. But, most frequently, they broke out in years of bad harvests and rising prices: no fewer than 175 outbreaks out of 275 noted between 1735 and 1800 were of this kind; and, in the year 1766 alone, cases of popular price-fixing by riot were reported from twenty-four towns and districts.

Strikes and industrial disputes, too, became more frequent as wage-earners became more conscious of their particular economic interests. Parallel with the Wilkite movement in London in 1768-69, there were strikes of weavers, hatters, sailors, watermen, glass-grinders, sawyers, coopers, tailors and coal-heavers; and, over England as a whole, such disputes were noticeably increasing after 1780. In France, the Lyons silk-weavers were involved in strikes and bloody riots in 1744, 1779 and 1788; and, in Paris, there were strikes of bookbinders, building workers, carpenters, farriers, locksmiths, bakers, stonemasons, porters and hatters between 1776 and

1789. Yet, even so, for reasons noted in the last chapter, workers were, at this time, more often concerned with the price of food than with their money-wage and food riots were more frequent than industrial disputes. This was so even in cities and in Vienna, Rome and Naples they may have been the most familiar cause of popular disturbance. It was less frequently the case in Paris, where special measures were taken to feed the population; but, even here, there were half-a-dozen major outbreaks of the kind between 1709 and 1775. In London, food-rioting was the exception rather than the rule, and the targets of popular violence were more often "outsiders" like Roman Catholics, Jews, Scots, Irish and Dissenters, or press-gangs and unpopular politicians. Nevertheless, such riots often involved an element of deeper social protest; and the "Wilkes and Liberty" movement, by providing London's "lower orders" with a political slogan, marked a new stage in their political development.

But, whatever their nature, the protest movements of the common people were, generally, severely repressed by the authorities and frowned on, or actively condemned, by those of the "middling sort", even when they were themselves engaged in encounters with Crown or aristocracy.[4] In France, the bourgeois militias of country towns joined royal troops and *maréchaussée* in quelling peasant disturbances and food-riots. In London, the City's householders, in 1780, enrolled in the militia or formed "voluntary associations" to protect themselves against the Gordon rioters, once their activities took on the form of a wider social protest; and we saw that Dutch Patriots, like Genevan Burghers, were "too inattentive to the sense of the common people". We have noted a small exception in England in the 1760's and early seventies, when middle-class radicals joined with London's "lower orders" in

[4] It is also notable that, in the Habsburg dominion, Joseph II, in the last years of his reign, ordered troops and police to crush those very movements of peasants and urban workers that his earlier "enlightened" reforms had provoked and stimulated (E. Wangermann, *From Joseph II to the Jacobin Trials* (London 1959), p. 36).

promoting the cause of John Wilkes; but the experience was short-lived. The dilemma of many would-be middle-class reformers at this time was reflected in the anguished question of a correspondent of the *Gloucester Journal* in September 1769: " Are my apprehensions of Tyranny of Government equal to those I have from the Licentiousness of the People?" Twenty years later, the French Third Estate, faced with a similar problem, were prompted by circumstance, rather than by their reading of Rousseau, to turn to the people for support. And that is not the least of the reasons why it was the French alone who, in 1789 and in the years to come, carried through a " democratic revolution ".

Chapter III

THE CONFLICTS BETWEEN STATES

War was still the normal arbiter between European States once the niceties of diplomacy had been exhausted. It was usual, and considered proper, to precede hostilities by a formal declaration of war; yet this practice was sometimes dispensed with : England, for example, opened her hostilities against France in the Seven Years' War by seizing several hundreds of her vessels before making a declaration. While such irregularities were frowned on, there was little evidence as yet of any widespread body of opinion ready to condemn war as an instrument of national policy. Where denunciations of this kind were voiced, they were dismissed as Utopian by those who read them and aroused little sympathy among governments or peoples. The notion of a " social contract " between States and of an underlying " law of nations " that should govern relations between them had, however, begun to be discussed in a small circle of international jurists and advanced thinkers. Among the latter was the Abbé de Saint-Pierre, whose *Project for settling an Everlasting Peace in Europe* (1713) by means of an international federal authority was later recommended by Rousseau. There was also Richard Price, the English radical, who, in 1776, proposed the creation of a Senate, representing all the States of Europe and armed with powers to intervene in and settle their disputes. The Swiss jurist, Emmerich Vattel, while not subscribing to these visionary designs, condemned war as a scourge that was unjustifiable " on any other ground than that of avenging an injury received, or preserving ourselves from one with which we are threatened ". French Physiocrats and English economists, who were beginning to link peace with free trade, saw the problem in different terms. " Nothing is so evident," wrote

Sir James Steuart in 1767, "as that war is inconsistent with the prosperity of a modern state." Writers as varied as Pope, Hume and Herder ridiculed the military virtues and were contemptuous of conventional notions of heroism and honour.

But such views went largely unheeded. A few statesmen, it is true—among them Turgot and Vergennes in France and the younger Pitt in England—responded to their arguments; but for the absolute rulers of Prussia and Russia and the more "enlightened" Joseph II of Austria—all of whom were busy enlarging their territories—they had no message whatsoever. Philosophical sceptics were equally unimpressed. "The times," wrote Voltaire, "the occasion, custom, prescription and force . . . it is from these that the rights (of nations) derive"; and Guibert, prophet of the citizen-army of the future, thought that "to declaim against war . . . is to beat the air with vain sounds". Gentry and merchants, over-taxed or sated with earlier spoils, might momentarily protest against the mounting cost of a protracted war, but public opinion, in general, remained unmoved. Nor was this altogether surprising when war, in many countries, touched but a small part of the population and when the profits that it brought to some might easily appear to outweigh the hardships that it brought to others. Even Adam Smith, who condemned the wastefulness of war, argued in 1763 that "war is so far from being a disadvantage in a well-cultivated country that many get rich by it. When the Netherlands is the seat of war, all the peasants grow rich, for they pay no rent when the enemy is in the country, and provisions sell at a high rate." In France and England, peasants and townsmen rioted against press-gangs and Militia Acts—like those 5,000 Hexham colliers in the north of England who, in March 1761, lost 42 dead and 48 wounded in a bloody encounter with the militia. But, in England at least, there was little popular opposition to war as such. The opposite might even be the case: the jingoism of William Pitt, the great war-minister of the 1750's and sixties, was matched by that of his supporters of both the "middling" and "inferior" sort; and, in 1780, after five years of the disastrous American War, there were ample signs of popular hostility to Catholics, Frenchmen and Spaniards—the traditional national enemies—but there appeared to be little popular revulsion against the war itself. The same mood, however, might not prevail in countries like Prussia and Austria, where war imposed heavier burdens in terms of peasant-conscripts, taxes and rising prices. In Austria, for example, Joseph II's war against Turkey in 1788 was universally unpopular, while the conclusion of peace a year later was met with demonstrations of joy and relief.

While, then, the belief of rulers in the efficacy of war remained constant, the objects that they sought to achieve by its prosecution were slowly changing. In the first place, as befitted an age of toleration and "enlightenment", little remained of the "ideological" preoccupations of the previous centuries. For Cardinal Richelieu and even for Cromwell, the narrower considerations of religious orthodoxy had, when it came to war-time alliances, tended to be overshadowed by the more pressing motive of "reason of state". To the rulers of the eighteenth century they were things of the past and the State, or "national", interest, had taken over entirely. Exceptionally, such slogans as the defence of "the Protestant interest" might be invoked to justify England's alliance with Frederick of Prussia in 1756, but they served a merely propagandist aim and were not considered seriously as guides to conduct by kings, ministers or military leaders. "Holy alliances", or "concerts" of Europe were, in fact, to remain in cold storage until Europe's old rulers began, in the 1790's, to see their collective interests threatened by the progress of the revolution in France. On the other hand, as long as absolute monarchy remained the usual pattern of government, wars would continue to be fought over dynastic issues; and as long as feudal notions of land-tenure persisted, rulers would tend to see the extension of their territories in terms of a fresh acquisition of landed estates. In the eighteenth century, we see the survival of such concepts in the series of Wars of Succession—over the Spanish dominions, Poland, Silesia and

Bavaria; in the French monarchy's preoccupation with its Family Compact with the Spanish Bourbons; and in the lingering hostility of Bourbons and Habsburgs. In fact, it was France's long reluctance to abandon such aims that put her for so many years at a grave disadvantage in her struggle with Britain for colonial possessions.

Linked with this concept, but more universal and persistent, was that of the balance of power. In the seventeenth century, other states had sought to achieve the balance by forming successive coalitions to restrain the ambitions of the largest continental powers, Spain and France. England had fought against Louis XIV, as she had earlier against Philip II, to prevent the occupation of the Low Countries, facing her own south-eastern coastline, by a hostile great power. After France's defeat in 1713, no single state was powerful enough to dominate western Europe, and the pattern had become more flexible. In the first half of the century, the continental balance had generally been achieved by ranging France with Spain, Prussia and Bavaria on the one side against the Austrian Habsburgs, usually supported by Great Britain and the United Provinces, on the other; other states, in the East, in Italy and Germany, fitted in as the occasion might determine. But, during these years, the pattern had been rudely disturbed by the emergence of Russia as a great power dominating the East and the Baltic and, after 1740, by the meteoric rise of Prussia as a powerful counterweight to the Austrian Empire in the centre. Meanwhile, Sweden had ceased to be a power of military importance, Poland was virtually eclipsed, and the Ottoman Empire was being driven on to the defensive by the expansionist aims of Russia and Austria. The result was to shift the centre of the European balance away from the West, where it had remained so long, to bring to the fore such issues as Polish Partition and the " Eastern Question ", and to drive the western powers into new alignments.

The other important factor that altered the balance among European powers and provided new scope for international conflicts was the growth of trade and of colonial empires overseas. England had, in the War of the Spanish Succession, won the precious *asiento* from Spain, considerably extended her possessions in America and the West Indies, and emerged as the dominant colonial power. Her subsequent wars, fought against France and Spain in 1739-63, had tipped the balance further in her favour by conquests in India and North America. In these, England had had the advantage of naval ascendancy and the ability to concentrate her energies on overseas engagements, while subsidizing her European allies from a well-stocked Treasury. France enjoyed a more developed machinery for war and diplomacy, but she had continually been diverted from the colonial contest by her out-dated preoccupations with dynastic ambitions in Europe and the mirage of her Family Compact with the Spanish Bourbons. One result of Britain's colonial gains had been the re-appraisal of their value, not only in trade and treasure but in terms of foreign policy and the balance of power. Early in the century, Defoe had proclaimed that "to be Masters of the Marine Power is to be Masters of all the Power and all the Commerce in Europe"; and John Campbell, in *The Present State of Europe,* argued in 1750 that "the Interest and Commerce of the British Empire are so inseparably united that they may be very well considered as one and the same". In the scale of colonial values, it should be noted that contemporary opinion ascribed the place of first importance to the possession of the slave and sugar islands of the West Indies—and not without good reason, as the value of Britain's annual trade with her Caribbean possessions in 1783 amounted to no less than £4,250,000 (over half of this with Jamaica alone) compared with a little over £2 million with India and £882,000 with Canada and Newfoundland.

Nor is it surprising that this shift in the balance of colonial power should equally impress opinion in other countries, especially in those whose merchants and rulers had lost wealth and dominion through Britain's growing supremacy. And so, in the middle years of the century, we find a French pamphleteer arguing that "dominance of the sea would give a nation universal monarchy"; and the French minister Choiseul claiming that the English, "while pretending to protect the balance on land which no one threatens . . . are entirely destroying the balance at sea which no one defends". Such considerations played their part in bringing about a change in France's foreign policy: she began to abandon her dynastic ambitions (she even held herself aloof from the problems of Poland and Bavaria), "reversed" her traditional alliance against the Habsburgs, and kept her hands freer for settling her overseas account with England. In this, she had the advantage, too, that other European countries, whose merchant shipping had been searched at sea by the English for contraband, were easily persuaded that both the freedom of the seas and the balance of commerce were being endangered by Britain's highhanded methods and increasing domination. So Britain, from 1763 onwards, found herself virtually isolated in Europe, and France, Spain, the United Provinces and the "neutral" Northern Powers combined with the Americans, in the war of 1775-83, to strip her of her North American colonies.

Other factors that, in the course of the century, were influencing the nature, scope and conduct of wars were the developments in military technique and organization and the growth, in some countries, of a middle-class public opinion. There was a tendency for armies to become larger; but this was not universally the case, and there was certainly no inclination to build "national" armies or to resort to the kind of massive mobilization effected by the French at the time of the Revolution. The greatest increase took place in the rising great powers, Russia and Prussia: Russia's military strength rose from 132,000 men in 1731 to 458,000 in 1796 and Prussia's from 38,000 in 1714 to 80,000 in 1740; and Prussia's forces accounted, at one stage of the Seven Years' War, for 4.4 per cent of her population, which was a far higher proportion than was considered practicable elsewhere. France's armies were little larger than they had been during the wars of Louis XIV, and the Maréchal de Saxe, one of her greatest military theorists, held the view that, in battle, "multitudes serve only to perplex and to embarrass ". Another limiting factor was the persisting notion that the productive classes should be used only sparingly in warfare : foreign levies, deserters from other armies, or social misfits would serve the purpose better. In England, a considerable part of those recruited at home were vagrants and criminals, the latter faced with the choice of enlistment or transportation. France's great war-minister, the Count of Saint-Germain, believed that " as things are, the army must inevitably consist of the scum of the people and of all those for whom society has no use "; and even Frederick the Great had argued that " in wartime recruits should be levied in one's own country only when the bitterest necessity compels ". But limitation in numbers was, to some extent at least, compensated for by an improvement in military techniques and organization. Rulers were taking a more personal and informed interest in the equipment and direction of their armies : the military exploits of Frederick II have become legendary, and even George II of England and Hanover buckled on his sword to lead his troops into action at Dettingen in 1743. This growing concern of rulers was further reflected in the founding of schools and academies of military education : it was during this period that the Russians established their Noble Cadet Corps at St. Petersburg, the French their Royal Military School in Paris, and the English their academy for engineers at Woolwich. From such institutions flowed a spate of manuals on military problems, leading to an increase in the fire-power of armies and in the manœuvrability of weapons. The bayonet came into general use; shrapnel was first demonstrated, in 1787, at Gibraltar; and Gribeauval's radical reforms in France, which provided her armies with lighter and more mobile artillery, left a priceless legacy to the armies of the Revolution and Empire.

In absolute monarchies, the issues of war and peace, as all matters relating to the higher policies of State, were the sole province of the ruler, advised by a small circle of his intimates.

Discussions on such matters were carried on behind the closed doors of the royal closet, the cabinet or chancellery, and decisions were a tightly guarded secret. In France, under Louis XV, secrecy had reached almost ludicrous proportions: as government became more faction-ridden, the King had adopted the habit of private consultation with an inner cabal of advisers (the *secret du Roi*) to promote his own private dynastic policies, that were often at variance with those practised and proclaimed by his ambassadors and Secretaries of State. In England, George III was strongly suspected by the opposition of carrying on similar backstairs intrigues with a small group of "King's Friends"; but such a practice, whether contemplated or not, could hardly have stood up for long against the blast of parliamentary questions and debates. Yet Parliament had never claimed full control of the conduct of foreign affairs; and, in the debate on the Treaty of Aix-la-Chapelle in 1748, Henry Pelham had reminded the Commons that "the power of making peace and war is by our Constitution most wisely lodged solely in the Crown, because in both it is absolutely necessary to keep our designs secret, till the moment of their execution". Nevertheless, England differed from other countries in that Parliament, by debating and seeking information on foreign policy, in effect determined its outcome and direction; and no minister, however staunchly supported by the Crown, could long survive its active displeasure. Thus, Walpole had been forced into war with Spain against his wishes; Carteret had been driven from office owing to the failure of his anti-Bourbon policy; and, above all, Lord North, though promoting a policy in the American War that accorded with the wishes of the great majority in Parliament, was hustled out of office in 1782, when this policy proved to be an inglorious failure. In all this, what was new was not so much the assertion of Parliament's rights against the King as the growth of an informed middle-class public opinion outside Parliament itself, that compelled the House of Commons to take notice of its wishes. It was the pressure "without doors" of the rising class of " interloping " merchants of London and the great commercial cities, eager to settle accounts with France and Spain, that made Walpole change his policies before resigning office. By a reverse process, William Pitt was carried to office in 1757, not by the wish of George II or of the majority in Parliament but by the influence of the powerful merchant-interest outside. A similar body of opinion supported Pitt when he resigned office in 1761 and considerably embarrassed George III's government in its conduct of the peace preliminaries, believed to be too soft with France and Spain, that culminated in the Paris Treaty of 1763. In the concluding stages of the American War it was the peace-party rather than the war-party that received the support of this outside public, and it was with its blessing that the Rockingham-Shelburne Ministry took office, on the resignation of North, in 1782. Such pressure had become the more effective with the growth of an independent political press. By 1782, London's eighteen newspapers were devoting considerable space to " foreign intelligence "; and the *Annual Register*, for one, had, for years, been instructing its readers in the complexities of European politics. Other countries, too, had their newspapers; but wherever the conduct of foreign affairs was a closely guarded secret, they could not hope to be so well informed; and, wherever parliamentary institutions were lacking, middle-class opinion would have little opportunity of influencing the policies of governments. Exceptionally, in France, a powerful financier like Pâris-Duverney might, earlier in the century, persuade Cardinal Fleury, the King's minister, to heed his warnings against costly military adventures. But it was not until the American War that the veils of secrecy in diplomatic and military affairs began to be pierced by the insistent intervention of a wider reading and thinking public. One reason, no doubt, why the French government was willing to engage its forces in America was the popularity that the American cause had aroused among politically-minded Frenchmen; and there were similar echoes, as we have seen, in Germany and other countries. This factor was to be one of increasing importance in the years ahead.

The Versailles Treaty of September 1783, which ended the American War, proclaimed between "their Britannic and most Christian Majesties" of England and France "a Christian, universal, and perpetual peace". These noble sentiments were the easier to utter and even, to some extent, to translate into practice, owing to the exhaustion of both countries from their recent exertions. Thus, the initiative in European affairs tended, in the years between the American and French Revolutions, to be taken by the three eastern "despots" of Austria, Russia and Prussia. While the western powers were, in various ways, trying to pick up the pieces and to recuperate from mutually inflicted wounds, new opportunities for expansion lay open in the East.

Strangely enough, England's main problems did not arise from any continued animosity on the part of France or the United States of America, who had been mainly responsible for her defeat. France was approaching a state of national bankruptcy (of which more will be said in the next chapter) and made only half-hearted attempts to embroil herself in the wider affairs of Europe; and England, though losing her American colonies, was soon able to restore her trade with them on a new foundation; so that France, which had entered the war to gain India and the West Indies, proved to have gained little from it in practice. For England the main problems were to restore her financial position (she had spent £100 million on the war) and to end her 20-year-old isolation in Europe by re-forming old friendships, as with the Dutch, and entering into new alliances. Pitt, the Prime Minister, who had read Adam Smith and been convinced by many of the arguments of the new school of political economy, set about the work of peaceful reconstruction in vigorous style: he increased the annual revenue, reduced the national debt, kept public expenditure on a tight string, and even signed a highly advantageous "Free Trade" agreement (the

Eden-Vergennes Treaty of 1786) with the French: thus manufactures and commerce prospered. But Pitt's financial system could only work and bring further benefits to the business and trading community as long as the peace was kept and rumours of war remained in abeyance. His good fortune here was the enforced passivity of France and the increasing difficulties of Austria; and as long as he could restrict his active interventions to the West, while keeping a watchful eye in the East, he might weather the dangers and keep his powder dry.

Though Pitt's chances of finding an ally in Europe seemed at first to be slim, he was favoured by the restless activity and thwarted ambitions of the Austrian Emperor. Among Joseph's plans was that of exchanging his Belgian provinces for Bavaria. This roused against him the hostility of the German princes, who found a champion in Frederick of Prussia. The League of German Princes that ensued under Frederick's direction compelled Joseph to abandon Bavaria and prompted him to put into operation his alternative plan for the economic development of Belgium. With this end in view, he tried to force the Dutch to open the River Scheldt for free transit to Antwerp. Though England was alarmed by this challenge to her trading interest, she was still on bad terms with the Dutch; and it was the French who, when called upon for assistance, were able to persuade Joseph to give up his plan for the Scheldt and signed a treaty of alliance with the United Provinces (1785). This was a temporary set-back to England's diplomacy; but Joseph's mounting difficulties in Belgium, the financial problems of France and the internal conflicts within the United Provinces combined to promote her advantage. The French alliance had strengthened the Dutch urban patriciates and the rising Patriot groups in the provinces in their opposition to the pro-English party of the Stadholder, William V. The Stadholder was suspended from his offices by the estates of Holland; but the revolutionary agitation of the Patriots alarmed the patricians who, to defend their threatened privileges, turned to the House of Orange for protection. Prussia, too, was an interested party as the Princess of Orange, the Stadholder's wife, was the sister of the new Prussian King, Frederick William II. While Sir James Harris intrigued at The Hague in England's interest, the Prussians intervened actively with an army of 20,000 men after the Princess of Orange had been publicly humiliated by the Patriots of Utrecht. By October 1787, Amsterdam had been taken and the Stadholder was fully restored to his offices. France, being bankrupt and faced with an "aristocratic" rebellion, was unable to support her Patriot allies; and Joseph II had a revolution in Belgium on his hands. The outcome was a Triple Alliance between the English, the Prussians and the Dutch for common defence and the maintenance of the *status quo*. So, after twenty years of isolation, England had regained a foothold in Europe.

But the main focus of diplomatic interest, as of great power expansion, lay in the East. In 1772, the three eastern powers had, on Prussia's initiative, settled their prevailing differences by sharing among themselves one-third of the territories of Poland. In 1774, Russia had reached the Black Sea and gained the port of Azov. In 1780, Russia and Austria had opened negotiations for an alliance whose main object was to divide up the Ottoman dominions in Europe. Meanwhile, Sweden had her eyes on Finland and Carelia, Denmark on Swedish Göteborg and Prussia on Polish Thorn and Danzig. In 1783, Catherine annexed the Crimea and compelled Turkey, a year later, to recognize the fact. In 1787, hostilities broke out again in the Caucasus and the Crimea; and, as a Russian army under Potemkin laid siege to Oczakov, near Odessa, Joseph II, summoned to Catherine's aid, engaged the Turks along the Danube. The war looked like becoming another general conflagration when Sweden, taking advantage of Russian preoccupation in the south, opened an offensive against her in the north by marching into Finland, while Denmark joined the Russians and invaded Sweden. At this point, the Triple Alliance, being anxious to limit the scope of the conflict, intervened on Pitt's initiative and forced an armistice on Denmark. A year later, the Swedes, weakened by mutiny and defeated in Finland, made peace with Russia and accepted the *status quo*.

Austria's intervention, too, was short-lived. Joseph died in February 1790; and his brother, Leopold II, concerned to recover Belgium and to restore his authority in his disintegrating dominions, accepted the mediation of the Triple Alliance and, by the Treaty of Reichenbach with Prussia (October 1790), agreed to withdraw from the Turkish War. But the Russians had no such compelling reasons for responding to the wishes of the Anglo-Prussian alliance; so Catherine, having disposed of the Swedes in the north, concentrated her efforts more fully against the Turks. Potemkin had reduced Oczakov; now the fortress of Ismail on the Danube fell to Suvorov; and his armies occupied all the territory between the rivers Bug and Dniester. The Russian drive towards Constantinople and the Mediterranean had, by this time, thoroughly alarmed the English, who demanded that Catherine make peace with the Turks and restore her conquests. When Catherine refused to return Oczakov, which she valued as a Black Sea base, England was, for a month, on the brink of war with Russia (March 1791). But the Triple Alliance was already breaking up; and while England had nothing to fear from France, she feared that she could achieve no decisive result in the East without the support of Prussia. Poland proved to be the stumbling-block. In 1790-91, while Russia's attention was otherwise engaged, the Poles had carried out a minor revolution led by the more liberal of their nobles. One of their aims was to weaken the influence of Russia and to protect themselves against further Russian encroachments; so they turned to Prussia for help. The Prussians were willing to give it— but in return for Danzig and Thorn. The demand led, in turn and by stages, to renewed demands on Poland by Russia and Austria. Thus the Triple Alliance broke up and Prussia, Russia and Austria—though deeply divided over Germany, the Netherlands and Turkey—were able once more, by further partitions in 1792 and 1795, to compose their differences at the expense of the unhappy Poles.

But, meanwhile, a revolution of infinitely greater consequence was convulsing France. In its early stages, it could not but benefit from the entanglements of Europe's rulers and from the conflicts that they had to face at home and abroad. Yet, sooner or later, they were compelled to face the new problems that it posed and to concert their efforts to meet them. How they, and their peoples, responded to the challenge will be the subject of later chapters.

PART TWO

The French Revolution

Chapter IV

WHY WAS THERE A REVOLUTION IN FRANCE?

From the foregoing chapters it must be evident that there can be no simple answer to the question : why was there a full-scale revolution in France in 1789—and not elsewhere? How far the Americans had a social as well as a national and political revolution in 1776 will not be argued here; certainly in Belgium and in Poland there was something like a national revolution against the Austrians in the one case and against the Russians in the other; in the United Provinces, there was an attempted (though still-born) political revolution by the Patriot party; and, in Geneva in 1768, a *coup d'état* by the city's Burghers which, for a few years, redressed the balance of the constitution in their favour. But in none of these conflicts was there a decisive victory for any social group over another; none was " democratic ", in so far as none transferred, or was intended to transfer, the weight of political authority to the people at large; and none went on, by progressive stages, to effect a thorough transformation of existing society. This happened only in France; and while some of these countries, and some others besides, later followed in the wake of the revolutionary changes taking place in France, this is not the question we are concerned with at present.

Why, then, was there such a revolution in France? Historians, being adepts at reading history backwards, have answered the question in very different ways according to their own prejudices and to those of their contemporaries. It may perhaps be interesting to see how certain of the great chroniclers and historians of the past have viewed the problem before offering an explanation that may, possibly, appear to be valid and reasonable to-day.

The first person of note to comment on the matter was Edmund Burke who, though not a historian, was an observer of the Revolution and has greatly influenced the thinking of some people about it since. To Burke, the society described in our first chapter was by no means undesirable and, therefore, required no thorough transformation. Its political institutions, too, he considered, were susceptible of gradual improvement but, by and large, they had stood the test of time and should not be tampered with. As an Anglo-Irishman, he held English institutions to be superior to the French; but for France the existing absolute monarchy, aristocracy and higher clergy, though by no means perfect, were nearly as good as could reasonably be expected. The Revolution, therefore, could not in his opinion be the outcome of a genuine and widespread feeling for reform, but rather of the evil machinations of selfish and socially disruptive groups. He instanced, in particular, the clique of literary men and *philosophes*, who had long been sniping at the established Church, and the jumped-up moneyed interest, eager to settle accounts with the traditional aristocracy. In the wake of these sinister influences, he argued, followed the poor benighted "mob", or "swinish multitude", owning little or no property and incapable of political thinking or discernment. Thus the Revolution, having no roots in legitimate dissatisfaction, was the child of the "conspiracy" of a few. This "conspiracy" explanation was further elaborated by *émigrés* of the 1790's, like the Abbé Barruel; and has, with its later modifications, been popular ever since with all those to whom the Revolution has seemed a bad thing from start to finish.

Those who favoured the Revolution, however, have naturally tended to explain it in somewhat different terms: it could be explained either as a legitimate political protest against the tyrannies and restrictions of the Old Régime, or as a social protest of depressed or impoverished classes. The liberal historians of the French Restoration—men like Thiers and Mignet—saw it mainly in the former light. The motives that prompted them in their day to demand a more liberal constitution, or Charter, from Louis XVIII and Charles X were basically the same as those which, a generation earlier, had prompted the revolutionaries of 1789 to draft a Declaration of the Rights of Man and to demand a constitution from Louis XVI. Thus, the Revolution was seen essentially as a political movement promoted by the "respectable" classes of the nation for the redress of long-standing grievances and the reform of outmoded institutions. "When a reform becomes necessary," wrote Mignet, "and the moment to achieve it has arrived, nothing can stand in its way and everything serves its progress." Like Burke's conservative explanation, this liberal or Whiggish explanation of the Revolution has been modified and improved upon by later historians, but it carries influence even today.

Jules Michelet, the great historian of the 1840's, also sympathized with the revolutionaries of 1789; but, being a Republican and a democrat, he saw the Revolution as a far more drastic surgical operation than either Mignet or Thiers. In his pages it becomes a spontaneous and regenerative upsurge of the whole French nation against the despotism, grinding poverty and injustice of the Old Régime: something, in fact, like the spontaneous outbreak of popular hope and hatred portrayed by Dickens in the opening chapters of *A Tale of Two Cities*. And as it is the common people—the peasants and city poor—that have suffered most from the cruelty and injustice of kings and aristocrats, for Michelet "the people", far from being a merely passive instrument in the hands of other interested parties and social groups, is the real and living hero of the piece. This view of the Revolution as a spontaneous angry outburst of a whole people against poverty and oppression has, until recent times, probably been more influential than any other.

But none of these widely varying interpretations, as Alexis de Tocqueville recognized over a hundred years ago, really gives a satisfactory answer to the question why there was a revolution in France. Tocqueville, who wrote his own explanation, goes a part of the way with Burke. He writes, for example, that, in France, " irreligion . . . produced an enormous public evil "; and that " all the spirit of political opposition engendered by the vices of government, unable to find an opening in action, had taken refuge in literature, and that the writers had become the true leaders of the party which had as its aim to overthrow all the social and political institutions of the country ". So Tocqueville, like Burke and many others, acknowledges the importance of the writings of the Enlightenment in helping to undermine traditional beliefs and loyalties, thus leaving the whole system weakened and exposed; yet, unlike Burke, he does not see this as part of an organized conspiracy, but rather as the outcome of " the vices of government " and of widespread dissatisfaction with things as they were. In fact, he agrees with Mignet and Thiers that government was despotic, rotten and in need of reform : " for a long time past (he writes) the old edifice of government had begun to shake; it already tottered ". But, having said as much, he goes on to argue that the royal Council and officers of State, far from being impervious to the repeated demands for reform, were highly sensitive to them and that, under Louis XVI in particular, an " administrative revolution " was taking place, which extended the powers of the Council and the activities of the Intendants, integrated the Gallican Church more completely with the machinery of government, and was creating a whole new apparatus for the exercise of administrative justice. And not only that : France had the best roads in Europe; social welfare was being extended; torture was being abolished; the *lettres de cachet* were falling into disuse (there were 14,000 under Louis XVI compared with 150,000 under Louis XV); and the Bastille was being emptied of its prisoners. But Tocqueville added with a remarkable flash of insight : " The social order destroyed by a revolution is almost always better than that which immediately preceded it, and experience shows that the most dangerous moment for a bad government is generally that in which it sets about reform!" Thus, it was not so much the absence of reform as the nature and tardiness of it which, in opening the eyes of men to better things, served to precipitate a revolution rather than to avert it.

Tocqueville applies a similar argument in criticizing Michelet's notion of a spontaneous revolt of "misery". Was France, in fact, poor or becoming poorer? We saw in an earlier chapter that her trade, national income and the production of her industries and agriculture were rapidly expanding; that the middle classes were becoming more prosperous; that Paris was being rebuilt, largely by the enterprise of the up-and-coming bourgeoisie; and that Bordeaux—like Nantes and Le Havre—could, on the eve of the Revolution, rival and outmatch the wealth and trade of Liverpool. The peasants, too, far from grovelling in abject poverty, backwardness or unrelieved squalor, or being bound by servitude to their lord's domain, had (in most cases) won their freedom, were becoming literate and had already become proprietors of one-third of the land of France. Why, then, asks Tocqueville pointedly, was there a revolution in France, and not in Austria, Bohemia, Prussia, Poland or Russia, where the people—and the peasants, in particular—were far more impoverished and oppressed? It was precisely, he argued, because the middle classes were becoming richer and more conscious of their social importance and because the peasants were becoming free, literate and prosperous that the old feudal survivals and aristocratic privileges appeared all the more vexatious and intolerable. So he concludes, in a passage from which we have already quoted :

It is not always by going from bad to worse that a society falls into a revolution. It happens most often that a people, which has supported without complaint, as if they were not felt, the most oppressive laws, violently throws them off as soon as their weight is lightened. . . . Feudalism at the height of its power had not inspired French-

men with so much hatred as it did on the eve of its dis-
appearing. The slightest acts of arbitrary power under
Louis XVI seemed less easy to endure than all the despotism of Louis XIV.[1]

Tocqueville's comments are illuminating because they re-
mind us that revolutions—as opposed to peasant rebellions or
food riots—seldom, if ever, take the form of mere spontaneous
outbursts against tyranny, oppression or utter destitution : both
the experience and the hope of something better are important
factors in the story. This is, of course, why the unrest provoked in the Austrian dominions by the well-intentioned reforms of Joseph II were, in the long run, a far greater danger
to absolute monarchy than all the peasant outbreaks against
Catherine of Russia. But, nonetheless, recent research and our
own experience of later revolutions suggest that Tocqueville's
analysis, brilliant as it is, does not go far enough and does not
take account of all the factors that made for the revolution in
France. If Kings and ministers were of so reforming a
disposition, why did their reforms stop short—and *have* to
stop short—of giving a more general satisfaction? If the
middle classes were becoming gradually more prosperous and
more confident of their role in society, why should they sud-
denly feel the urge to resort to open rebellion against a
system which they had hitherto supported? If the peasants
were acquiring land and gradually freeing themselves of the
last vestige of personal servitude, why should they, in 1789,
revert to forms of rebellion that had not been seen in France
for the past eighty years? How did the ideas of the Enlightenment, propagated by the writers, journalists and fashionable
clientèle of the salons, begin to grip the minds of the poorer
townsmen, if not the peasantry? What were the actual circumstances out of which the Revolution arose, and how did a
revolt of disgruntled magistrates and aristocrats become transformed into a revolution of the " middling " and lower classes

[1] A. de Tocqueville, *L'Ancien Régime* (Eng. trans. Oxford, 1937),
p. 186.

of town and countryside? These are some of the further questions to which we must attempt to find an answer.

We saw, in an earlier chapter, that the system of government devised by Louis XIV had, under his successors, lost a great deal of its vigour and its ability to maintain the loyalty and respect of their subjects. This, as we saw, was due in part to the indolence and personal failings of Louis XV and, in part, to the tendency of the bureaucracy, staffed by privileged office-holders, to become almost a law unto itself. Meanwhile, as the middle classes became more prosperous and more self-important, they could hardly fail to become more resentful of the extravagance, inefficiencies and petty tyranny of a Court and government to whose upkeep they largely contributed but over which they had no control. Yet Louis XVI, on ascending the throne, was eager to bring about substantial reforms in the administration, to reduce the expenditure of the Court, to free trade of petty restrictions, to ease the tax-burdens on the peasantry and promote a measure of self-government, by means of local assemblies, in the provinces. Unlike his predecessor, he had a high sense of personal responsibility; besides, in Turgot, he had a minister who enjoyed the esteem and affection of both the "enlightened" and the industrious middle classes. Yet the whole scheme collapsed and Turgot was out of office after a couple of years. Why? Because Turgot's reforms, though welcome to the middle classes, ran counter to the vested interests of the *Parlements,* the higher clergy and aristocratic factions at Court. In this his experience was similar to that of Machault and Maupeou before him and of Calonne, Brienne and Necker after him; and it proved once more that no far-reaching measures of reform were possible, however well-meaning the King or honest and able his minister, so long as the privileged orders were left in possession of their powers, through the *Parlements* or their influence at Court, to obstruct their operation. These, then, were the limits beyond which reform could not go—sufficient to whet the appetite of some, to irritate others and to satisfy none.

Sufficient, too, to draw further hatred on the privileged orders and contempt on the monarchy that appeared to shield them.

Besides, if the middle classes were growing richer, their hopes of achieving their social ambitions were becoming more slender. The obstacles to the free exercise of trade and manufacture by onerous internal tolls, *péages* (private tolls on rivers, canals and bridges), and the inquisitions of government inspectors were long-standing grievances; but now a new grievance was being added, as during a period of " feudal reaction " the avenue to social and political advancement was becoming progressively closed. The merchant or financier, enriched by banking, manufacture or colonial trade, could no longer count, after (say) the 1750's, on crowning his career by the purchase for himself or his children of a hereditary office of State or a commission in the army. Such posts, as we have seen, were becoming the sole preserve of the aristocracy : the *Parlements* were closing their doors against middle-class intruders; and, with few exceptions, noble birth had, by 1789, become the sole essential qualification for holding high office in the army, Church or administration. It is perhaps the more remarkable that the French middle classes—if we except the writers, lawyers, pamphleteers and journalists among them—waited so long before fully venting their grievances. It was only when prodded into action by the *Parlements,* the higher clergy and nobility that, as we shall see, they began seriously to lay claim to social equality and a share in government.

Again, the picture of growing peasant prosperity painted by Tocqueville was by no means universal. While one in three of the French peasants owned their land outright, the larger part of these proprietors owned tiny parcels of land that, even in years of good harvest, were quite insufficient to feed their families : Arthur Young wrote that, in Champagne and Lorraine, he had, " more than once, seen division carried to such an excess that a single fruit tree, standing in about 10 perch of ground, has constituted a farm, and the local situation of a family decided by the possession ". There were, too, the even greater number of share-croppers and landless labourers, who purchased their bread in the market and who could never, under the most favourable of circumstances, hope to have more than the most meagre of shares in rural prosperity. The small proprietors, poor tenants and cottagers had the added griev-ance that improving landlords and wealthy peasants, stimu-lated by the urge to increase agricultural production, were enclosing fields and common lands, and encroaching on the villagers' traditional rights of gleaning and pasture. A more general grievance was one already noted in an earlier chapter : the recent tendency of landlords to rake up old rights attach-ing to their lands and to impose new or added obligations to those already exacted from their peasants. What Tocqueville had not noted, and only recent research has brought to light, is that it was precisely in these closing years of the Old Régime that the general prosperity of agriculture was grinding to a halt, and that a prolonged depression was beginning to take its place. This developed in two main stages. After 1778, the year France entered the American War, there was a reces-sion as the result of which prices fell—gradually in most in-dustrial and farm products, but reaching crisis proportions in wines and textiles. During these years, the net profits of small tenant farmers, peasant proprietors, wine-growers and other share-croppers tended, because of the heavy and sustained toll of tax, tithe and seigneurial exaction, to fall out of all propor-tion to the fall in prices, while large landed proprietors were cushioned against loss by means of their feudal revenues. Then, on top of this cyclical depression, came the sudden economic catastrophe of 1787-89, which took the form of bad harvests and shortage, with the price of wheat doubling within two years in the main productive regions of the north and reaching record levels in 27 of the 32 *généralités* in mid-summer 1789. The crisis hit the bulk of the peasantry both as producers and as consumers; as proprietors, tenants, share-croppers or labourers; as wine-growers, dairy-farmers or wheat-growers. From agriculture it spread to industry; and unemployment, already developing from the " Free Trade " treaty of 1786 with England, reached disastrous proportions in Paris and the textile centres of Lille, Lyons, Troyes, Sedan, Rouen and Rheims. Another result was that wage-earners and all small consumers, in both town and countryside, were compelled by the rapid rise in food-prices to increase their daily expenditure on bread from perhaps half to three-quarters, or even four-fifths, of their earnings.[2] Thus, peasants and urban craftsmen and workers were drawn together in common hostility to government, landlords, merchants and speculators; and these classes entered the Revolution in a context of increasing poverty and hardship rather than of "prosperity". In this sense at least, modern research has tended to justify Michelet rather than Tocqueville.

But, of course, it needed more than economic hardship, social discontent, and the frustration of political and social ambitions to make a revolution. To give cohesion to the discontents and aspirations of widely varying social classes there had to be some unifying body of ideas, a common vocabulary of hope and protest, something, in short, like a common "revolutionary psychology". In the revolutions of our day, this ideological preparation has been the concern of political parties; but there were no such parties in eighteenth-century France. In this case, the ground was prepared, in the first place, by the writers of the Enlightenment. It was they who, as Burke and Tocqueville both noted, weakened the ideological defences of the Old Régime. The ideas of Montesquieu, Voltaire and Rousseau, and those of many others, were, as we have seen, being widely disseminated and absorbed by an eager reading public, both aristocratic and middle class. It had become fashionable, even among the clergy, to be sceptical and "irreligious"; and the writings of Voltaire had combined with the struggles within the Church itself (Gallicans against Jesuits, Richerists and Jansenists against the increasing authority of the bishops) to expose the Church to indifference, con-

---

[2] C. E. Labrousse, *Esquisse du mouvement des prix et des revenus en France au XVIIIe siècle* (2 vols. 1933), ii, 637-41; *La Crise de l'économie française à la fin de l'ancien régime et au début de la Révolution* (1944), pp. ix-xli, 625.

tempt or hostility. In the 1750's, Parisians had demonstrated against their Archbishop's refusal to allow priests to administer the sacrament to dying Jansenists; and Hardy, the bookseller-diarist of the University quarter in Paris, reported similar expressions of anti-clericalism in his Journal in the 'eighties. Meanwhile, such terms as " citizen ", " nation ", " social contract ", " general will " and the " rights of man "—soon to be followed by *"tiers état"*—were entering into a common political vocabulary. As Tocqueville observed, it was often the pillars of the administration itself—ministers and Intendants —that first initiated a wider public in the use of these phrases; but it was neither they, nor the *philosophes* themselves, nor the fashionable society and men of letters of the salons, that brought them down to street-level and transformed abstract speculations into popular slogans and rallying-calls for political action. This was partly the work of the pamphleteers of the Third Estate in 1788 and 1789; but, long before that, the ground had been well and truly prepared by the tracts and remonstrances published by the *Parlements* who, in their prolonged duel, from the 1750's onwards, with ministerial " despotism ", quoted freely, and almost indiscriminately, from the writings of the *philosophes*. So we find the *Parlement* of Paris, in its grand remonstrance of 1753, asserting its right, as an " intermediate body ", to be the guardian of a " kind of contract " between the King and his people. The law, claimed the *Parlement* of Toulouse in 1763, must be subject to " the free consent of the nation ". In 1760, the *Parlement* of Rouen had insisted that " the right of acceptance (of laws) is the right of the nation "; and, in 1771, it repeated that the fundamental laws of the realm should be " the expression of the general will ". And, in 1788, the *Parlement* of Rennes quoted almost textually from Rousseau and the American Declaration of Independence in proclaiming: " That man is born free, that originally men are equal, these are truths that have no need of proof." What was new in all this was that the *Parlements* were not just writing political tracts, as the *philosophes* had done before them, but were deliberately setting out to influence public opinion and to marshal active public support in their struggles with the Crown.

But, when all this has been said, it is still doubtful if, (say) in January 1787, any intelligent Frenchman or foreign observer could have found good reason to predict that a revolution was close at hand, and still less to foretell the form that such a revolution would take. It is easy for us, with our superior knowledge after the event, to see that such reasons existed; yet, even so, there was still an important element lacking. It still needed a spark to bring about an explosion; and it needed a second spark to bring about the particular alignment of forces that ushered in the revolution of 1789.

The first spark was the government's declaration of bankruptcy following the American War. Opinions may vary as to the extent of the influence of the American Revolution and of its Declaration of Independence on the course of events in France; but there can be no two opinions about the cataclysmic results that flowed from France's participation in the war. In 1781, Necker, the Controller General, had, in a famous *compte rendu* of the nation's finances, assured the government's creditors that there was a favourable balance of 10 million livres; in 1786, three years after the war ended, his successor, Calonne, estimated a deficit of 112 million livres. The sum represented nearly a quarter of the total State revenue and called for drastic remedies. Calonne decided that it would be useless to resort to the old time-worn expedients : short-term loans already amounted to 400 million livres; the *taille* had been fixed at its present level in 1780 and was already high enough to provoke peasant discontent; and it seemed unwise to increase the taxes on consumers' goods at a time of recession and of falling industrial profits. The minister, therefore, proposed to the King that government expenditure should be cut (always a popular measure with all but those at Court); that the operation of the stamp duty should be extended; and that the *vingtième* (which many landowners evaded) should be replaced by a land tax on the annual production of the soil, to be paid in kind by all landowners and assessed and collected by local assemblies of owners representing all three estates. As a sop to large cultivators, it was further proposed to revive Turgot's former measures for free trade in grain, and to extend them to the export market.

The proposals had much to recommend them : if put into operation, they would have wiped out the deficit and assured the Treasury of a regular income. But, having learned wisdom from experience, the King and his minister knew that they would meet with resistance from the privileged orders : they were being asked to surrender a part of their fiscal immunities; the Church, in particular, valued its right to be taxed by means of the *don gratuit* (voluntary gift); and the provincial *Parlements* might resent any encroachment by the new local assemblies on their own jurisdiction. Besides, the business community—and, therefore, the Third Estate—might equally object to the stamp duty, whose main burden would fall on their shoulders. To forestall trouble it was, therefore, decided to submit the proposals not to the Paris *Parlement,* as was usual in such cases, but to a specially convened assembly of Notables—a mixed body of all the estates, which was composed of prelates, nobles, members of the *Parlements,* Intendants, councillors of State and members of provincial estates and urban corporations; and which had the advantage of being hand-picked by the King and of not having met for 160 years. Furthermore, it was convened in both haste and secrecy, and the objects of the meeting were not made public in advance.

The results were far less encouraging than was hoped. Calonne succeeded in estranging all parties. The die-hards, though in a minority, naturally resented the attacks on privilege; and the majority opposed the proposals on other grounds. The liberal aristocracy in particular (among them the Marquis de Lafayette), who played a large part in the proceedings, were not opposed to a more equitable distribution of taxes and made no objection, in principle, to the stamp duty, the land tax and the provincial assemblies; but they profoundly distrusted Calonne, whom they suspected of trying to buttress ministerial authority by means of the new assemblies and by manipulating a tax whose amount and means of assessment had not been sufficiently circumscribed. When Calonne tried to break the deadlock by an open appeal to public opinion, the King was appalled by such a breach of decorum, dismissed the minister and replaced him by Loménie de Brienne, Archbishop of Toulouse. Brienne was a *protégé* of the Queen and had the further advantage of popularity (he was known for his liberal, Physiocratic opinions) and of enjoying the confidence of the Notables and the clerical order. Yet, though he had been one of Calonne's sternest critics, circumstances compelled him to present a programme that differed only in detail from that of his predecessor: he modified the stamp duty and made the important concession of fixing an upper limit of 80 millions to the estimated yield of the land tax. The proposals were well received, but he failed to win the full authority for their enactment that he had hoped for. The Notables, possibly encouraged by the spate of pamphlet literature which their meeting had evoked, decided that such radical fiscal measures lay beyond their full competence and should be referred to the Paris *Parlement* for their approval—or, better still (the suggestion was Lafayette's), to the States General, which had not met since 1614. On 25 May, the Notables were dismissed and Brienne had to face the *Parlement*, after all.

It was, in fact, once more the judicial oligarchy of *parlementaires*, and not the Notables or the older aristocracy, that raised the banner of rebellion and provoked what has been called the " aristocratic revolt ". Not that the *Parlement* at this time represented a solid body of reaction. Its main court —the *cour des pairs*—consisted of 144 members, including 7 Princes of the Blood, 7 ecclesiastical peers and 27 lay noblemen; the rest were the rank-and-file *conseillers* of the *Enquêtes* and *Requêtes*, mainly young men: of 72 whose ages have been recorded, 59 were under thirty-five years of age.[8] They were divided between those who sought every favourable

[8] J. Egret, *La Pré-Révolution française* (Paris, 1962), p. 154. I have drawn substantially on M. Egret's new account of the " aristocratic revolt ".

opportunity of asserting the privileges (ancient or usurped) of the *Parlement* and other "intermediate bodies" against the increasing claims of government and a smaller group, who, inspired by the *philosophes* and the American Revolution, were eager for far-reaching constitutional reform. The spokesman of the former, in the debates that followed, was Duval d'Eprémesnil; and of the latter Adrien Duport, supported, on occasion, by Lafayette's friend, the Duke of La Rochefoucauld among the peers, and the King's cousin, the Duke of Orleans, among the Princes of the Blood; all three were to play a prominent part in the Revolution of 1789. Though divided as to their ultimate aims, the two groups were drawn together by the circumstances of the moment: they were both suspicious of ministerial "despotism" and both hoped to realize their various purposes by means of the States General. So when Brienne turned to the *Parlement* to register his decrees, it raised no objection to the liberation of the grain trade and welcomed the new provincial assemblies; but it rejected the stamp duty and land tax and insisted that the States General be summoned to deal with the financial crisis. Brienne was equally obdurate: he had other reforms in mind—a reform of local government, the restoration of the provincial estates, judicial and army reform, and civil rights for Protestants—and he feared (with some justice) that the States General, if convened, would either serve as a diversion or submerge his own moderate measures in others of a far more radical intent. So the King's authority was invoked to call a *lit de justice,* which overrode the *Parlement's* objections, promulgated the fiscal decrees and exiled the Paris magistrates to the northern town of Troyes.

But it was the *Parlement* that won the day. The provincial courts, to whom Brienne now turned, were far more consistent than the Parisians as champions of aristocratic privilege and local immunities; they rejected almost every one of the minister's proposals and rallied to the support of their Paris colleagues; and Brienne had no option but to yield. The *Parlement* was reinstated in September, the decrees on the stamp duty and land tax were withdrawn, and if was agreed by all concerned that the existing *vingtième* (though expected to yield a substantially lower revenue) should be prolonged until 1792. The magistrates' return from exile was acclaimed by noisy and enthusiastic demonstrations in the City of Paris, anti-royalist tracts began to circulate, and Arthur Young reported the opinion that France was "on the verge of some great revolution in the government".

The "revolution" that Young predicted was, however, not so much one of the middle classes and the people as one that would be likely (as he put it) to "add to the scale" of the nobility and clergy. And such a view seemed amply justified by the events of 1788. In the previous October, the Paris *Parlement* had agreed to register further loans in return for the government's promise that the States General should meet in 1792. But negotiations broke down again in November, and the Duke of Orleans, by now a popular figure, and two other magistrates, who had been particularly outspoken in the debates, were exiled. This prompted the *Parlement*, in May, to court further popularity by issuing a declaration condemning the whole system of arbitrary government, including the obnoxious *lettres de cachet*. Brienne replied by ringing the law courts with troops and forced the *Parlement* to surrender two of its leaders (d'Eprémesnil was one) to royal justice. Meanwhile, the Keeper of the Seals, Lamoignon, issued six edicts, which suspended all the *Parlements*, vested the greater part of their appellate jurisdiction in forty-seven new tribunals, and transferred their powers of registering royal edicts to a "Plenary" Court. Thus it was intended not only to punish the *Parlements* for their disobedience, but to drive a wedge between them and the rest of the "political nation"— particularly the liberal aristocracy and the host of middle-class *avocats* and lawyers, to whom the new measures would open new avenues of preferment.

But the plan miscarried and, far from dividing its critics, stirred up something like a nation-wide rebellion against the government. The clergy, when invited to vote an extraordinary *don gratuit*, re-asserted their own immunity from taxation and protested against the suspension of the *Parlements*. The dukes and peers of the realm added their protesting voices to those of the clergy; and the general order of the nobility, though long resentful of the social pretensions of the *noblesse de robe*, found the moment opportune for declaring their support. In Paris and the provinces, both middle classes and " lower orders ", fired by the militant declarations of the *Parlements*, joined in the common hue and cry against the " despotism " of ministers. The " patriots ", as champions of " the nation " against both privilege and " despotism ", had been inclined, like Mirabeau and Lafayette (but unlike Duport and Barnave), to pin their hopes on ministerial reform; but now, seeing Lamoignon's *coup d'état* as a veiled threat to the coveted States General, they tended to line up behind the *Parlements* instead. Besides, many of the Third Estate had been disappointed by the half-heartedness or alienated by the illiberalism of ministerial reforms; and of 500 protesting pamphlets published in the four months following the edicts of May 1788, one half were the work of " patriot " scribes. Meanwhile, riots broke out at Bordeaux, Dijon, Grenoble, Pau, Rennes and Toulouse—all cities with a tradition of provincial separatism and aristocratic self-rule. In Dauphiné, where Barnave and Mounier were active, *noblesse* and Third Estate co-operated in reviving the long-moribund estates of the province; in Brittany, the estates united in common protest against ministerial " despotism ". At Grenoble, massive riots, launched by the lawyers' clerks and supported by the townsfolk and visiting peasantry, prevented the suspended magistrates from leaving the city for five days. At Rouen, where the nobility exploited the people's anger over the high prices resulting from the restoration of free trade in grain, the Intendant and military commander were attacked in the streets and besieged in their houses. In both cities, the army proved unreliable : egged on by young officers of the provincial *noblesse* and irritated by Brienne's new disciplinary regulations, it refused to fire and fraternized with the riotous townsmen.

Overwhelmed by this national movement of protest, the government was compelled to surrender. The States General were promised for May 1789; Brienne was replaced by Necker; Lamoignon's judicial reforms—and, for that matter, all other projected reforms—were withdrawn; and the *Parlements* were recalled soon after. The result was hailed as a triumphant victory for the people at large—not least by the Paris tradesmen, journeymen and apprentices of both City and *faubourgs,* who had found an additional cause for demonstration in the sudden upward movement in the price of bread. The " aristocratic revolt " (for such it was in essence) had triumphed all along the line: with the support of the non-privileged classes, it had forced the government to withdraw its taxation proposals and to reinstate the *Parlements*; the States General would meet in May; and the States General, it was confidently believed, would solve all the nation's problems. But many believed (and some hoped and others feared) that, by striking further blows at the " despotism " of ministers, it would proportionately increase the authority, status and advantage of the privileged orders.

Yet these calculations proved to be ill-founded, and the revolution that emerged from the convening of the States General turned out to be of a very different kind from that envisaged by many of the pamphleteers of 1788 and Arthur Young's informants of October 1787. Chateaubriand later wrote that " the patricians began the revolution and the plebeians completed it "; and Robespierre said something similar. In a sense it was true, and many historians have accepted the verdict. But the revolt of the nobility was, perhaps, a curtain-raiser rather than a revolution, for it was the prelude of a revolution which, by associating the middle and lower classes in common action against King and aristocracy, was unique in contemporary Europe. This was by no means what liberal aristocrats or middle-class " patriots ", or anyone else, had intended or foreseen. Why and how it came about, nonetheless, will be told in the next chapter.

Chapter V

1789

In January 1789, four months after the triumphant return of the *Parlement* to Paris, Mallet du Pan, a shrewd Swiss observer, noted that the position in France had radically changed. The question at issue, he wrote, was no longer a constitutional contest between the King and the privileged classes but " a war between the Third Estate and the two other orders ". Not only that; but a nation-wide movement against the royal government, led by the aristocracy and clergy, was becoming transformed into one that lined up the monarchy and people against the very forces that had unleashed the " aristocratic revolt ".

How had this change come about? Partly it was due to the deepening economic crisis, in the course of which the peasant was likely to see the landlord as a greater menace than the King or his ministers at Versailles. Partly it was due to the newly-found confidence of the middle classes, whose scribes and pamphleteers were already proclaiming their readiness to lead and represent the nation: already in August 1788, Mirabeau, himself a nobleman, had declared war on " privilege " as the mortal enemy of the " nation ". Again, Brienne's defeat and the collapse of his reform-programme had brought " patriots " ranged on opposing sides during the " aristocratic revolt " together: now the only hope for reform lay in strengthening the hand of the Third Estate within the coming States General. And perhaps even more important was the sudden realization that the *Parlements* and *privilégiés*, the professed champions of the nation's " liberties ",[1] far from

[1] Nor was this mere hypocrisy or double-talk: in aristocratic parlance, as for Burke in England, " liberties " and " privileges " were often virtually synonymous terms.

envisaging radical reforms, were at all costs eager to cling to
their old privileges and immunities. Once the States General
had been definitely promised, the great question was: how
should they be constituted—as in the distant past (in Richelieu's day), when the Third Estate had been willing to play
second fiddle to the other two orders; or should some new
formula be found that would take account of the increased
importance of the middle classes within the nation? According to the formula of 1614, the three orders should be composed of an equal number of deputies and should deliberate in
their three separate assemblies; thus ensuring that the Third
Estate would be in a permanent minority in its relations with
the other orders. But the Third Estate of 1789 was not willing
to accept this humble role any more; and once the date of the
States General's meeting had been declared, its spokesmen
began to insist that it should have double representation and
that the orders should meet in a single deliberative assembly:
thus the Third Estate would at all times be assured of a
majority. After all, it was argued, the representatives of
France's 24 million commoners should have voting equality,
at least, with the mere 200,000 of the privileged minority. The
Abbé Sieyes, whose pamphlet *What is the Third Estate?*
appeared at the end of January, went further and claimed that
the Third Estate was the nation itself and that, therefore, the
wishes of the 200,000 could be conveniently ignored altogether. But this was not yet the general view.

The privileged orders had a very different conception of
how the States General should be constituted and of the role
that the Third Estate should play within it: why else, in fact,
should they have taken the initiative in demanding that the
estates be summoned to meet? Already at the end of September, 1788, when its popularity was at its height, the Paris
Parlement had insisted that the precedent of 1614 should be
followed to the letter: that the three estates be equally represented and that voting be by separate assemblies. A month
later, a second assembly of Notables, less liberal than the first,

when convened to express its opinion on the matter, gave a similar reply; and, in December, the Princes of the Blood denounced the pretensions of the commons as a danger to the safety of the State. Yet the privileged orders were no longer firmly united : leading *parlementaires* like Adrien Duport and Hérault de Séchelles, and the Duke of Orleans among the Princes, supported the claims of the Third Estate; and the *Parlement* of Paris had, in a recent decree carried by the votes of its younger members, incensed the older landed *noblesse* by resolving that its feudal rights be ended; and—most bitter blow of all—advised by Necker, the royal Council, on 27 December, while suspending judgment on the question of voting procedure, decided to allow double representation to the Third Estate. So, for a while, the monarchy, outraged by the disloyalty of the privileged orders, once more assumed the guise of the champion of reform; while the aristocracy and *Parlements,* so recently the acclaimed custodians of the nation's "liberties" against ministerial oppression, appeared as its bitterest enemy. From this simple realization was born the "great hope" that the nation might be regenerated through the convening of the estates; and, with this "hope", the fear that it might be shattered by the evil machinations of an "aristocratic plot".[2]

Meanwhile, the preparations for the States General's meeting went ahead. On 24 January, regulations were issued governing the election of deputies; and, as an earnest of the government's concern for reform, the people were invited to prepare their own *cahiers de doléances*, or lists of grievances, to guide the estates in their deliberations. In general, electoral districts were formed from the ancient sub-divisions used for administering justice, the *bailliages* and *sénéchaussées*; but Paris was treated as a separate electoral division and the

[2] There were, however, at Rennes (Brittany), as late as 26-27 January 1789, bloody riots in which local domestic servants and chairmen, supported by the provincial *noblesse,* were engaged against the law students and lawyers' clerks of the Third Estate.

revived estates of Dauphiné were accorded the right to appoint their own deputies. Deputies were to be elected in separate orders. The privileged orders enjoyed direct male adult suffrage; all lay nobles, aged twenty-five and above, had the vote in their electoral assemblies, either in person or by proxy; the same right was enjoyed by bishops and parish clergy, whereas canons and monks were only entitled to send representatives. Deputies of the Third Estate, on the other hand, were chosen by a rather more restricted franchise and by a more complicated system of indirect election. Except in Paris, where the suffrage was limited to those paying six livres per annum in *capitation*, Frenchmen of twenty-five years of age and over, whose names were inscribed in the taxation rolls (for however small an amount), were eligible to vote in their primary assembly—either in that of their parish or of their urban guild. In brief, all male adult commoners had the vote with the exception of domestic servants, non-householders (*non-domiciliés*), sons living in their father's house, the poorest labourers and downright paupers. But the finally elected representatives of their estate only emerged after two, three or four stages of the electoral process, depending on whether the constituency was urban or rural and whether a principal or secondary *bailliage* (or *sénéchaussée*).

Whatever had been the government's intention, the system most definitely favoured the urban and professional bourgeoisie, who dominated discussions and voting in the assemblies of the Third Estate, took full advantage of their practical monopoly of literacy and vocal expression, and enjoyed the means and leisure to concert common action among "patriots", to print circulars and pamphlets, and to conduct electoral campaigns denied to the rural craftsmen and peasantry, let alone to the labourers and village poor. It is, therefore, no accident that the urban bourgeoisie captured the great bulk of the seats among the deputies of the Third Estate: of the 610 that went to represent their order at Versailles, some 25 per cent were lawyers, 5 per cent were other professional men, 13 per cent were industrialists, merchants and bankers; at most 7 to 9

per cent were agriculturists—and, even of these, only a handful were peasants.[8]

And, even before the campaign had started, a "patriot"
party had been emerging among the promoters of constitutional reform. Though mainly voicing the hopes of the Third
Estate, it included such wealthy aristocrats as the Marquis de
Lafayette, the Duke of La Rochefoucauld, and the Marquis de
Condorcet, and noted *parlementaires* such as Adrien Duport,
Hérault de Séchelles and Lepeletier de Saint-Fargeau : some
had taken part in the "aristocratic revolt" and all were to play
a prominent part in the Revolution. Some belonged to
Masonic lodges; others to the famous *Comité des Trente,*
which met at Duport's house and was composed of lawyers,
liberal aristocrats and clerics (Talleyrand and Sieyes were of
their number); others, again, such as Sieyes and Mirabeau,
acted as a link between the *Comité des Trente* and the Duke
of Orleans, who conducted his own separate campaign. Such
facts have led some historians to lay too much stress on the
existence of a central direction of all revolutionary agitation
and to exaggerate the part played by Freemasons and "the
Thirty", whose operations have been seen as evidence of a
concerted "conspiracy" to undermine the institutions of the
Old Régime. Yet it must be remembered that the Masonic
lodges recruited men of every shade of opinion; and com-
munications were as yet not sufficiently developed to allow of a
highly organized direction by comparatively unknown men.
Even so, it is certainly true that leaders were now beginning
to emerge from among both bourgeois and liberal aristocrats,
who were able to give some guidance to the nation-wide discussions and impress their personalities and ideas on the
spontaneous actions of many thousands that broadly shared
their views, or were willing to adopt them, in every part of
the country.

The electors, meanwhile, had been drafting their *cahiers de
doléances.* They were of two main kinds : those drafted in the
preliminary assemblies of the parishes and guilds for sub-

[8] A. Cobban. *A History of Modern France,* vol. I (1957), p. 140.

mission to the assemblies of the *bailliage*; and those drawn up in the *bailliage* for direct submission to the States General. Of the latter kind most have survived and are fairly evenly divided between the three orders. As might be expected, the *cahiers* of the clergy and nobility generally stress their attachment to their traditional privileges and immunities, though they frequently concede the principle of fiscal equality. At the same time, they join with those of the Third Estate in demanding the removal of many of the more oppressive and wasteful practices of the absolute monarchy. They roundly condemn fiscal abuse and extravagance, the arbitrary acts of ministers, the system of *lettres de cachet,* the anomalies and vexations of the internal customs and the prevailing chaotic system of weights and measures. More positively, they demand freedom of the press and of the individual (though not that of conscience) and a constitution that, while upholding the traditional power and authority of the monarch, will invest a periodically convened States General with the right to frame laws and vote taxes, whose assessment and collection will be entrusted to elective provincial and municipal assemblies. In brief, on matters affecting political and administrative reform, there was a considerable measure of agreement among the three estates.

But the general *cahiers* of the Third Estate, drawn up in nearly every case by the bourgeoisie, go much further. They not only demand liberty of speech, writing and assembly, freedom of trade and freedom from arbitrary arrest; but they generally insist on the complete civil equality of all three estates—that is, that the clergy and nobility must surrender not only utterly discredited relics like serfdom, but they must give up such age-old privileges as tithe, *banalités* (local monopolies), *champart* (feudal rent in kind), hunting rights and seigneurial jurisdiction. So much the bourgeoisie had learnt, if not from their own experience, at least from a study of peasant grievances; but the most urgent peasant demand of all— for land—is seldom, if ever, voiced in these *cahiers*.

Of the local *cahiers* drafted in parishes and guilds a far

smaller portion has survived. Some are set pieces based on circulated models and, therefore, tell us little of the real intentions of their reputed authors; others (and there are several among the parish *cahiers*) are genuine enough and illustrate two truths: the one, that the villagers taking part in the debates supported bourgeois criticisms of the absolute monarchy and of the feudal survivals in land-tenure and justice; and the other, that they had often social claims of their own that, in other respects, divided them sharply from the capitalists and large proprietors within the Third Estate. The voice of the urban wage-earners, however, is rarely heard. In Paris, none but the wealthiest merchant-guilds were invited to air their grievances; elsewhere, the *compagnons*, or journeymen, were generally excluded from the assemblies of the master craftsmen. There were exceptions, as at Rheims, Troyes, Marseilles and Lyons, where the workers protested against the rise in prices, but otherwise accepted the lead given by their employers. The peasant *cahiers* tended to be more outspoken. In addition to the general grievances of the whole rural community, we occasionally hear the particular complaints of the small proprietor, share-cropper or labourer. In the Rouen district, where the price of the 4-lb. loaf had risen to 16 sous, villagers demand that it be reduced to a half. In Brittany, small peasants around Rennes complain that such are the burdens of taxation and seigneurial exaction that a strip of land with a gross yield of 40 livres per annum scarcely brings its owner, once the demands of tax-collector and landlord have been met, a net income of a quarter of that amount. In the parish of Pierreville (Cotentin), the *laboureurs* (peasant proprietors) are so forthright in their condemnation of royal officials and of tithe and hunting rights that the *bailli* refuses to accept their grievances and dictates a *cahier* of his own! In Lorraine and Hainault, landless peasants and small *laboureurs* join forces in opposing enclosure edicts and land clearance schemes promoted by the more prosperous members of their community. In the Vosges, on the other hand, a parish *cahier* protests that the allocation of

land to landless labourers, following the division of the
commons, has disturbed the harmonious relations existing
hitherto between labourers and proprietors! In short, the
parish *cahiers* reflect both the common bonds of interest linking all members of the peasant community in opposition to
royal tax-gatherer, tithe-owner and landlord, and those further
divisions separating small consumer from large producer and
landless labourer from tenant farmer or proprietor. The
revolution in the village was to be compounded of all these
elements.

The States General met at Versailles on 5 May 1789 against
a background of mounting crisis and popular unrest: in Paris,
the price of bread was at nearly twice its normal level; there
had been bloody riots in the Faubourg St. Antoine and, in the
provinces, peasants were already beginning to pass from words
to deeds by stopping food-convoys, raiding markets and destroying game-reserves. As the great assembly opened, nothing
was done to spare the commons' susceptibilities or to realize
their high hopes of early reform. They were ordered to wear
the traditional black, to enter the meeting hall by a side door
and, in every way, made mindful of their inferiority of status.
The royal Council, though it had agreed to grant the commons double representation, was unwilling to concede their
further demand to deliberate in common. Necker was sympathetic but, being strongly opposed within the Council by
Barentin, the Keeper of the Seals, felt unable to give a lead.
He merely advised the Third Estate to show forbearance,
while asking the privileged orders voluntarily to renounce
their fiscal immunities. Meanwhile, the estates were invited
to meet in separate assemblies and to recommend which subjects should be discussed and voted in common. The King
had no settled policy and was pulled from one side to the
other. But to the commons it seemed that he had decided to
throw in his lot with the clergy and nobility; for double representation would be a hollow victory without the union of
the orders: without the support of like-minded deputies of
the other estates, they could always be outvoted by the com-

bined strength of their opponents. So they refused to deliberate as a separate assembly, and they demanded a joint
session to consider the validity of mandates—as a first step to
holding common sessions on more fundamental questions.
The nobles and bishops naturally saw the danger and resisted
the suggestion, though the bishops had difficulty in dissuading
the parish priests (who outnumbered them by five to one)
from joining their fellow-commoners. So, behind the
five-week procedural wrangle that ensued, lay a struggle over
a basic principle.

On 10 June, the Third Estate, encouraged by the growing
support from " without doors ", decided to take the bit between
its teeth. It invited the other orders to a common verification
of powers : if they refused to attend, it would proceed without
them. Joined by a few parish priests, it completed a check of
election returns, elected two secretaries and a president (Jean-
Sylvain Bailly), and, on 17 June, by a majority of 491 to 89
votes, arrogated to itself the title of National Assembly. This
first revolutionary act of the commons was followed by the
issue of two decrees, of which one provided that a dissolution
of the new Assembly, for whatever cause, would invalidate all
existing taxes; and the other that, as soon as a constitution had
been determined, the public debt should be consolidated and
underwritten by the nation as a whole. On 20 June, a
further challenge was thrown down when the Assembly found
itself—accidentally, it seems—locked out of its usual meeting
hall : following President Bailly into an adjoining tennis
court, every deputy except one took a solemn oath that the
National Assembly should not disperse until the constitution
had been firmly established. By this time the clergy had, by a
narrow majority, decided to throw in its lot with the new
Assembly, and 150 clerical deputies, headed by two arch-
bishops, joined it a few days later.

Even before this last act of defiance, Necker had urged the
King to assert his authority, break the deadlock between the
orders and take the initiative in legislative form. To this end,
he suggested that a royal session (*séance royale*) be held, where

it should be announced that such matters as the future constitution of the States General should be discussed in common assembly, whereas matters affecting the vested interests of individual estates should continue to be separately considered. After bitter arguments within the Council, a first decision was taken on 19 June to hold a *séance royale* on the 22nd—presumably on the basis of Necker's proposals. But, meanwhile, the King, indecisive as ever, had been prevailed upon by other counsels. Surrounded at Marly (where the Court had retired on the death of the young Dauphin in early June) by a group of courtiers, led by his younger brother, the Comte d'Artois, whose arguments were supported by the Queen and leaders of the privileged orders, he was persuaded to agree to quash the self-styled Assembly's decree of 17 June, to refer discussion on the future organization of the States General to each of the separate orders, and to overawe the Third Estate by a display of force. The session was deferred until 23 June; Necker, whose removal had been secretly decided upon, decided to stay away. Once more, nothing was done to spare the feelings of the Third Estate: they were kept waiting in the rain while the privileged orders took their seats; the hall was ringed with troops; and the proceedings had all the arbitrary atmosphere of a *lit de justice*. The main business was devoted to the reading of two royal declarations by Barentin. The first pronounced the National Assembly's resolutions null and void and, while recommending the acceptance of the principle of common sessions for matters of common concern, expressly reserved for separate deliberation all questions relating to the special privileges and immunities of the first two estates. The second declaration outlined the Council's legislative programme. It provided, broadly, for a reform of the instifutions of the Old Régime along lines already advocated by all three estates in their respective *cahiers*; but the social fabric of the old order was to remain intact: it was categorically stated that tithes and feudal and manorial dues were to be treated as proprietary rights and that no surrender of fiscal privilege would be called for without the consent of the parties concerned.

Finally, the estates were ordered to disperse and to resume discussion in their separate chambers on the morrow.

Yet the plans of the Court party miscarried. Thousands of Parisians invaded the courtyard of the *château* to demand that Necker be retained in office; soldiers under the command of the Prince de Conti refused to obey the order to fire; the deputies of the Third Estate, having declined to disperse after the termination of the *séance,* were rallied by Mirabeau in an historic speech. The King was compelled to yield. Necker remained in office and not only was the National Assembly (whose numbers had now risen to 830 deputies) left in possession of its chamber; but, on 27 June, the remnants of the other orders were expressly ordered to merge with it.

Up to now the revolutionary temper developing in Paris had been without effective leadership. With the latest news from Versailles, however, the professional and commercial classes, who had been prepared to await events and had viewed the simmerings in the *faubourgs* and markets without sympathy, began to give a direction to affairs without which the July revolution could hardly have taken place. From this date the pamphleteers and journalists in the entourage of the Duke of Orleans (who had joined the new National Assembly at Versailles) began to establish a permanent headquarters at the Palais Royal; here thousands congregated nightly and acquired the slogans and directives—and, possibly, too, the funds—of what the diarist Hardy called " the extreme revolutionary party ". Also at this time, the 407 electors of the Paris Third Estate, whose original task it had been to appoint the Parisian deputies to the Third Estate at Versailles, began to meet regularly at the City Hall in the heart of the capital. These two bodies were to play distinct, yet complementary, parts in the events of July. In the earlier days, however, it was the Palais Royal alone that gave a positive direction to the popular movement. Whereas the City Hall contented itself with drafting paper schemes for a citizens' militia, the Palais Royal took steps, by public agitation and liberal expenditure, to win over the troops—above all, the Gardes Françaises—

from their loyalty to the Court. Tracts supporting the stand of the Third Estate were distributed among the Paris garrisons; and, by the end of June, the Guards, who had loyally shot down rioters two months before in the Faubourg Saint-Antoine, were parading the streets of Paris to shouts of "Long live the Third Estate! We are the soldiers of the nation!" On 10 July, eighty artillerymen, who had broken out of their barracks in the Hôtel des Invalides, were publicly fêted in the Palais Royal and the Champs Elysées.

Responding to these developments, the Court, which had been steadily summoning loyal Swiss and German regiments to Versailles, attempted a further show-down. On 11 July, Necker was sent into exile and replaced by a nominee of the Queen, the Baron de Breteuil. This proved to be the spark that touched off the insurrection in Paris. The news reached the capital at noon on the 12th. During the afternoon Parisians flocked to the Palais Royal, where orators—the young Camille Desmoulins among them—gave the call to arms. Groups of marchers quickly formed; the busts of Necker and the Duke of Orleans, the heroes of the hour, were paraded on the boulevards; theatres were compelled to close as a sign of mourning; in the Place Louis XV (the Place de la Concorde of today), demonstrators clashed with cavalry commanded by the Prince de Lambesc, who had been ordered to clear the Tuileries gardens. Besenval, commander of the Paris garrison, withdrew to the Champ de Mars. The capital was in the hands of the people.

As the tocsin sounded—soon to become a familiar summons to Parisians—bands of insurgents joined those who, two days earlier, had begun to burn down the hated *barrières* (customs posts), whose exactions were bitterly resented by shopkeepers, wine-merchants and small consumers, and which had already been the scene of frequent disturbance and attempted smuggling. Forty of the fifty-four customs posts were systematically demolished in the course of four days' rioting; documents, registers and receipts were burned, iron railings were pulled down, offices and furniture were fired and customs officers expelled from their lodgings. The Palais Royal appears to have had a hand in the affair: it is perhaps significant that two posts said to belong to the Duke of Orleans were deliberately spared by the incendiaries. The main motive of the rioters was, no doubt, to settle accounts with an institution that added materially to the cost of food and wine entering the city; the organizers seem, however, to have been mainly concerned to destroy the monopoly of the Farmers General and to control the entry and exit of arms and persons to and from the capital. The same night, a similar operation was carried out on the northern fringe of the city, when armed civilians and Gardes Françaises, once more directed from the Palais Royal, broke into the monastery of the St. Lazare brotherhood, searched it for arms, released prisoners and removed over fifty cartloads of grain and flour to the central markets. This part of the proceedings was followed by an invasion of local poor and unemployed, who stripped the building of money, food, silver and hidden treasure.

But the main feature of the night of 12-13 July was the search for arms. Religious houses were visited and gunsmiths', armourers' and harness-makers' were raided in different parts of the capital. The Parisian gunsmiths eventually submitted to the National Assembly a statement of their losses, amounting to over 100,000 livres. They do not appear to have been paid and must be counted among the minor victims of the Revolution.

On the morning of the 13th, the Paris electors made a firm bid to gain control of the situation. They formed a permanent committee to act as a provisional government of the city and determined to put a stop to the indiscriminate arming of the whole population. To them the bands of unemployed and homeless, some of whom had played a part in the raids on the *barrières* and the St. Lazare monastery, were as great a menace to the security and properties of the citizens as the Court and privileged orders conspiring at Versailles. It was with both threats in mind that they now set seriously about organizing a citizens' militia, or *garde nationale*; and it goes without saying that it was on the former score alone that the King was induced, the next day, to give his consent. Householders were summoned to attend meetings in the sixty electoral districts into which Paris had been divided; each district was to provide 200 (later 800) men; and Barnave wrote, the same evening, to his constituents in Dauphiné, that there were already 13,200 citizens registered and equipped. From this body all vagrants and homeless persons (*gens sans aveu*) and even a large part of the settled wage-earners, were specifically excluded: it was, as Barnave said, to be *"bonne bourgeoise"*. Yet arms continued to fall into unauthorized hands as long as the insurrection lasted. Crowds besieged the City Hall, demanding arms and powder. Jacques de Flesselles, *prévôt des marchands* and acting head of the provisional city government, being anxious to limit their distribution, sent parties off on fruitless quests to the Arsenal and the Carthusian monastery: this "treachery" would cost him his life on the morrow. Meanwhile, the electors had deputed one of their number, the Abbé Lefevre, to guard the stocks assembled in the vaults of the City Hall; but so great was the pressure of the half-armed crowds surging round the building that he was compelled to hand out his powder with more speed and less discrimination than he would have wished.

The search for arms continued on the morning of the 14th, when a spectacular raid was made on the Hôtel des Invalides across the river. Here some 30,000 muskets were removed by the 7-8,000 citizens taking part; and from here the cry went out, "To the Bastille!" The object was not to release prisoners (there were, in fact, only seven of them), but to seize the powder that, as was known, had lately been sent there from the Arsenal. Besides, the fortress was widely hated as a symbol of past tyrannies and had figured as such in the *cahiers* of all three estates. It was believed to be heavily armed and its guns, which that morning were trained on the Rue St. Antoine, could play havoc among the crowded tenements. In the night, too, it had been rumoured that 30,000 royalist troops had marched into the Faubourg St. Antoine and had begun to slaughter its citizens. Yet there does not seem to have been any serious intention, at the outset, of taking the Bastille by storm—least of all on the part of the committee of electors, who had thrust on them the task of directing operations from the City Hall.

From the electors' own account of the event, we learn that they proposed to negotiate with the governor, de Launay, for the surrender of the gunpowder in his keeping and for the withdrawal of the guns from his battlements. De Launay received their deputations and promised not to fire unless attacked. Nevertheless, the besieging crowds, already filling the outer courtyard, managed to lower the drawbridge leading into the inner *cour du gouvernement*; and the governor, believing a frontal assault to be imminent, ordered his men to fire. In the ensuing affray, the besiegers lost 98 dead and 73 wounded. Tempers were roused and the electors lost control of operations. The decisive blow was struck by two detachments of Gardes Françaises who, responding to the summons of Hulin, a former N.C.O., marched to the fortress with five cannon removed that morning from the Invalides. Supported by a few hundred armed civilians—master craftsmen, journeymen and labourers of the St. Antoine and neighbouring districts[4]—they trained their cannon on the main gate. De Launay threatened to blow up the fortress, but, being dissuaded by the garrison, lowered his main drawbridge and surrendered to his assailants. He himself and six of the hundred defenders were massacred; de Flesselles met a similar fate. So the Bastille fell.

Though of little military importance, its fall had far-reaching consequences. The National Assembly, for the time being at least, was saved and received royal recognition. The Court party began to disintegrate and Artois, Condé and Breteuil went into exile, while Necker was recalled. In the capital, power passed firmly into the hands of the electors, who set up a municipal council, or Commune, with Bailly as mayor and

---

[4] The names of some 660 of these are listed, with their ages and addresses, in the Archives Nationales, T514 (1), in Paris.

Lafayette as commander of its newly-formed National Guard. On 17 July, the King himself made the journey to Paris, escorted by fifty deputies (Robespierre among them), was received by the victors at the City Hall and, in token of acquiescence in the turn of events, donned the red, white and blue cockade of the Revolution. It seemed as if now the National Assembly might proceed quietly with its work.

But the provinces had yet to have their say. The news from Paris, reaching the villages and market-towns by word of mouth and by deputies' letters during the third week in July, intensified and spread a peasant-movement that had already begun. It also provoked a series of minor municipal revolutions. Unlike the peasantry and small urban consumers, the provincial bourgeoisie had been resigned to await the outcome of events in Paris and Versailles. When the news of Necker's dismissal reached Nancy on 15 July, Arthur Young was told: "We are a provincial town; we must wait and see what is done in Paris." The "municipal revolution" took various forms. Sometimes, as in maritime Flanders, the old town corporation merely broadened its composition, adopted the tricolour cockade and carried on as before. Sometimes, as at Bordeaux, it followed the example of Paris and made way for the local assembly of electors. More often—as at Lille, Rouen, Cherbourg, Dijon, Rennes and Lyons—the old authorities were overthrown and replaced by entirely new bodies, sometimes pledged to reduce the price of bread. In nearly every case, the transfer of power was accompanied by the creation of a National Guard on the Parisian model, whose first object was, as in the capital, to meet the double danger of aristocratic reaction and popular disturbance. Meanwhile, the Intendants were either expelled or quietly disappeared; in either case, the royal authority was weakened.

It is one of the legends of history-books that the peasants, also, had waited on events. In fact, rural disturbance had been continuous, in many parts of the country, since December 1788. Starting, as in the grain riots of 1775, as a small con-

sumers' movement attended by assaults on millers, granaries
and food-convoys, it had, by the following spring and summer,
begun to assume the proportions of a widespread rural revolt
against game laws, hunting rights, royal taxes, tithes and seigneurial dues. The news from Paris gave this movement a fresh
stimulus, generalized it and gave it a more precise purpose.
It was accompanied by the strange phenomenon known as " *la
Grande Peur* " (the Great Fear), itself a product of the
economic crisis and of the revolution in Paris. The crisis had
increased the number of vagrants on the country-roads, as it
had increased the hostility of the peasants to their landlords.
On top of this came the intrigues of the Court and aristocracy
at Versailles and their defeat by the popular victory in Paris,
followed, in turn, by the emigration of Artois and Condé and
the dispersal of military units to country districts. From all
this had grown the belief that the aristocrats were preparing
to wreak summary vengeance with the help of armed vagrants, or " brigands ", who were reputed to be roaming the
countryside. So the peasants armed and awaited the invaders :
such incidents were reported from every province of France
with the exception of Alsace, Brittany and Lorraine. When
the imaginary " brigands " did not materialize, the defenders,
with true peasant thrift, often turned their arms against the
mansions of their landlords instead. Their targets were, in
fact, not so much the mansions as the hated manorial registers
on which their seigneurial obligations, both old and new,
were generally inscribed. And so, in July and early August,
the peasants left a trail of razed *châteaux* and burning manor-
rolls in many parts of the country. Often, they were led by
persons bearing orders purporting to come from the King
himself; and there seems little doubt that the peasants believed that, in settling accounts with their *seigneurs*, they were
carrying out the King's wishes, if not his specific instructions.[5]

The news of these events compelled the National Assembly
to pay immediate attention to feudal privilege and to the needs

[5] G. Lefebvre, *La Grand Peur de 1789* (1932).

of the peasants. It was bound to make concessions, and these took the spectacular form of the surrender of their feudal rights and fiscal immunities by the deputies of the liberal aristocracy and clergy on the famous night of 4 August. But the Assembly's claim that " the feudal régime had been utterly destroyed" was misleading : while the remnants of serfdom, the *corvée* and ecclesiastical tithes were abolished outright, some of the more onerous privileges and obligations—the *cens,* quit-rent, *champart, lods et ventes* among them—were made redeemable by individual purchase. The fact that the landlords never got their money (the total compensation has been estimated at 4,000 million livres) was due less to the foresight and generosity of the legislators than to the insist-ence and militancy of the peasants. Eventually, the Jacobin Convention faced the accomplished fact and, by a decree of July 1793, declared the outstanding debt null and void.

But, though saved by the people of Paris in July and prodded into " destroying feudalism" by the peasantry in August, the National Assembly was by no means yet secure. As long as the Court and King remained at Versailles and an active minority of deputies were able, in alliance with the Court, to frustrate the constitutional programme of the major-ity, effective power still remained divided between the revolu-tionary bourgeoisie, supported by a minority of aristocrats and bishops, and the adherents of the Old Régime. The gains so far made, substantial as they seemed, were precarious : Louis refused to assent both to the August decrees and to the Declaration of the Rights of Man (see next chapter); there were repeated royalist intrigues to abduct the King to a safe distance from the capital; and now determined attempts were made to persuade the Assembly to adopt an " English " con-stitution—by granting the King an absolute " veto " over legis-lation and creating an Upper Chamber.

These proposals were put forward in August by the so-called " *monarchiens* " or " English party", a group led by Mounier and Malouet among the commons and Lally Tollendal among the nobility. Their aims were to frame a "mixed" constitution on the English model, where powers would be divided, in more or less equal portions, between King, nobility and commons; only property-owners of substance would have the vote; and the rebellious peasants and urban *menu peuple* would be kept in their place. The proposal to form an Upper Chamber was easily defeated, as not only were the Left and Centre within the Assembly ranged against it, but it was strongly opposed by the provincial *noblesse* who feared their virtual exclusion from a Chamber dominated by the Court aristocracy. The "veto" proposal, however, was more tenaciously upheld and created sharper divisions, reaching beyond the confines of the Assembly itself. The Parisian "patriots", established at the Palais Royal, called for its outright rejection; but Barnave, who spoke for the "patriot" deputies (the Left) at Versailles, was prepared to negotiate with the Centre, who favoured a compromise. When, at the end of August, negotiations broke down, the Parisians' hands were strengthened and an attempt was made by a group of Palais Royal journalists to induce Parisians to march to Versailles and fetch the King back to his capital. This first attempt failed both because Barnave and his colleagues opposed it and because Parisians were not yet ready to undertake it.

They were ready to do so, five weeks later, as the result of the combination of three factors—their indoctrination with the ideas of the "patriots", the sharpening of the food crisis, and the provocative measures of the Court. That the common people of the capital were deeply influenced by the currents of advanced opinion had been evident during the electoral campaign, when rioters in the Faubourg St. Antoine and others had championed the claims of the *tiers état* against its opponents. The debates at Versailles were relayed with amazing speed to crowds in the Palais Royal and the Place de Grève, outside the City Hall. Already on 24 August, before the Declaration of the Rights of Man had been adopted, a journeyman gunsmith, when cross-examined by the police after arrest insisted that *" le droit de l'homme "* entitled him to a fair hearing. Chairmen at the gates of the National Assembly (Malouet tells us) freely discussed the rights and wrongs of the " veto "; and, in September, the unemployed workers of the *ateliers de charité* (national workshops) declared their readiness to go to Versailles to fetch the royal family to the capital.

Yet, once more, it was the food crisis that lent a particular insistence and intensity to popular agitation. The price of the 4-lb. loaf had, a week after the fall of the Bastille, been reduced from $14\frac{1}{2}$ to $13\frac{1}{2}$ sous; and, a fortnight later, after demonstrations at the City Hall, to 12 sous. But the calm that followed was short-lived. The harvest had been good, but a prolonged drought made it impossible for millers to grind sufficient corn. The shortage of flour and bread that resulted was a boon to speculators but a matter of deep concern to bakers, who were the most ready targets of popular vengeance. During August and September, there were constant bread riots in Paris, Versailles and St. Denis, in the course of which a baker and a municipal officer were killed by angry crowds and several others were threatened with the dreaded *" lanterne "*. It was noted by Hardy that, from mid-September, a leading part in the agitation was played by the women of the markets and *faubourgs*; and it was they who took the initiative and gave a lead to their menfolk in the great march to Versailles on 5 October.

But, as in July, it was developments at Versailles itself that brought matters to a head. On 11 September, Barnave had persuaded the Assembly to urge the King to agree to withdraw his objection to the August decrees. It was the Assembly's insistence on this latter point that determined the Court to break the deadlock by a further display of military force. On 15 September, Louis, having rejected the moderates' advice to transfer the Assembly to a provincial town, ordered the Flanders regiment to Versailles. It was welcomed by a banquet given by the royal Gardes du Corps (Life-Guards), in the course of which the national cockade was trampled underfoot

and the Queen and her children were received with almost
mystical fervour. The incident was widely reported in Paris
the next day and the "patriot" press called for vengeance.
This time, Barnave withdrew his objection to a resort to force;
so at least would appear from his comments after the event.
Danton carried a resolution in the Cordeliers Club in Paris,
urging Lafayette to go to Versailles with an ultimatum; and
Desmoulins repeated his summons to Parisians to fetch the
King to the capital. The call was echoed, on Sunday, 4
October, at meetings in the gardens of the Palais Royal.
Early next morning, women of the central markets and the
Faubourg St. Antoine invaded the City Hall, calling for bread
and searching for arms. They were joined outside by Stanislas
Maillard, a sheriff's officer who had distinguished himself at
the Bastille, and whom they persuaded to lead them to Versailles to present their demands to the King and the National
Assembly. So they set out in two great columns, in the rain,
chanting as they marched (or so tradition has it), "let us fetch
the baker, the baker's wife and the little baker's lad". They
were followed, a few hours later, by 20,000 National Guards-
men of the Paris Districts, who had compelled the reluctant
Lafayette to place himself at their head, and a motley band of
civilians armed with muskets, sticks and pikes. Faced with this
impressive array, the King needed little persuasion to give
orders for the provisioning of the capital and to sanction the
August decrees and the Declaration of Rights. But these concessions were not enough to satisfy the insurgents; and, the
next day, the King and his family, having thrown away their
last chance of seeking refuge in flight, were compelled to
accompany the marchers back to Paris, where they were joined,
ten days later, by the National Assembly. So the French
monarchy, after an absence of over a hundred years, returned
for a brief sojourn to its ancestral home.

By this second intervention of the people of Paris the gains
of the July revolution were consolidated. The King came
under the watchful eye of the Assembly, the Paris city government and Districts; the "English party" was discredited and

its leaders began to follow Artois and Breteuil into exile; while power passed firmly into the hands of the "constitutional" monarchists. Yet they had only survived and triumphed because, under the pressing compulsion of events, they had been willing to make common cause with the people who, though having aims and grievances of their own, shared their fears and suspicions of the aristocracy. In this sense, the revolution of 1789 was a merger of two distinct movements—the bourgeois and the popular—a merger that would leave its mark on the whole future course of the Revolution in France.

Yet, even with such divided aims, a merger of this kind could not take place in other countries in Europe—either because (as in Austria and Poland) the middle class was too weak to make any effective political challenge; or (as in England, Switzerland and the United Provinces) because it lacked the will or the motive to ally itself with the people. But, in France, too, the revolution of 1789 might have turned out differently. If the King had proved himself more trustworthy as a champion of reform, and if the aristocracy had been as willing to surrender privilege as to fight royal "despotism", the Third Estate might have settled for a compromise—something perhaps like the bourgeois-aristocratic-monarchist partnership proposed by Mounier or the alliance of King and people desired by Mirabeau. But, after July, it was too late: by his feeble intrigues with Court and nobility, the King had already lost all chance of being accepted as the leader of a national movement of regeneration; and the privileged classes were by now damned, in the eyes of "patriots" and people, as the declared enemies of reform.

Yet the alliance of bourgeoisie and people was by no means an easy, stable or unchequered one. Even among the victors of October, there were many who viewed it with misgivings; and once the insurrection had served its purpose, the Assembly took steps to curb the revolutionary energies of the Parisian *menu peuple* by imposing martial law, the death penalty for rebellion and a censorship of the radical press. The first victim of these restraints on liberty, Michel Adrien, a Bastille labourer, was hanged on 21 October for attempting to provoke a "sedition" in the Faubourg St. Antoine. Having won its double victory over aristocracy and "despotism", the bourgeoisie now wanted peace and quiet to proceed with its task of giving France a constitution.

Chapter VI

THE RECONSTRUCTION OF FRANCE

The men who laboured for the next two years to give France her first revolutionary constitution were by no means the starry-eyed dreamers or "ideologues" that they have sometimes been represented to be; nor were they as thoroughly committed, by inclination or precept, to re-shape society on entirely new foundations as Burke imagined. The Constituents, or constitutional monarchists, were essentially the lawyers, merchants, former government officers and landed proprietors of the old Third Estate, shorn of a small minority of *monarchiens* and reinforced by the addition of some fifty "patriot" nobles, forty-four bishops and 200 parish clergy. Their new leaders, after Mounier's and Malouet's departure, were men of the former Centre and Left—the triumvirate of Barnave, Duport and Charles Lameth; with Sieyes playing an important role and with a Left opposition formed by a small group of democrats like Robespierre and Pétion. Their thought and their language, it is true, were cast, like those of the Americans, in the mould of the new philosophy but, like them, they had a shrewd idea of which side of their bread was buttered. Owing to circumstances not entirely of their own volition, the Old Régime of aristocratic privilege and royal absolutism had collapsed, and something had to be put in its place. The constitution and the laws that they enacted during these years of comparative social peace bore, like the Declaration of Rights that preceded them, the mark of the current philosophy; but they were also conceived in their own particular image.

The Declaration of the Rights of Man and Citizen was adopted by the Assembly, while still at Versailles, on 27 August 1789. These "principles of 1789", which were later to enthrall and to divide the whole of Europe, were the outcome of hard bargaining between different groups of deputies. Both Mounier and Lafayette, respectively of the Right and Centre, played an important part in their drafting; but even the presence of Thomas Jefferson in Paris and their close kinship with the Virginian Declaration of 1776 do not prove that they owed their origin largely to American inspiration or experience: it is more sensible to conclude that both Americans and Frenchmen acknowledged a common debt to the " natural-law " school of philosophy, in particular to Locke, Montesquieu and Rousseau. The Declaration of Rights is remarkable in that it neatly balances a statement of universal principles and human rights with an evident concern for the interests of the bourgeoisie. In general, it voices the basic claims of the Third Estate, as expressed in the *cahiers*: protection of property, freedom of conscience, of press and from arbitrary arrest; equality before the law, equal taxation and equal eligibility to office; and, to show the deputies' appreciation of practical realities, it implicitly sanctions—*post factum* —the right of rebellion. On the other hand, its omissions and reservations are equally significant. Nothing is said of economic freedom, as the Assembly was still divided on the future of the guilds, and the resistance of small consumers to the " freedom " of the market had not yet become an urgent issue. Equality is presented in largely political terms: economic equality does not arise. Property is " a sacred and inviolable right ", and no attempt is yet made to define or to circumscribe it; nor is any mention made of the State's obligations to provide work or relief for the poor and unpropertied. There is silence, too, on the rights of assembly, of petitioning and association. Law is said to be " the expression of the general will " (memories of the *Parlements'* remonstrances of the 1770's!), but there is no guarantee that all citizens will have an equal right to enact it—least of all in the colonies: no mention is made of slavery and the slave trade. In matters of religion, Protestants and Jews are entitled to their opinions, " provided their manifestation does not disturb the public order ": there can be no question of complete and untrammelled liberty of conscience as long as the Roman Catholic Church remains the single State Church of France. The Declaration, then, for all its nobility of language and its proclamation of universal principles, is essentially a manifesto of the revolutionary bourgeoisie and its clerical and liberal-aristocratic allies. As such, it sounded the death-knell of the Old Régime, while preparing the public for the constructive legislation that was to follow.

The greater part of this legislation, though by no means all, became incorporated in the Constitution of 1791. Running through it all is the concern of the nation's new rulers that the system to be devised must be adequately protected against the triple danger of royal " despotism ", aristocratic privilege and popular " licentiousness ". There were no declared Republicans in the Assembly and it was generally agreed that the monarchy should remain; but it was to be a new constitutional monarchy, stripped of its former absolute control of government, legislation, army and justice. The " King of the French " would hold hereditary office, be granted a civil list of 25 million livres as the first servant of the State, and have the right to appoint his own ministers (from outside the Assembly), his ambassadors and military commanders. By the so-called " suspensive veto ", he would have the power to suspend or delay all laws, other than financial, initiated and adopted by the Assembly for a period up to four years, or the duration of two consecutive parliaments. But he had no power to dissolve the Assembly; ministers would virtually be answerable, not to himself but to the Assembly and its numerous committees; and, while he might take the first steps in declaring war or making peace, such measures would be subject to the approval of parliament. The armed forces, meanwhile, had already been largely removed from royal control : a great many of the old aristocratic officers had been purged, often by the troops themselves; commissions were declared open to all; all ranks were called upon to take an oath of allegiance to the " nation " as well as to the King; and local authorities had the disposal of their own citizens' militias, or National Guard. So Mirabeau, as much as Mounier, failed in his attempt to create a strong executive, centred on a monarch with an absolute power of veto, with an army at his command and served by ministers drawn from the Assembly.

The real power in the land was, in fact, to be the Legislative Assembly itself. It was to be a uni-cameral body, untrammelled by "checks and balances" on the English or American model, armed with unlimited powers over taxation and with initiative and authority in all legislative matters restricted only by the "suspensive veto" and the obligation to hold elections every two years. The majority took care, besides, to ensure that, if not they themselves, at least like-minded deputies should be returned at each subsequent election. Prompted by Sieyes, they adopted a formula whereby only citizens of some substance and property should be entitled to vote in two electoral stages. Though the Declaration of Rights had proclaimed the right of all citizens "to take part, in person or through their representatives, in the making of laws", it had been silent on the specific right of suffrage. Citizens were now to be divided into "actives" and "passives", of whom "actives" alone would have the vote. To qualify for active citizenship one had to be a male aged 25 years or above, domiciled for a year, not engaged in domestic service, and paying a direct tax equivalent to the value of three days' unskilled labour. Such citizens might vote, in the primary assemblies, at the first stage of the electoral process. But the secondary assemblies, which actually "elected" the deputies, were limited to one in 100 of all active citizens and excluded all but those who paid a direct tax equivalent to the value of ten days' labour. Finally, to qualify as a deputy, a citizen had to pay a silver mark, or 52 livres, in taxes. What limitations this system actually imposed, or was intended to impose, on the right of vote and representation has been hotly disputed by historians; it is a difficult question to resolve and all the more complicated because, in August 1791, the Assembly considerably tightened up the provisions restricting access to the electoral assemblies, while easing those relating to deputies. Formally, Professor Palmer may be right in concluding that, up to August 1791, almost 70 in 100 citizens had the right to vote in the primary assemblies, about 50 in 100 could qualify as electors, and one in 100 might qualify as a national deputy.[1] Yet published lists suggest that, in practice, both " active " citizens and electors—particularly the latter—tended to be men of greater substance than these figures would imply. Even so, it is undeniably true that these restrictions on the right to vote were far less stringent than those imposed by the unreformed Parliament of Britain : French bourgeois society of 1789-92 was decidedly more democratic than aristocratic society across the Channel.

The royal authority was further weakened by the reform of administration and of local government. The old hereditary offices, acquired by purchase, were swept away and their holders compensated : it could hardly be otherwise, as two in five of the Assembly's members were previous office-holders ! A similar fate befell the old complicated system of *généralités* and *intendances, bailliages* and *sénéchaussées, pays d'états,* and *pays d'élection,* privileged corporations and the surviving pockets of ecclesiastical and seigneurial jurisdiction. Following the Declaration of Rights, public office was made open, by election or appointment, to talent. In the place of the old patchwork of local authorities a uniform system was devised, based on departments, districts, cantons and communes, which, in its essentials, has survived to the present day. There were to be 83 departments of more or less equal size, whose boundaries, however, were drawn with careful attention to geography : in fact, their names, like those of the months in the later Revolutionary Calendar, were derived from natural phenomena—in this case, mainly from rivers, mountains and seas. The departments, like their subdivisions, the districts and cantons, were no longer, as under the old royal system, to be run by nominated officials but by committees elected from below. The base of the pyramid was formed by some 44,000 communes (or municipalities), whose mayors and councillors were elected by the active citizens and exercised considerable

[1] R. R. Palmer, *The Age of the Democratic Revolution,* I, 522-8.

powers of local administration. Paris was to have its own municipal council and to be further subdivided into forty-eight sections (replacing the sixty electoral districts of 1789), armed with powers of election, police and local justice. Thus, not only absolute monarchy but the whole old system of centralized government was dismantled; and France, at this stage of the Revolution, became virtually a federation of elective departments and municipalities, enjoying a wide measure of local autonomy and held together, at the centre, by a strong legislature but weak executive.

The same considerations governed the reform of justice and the judicial system. In the new bourgeois State, justice could no longer be subject to the royal prerogative or be dispensed by a local aristocracy of the sword, robe or mitre. So *Parlements, lettres de cachet,* and seigneurial and ecclesiastical courts followed the Bastille and the old venal offices into oblivion. As in England and America, the judiciary was declared to be independent of the executive: it was to become dependent on the "nation" (that is, on the enfranchised citizens) instead. Justice was made free and equal for all; a network of tribunals was created at municipal, departmental and national level, with elective judges and with juries elected to serve in criminal cases. At the apex were two national tribunals—a Court of Appeals and a High Court, of which the latter, concerned with the trial of ministers, public officials and enemies of State, looked forward to the Revolutionary Tribunal of 1793. And, in due course (after March 1792), the guillotine, the great leveller, would replace the aristocratic sword or axe and plebeian noose as the single instrument of execution for all capital offenders.

The old fiscal system had already been largely destroyed in the summer of 1789: then *taille, gabelle, aides,* tithes, customs-barriers, fiscal immunities and the authority of the Farmers General had been swept away by the nation under arms. Their replacement faced the Constituents with one of their knottiest problems. To meet immediate requirements, a land tax was introduced, assessed on all properties and calculated to raise 240 million livres a year. Further taxes were to be levied on personal incomes and movable property, and on commercial and industrial revenues; in addition, a "patriotic" contribution, proposed by Mirabeau, raised another 100 million livres. But these measures were quite insufficient to meet the mounting toll of debt, compensation payment and current expenditure, and they provoked violent hostility—particularly from the peasants who, complaining that they were once more being over-taxed, declared, in many districts, what amounted to a tax-payers' strike. So exceptional remedies had to be found, of which by far the most important was the decision to nationalize the estates of the Church and put them up for public auction. To finance the operation, interest-bearing bonds termed "*assignats*" were issued, which gradually came to be accepted as bank-notes and, after 1790, suffered steady depreciation. The assignat was a salutary shot in the arm and saved the Assembly from its momentary difficulties; but the inflation that it eventually brought in its train—under the impact of war and speculation—was to exact a heavy toll in terms of human suffering and of popular disturbance.[2]

The nobility had, as we saw, lost their rights of private justice, fiscal exemptions and feudal dues and privileges; in addition, titles and hereditary nobility were abolished and the aristocracy ceased to exist, with other corporations, as an estate of the realm. The abolition of titles, by reducing the former nobleman to the simple status of citizen, satisfied the commoners' demand for social equality. But more far-reaching in its consequences was the removal of feudal burdens from the land, proclaimed by the National Assembly in August 1789 and briefly mentioned in our last chapter. We then saw that the Assembly distinguished between one type of feudal obligation and another, thus betraying the deputies' anxiety not to transgress more than absolutely necessary against their own declared principle of the inviolability of property. They accepted the contention of Merlin of Douai that certain rights had been usurped or been established by violence: among

[2] S. E. Harris, *The Assignats* (Harvard Univ. Press, 1930).

these were the rights of conducting manorial courts, hunting and fishing rights, the right to maintain warrens, dove-cotes, mills and wine-presses, to collect tolls and market fines, to levy personal taxes and labour obligations (*corvée*) and, above all, to keep peasants in personal servitude. Such rights and monopolies, being deemed illegitimate, were abolished without compensation. But others, though often a heavier burden on the peasantry, were declared to be lawful rights of property: these were the various payments made in respect of the holding or transfer of land, such as the *cens,* quit-rent, *champart* and *lods et ventes.* Redemption was determined at a rate of twenty times the annual payment in cash and twenty-five times that in kind. The peasants, however, as we already noted, failed to appreciate the nicety of these distinctions and refused to pay any compensation whatsoever—until the Jacobin Convention, four years later, declared the debt to be null and void.

The abolition of tithe also benefited the peasant proprietor; but there remained the great mass of share-croppers and land-less labourers, who were largely untouched by these arrangements. The nationalization and sale of Church lands provided a possible solution; but sale by auction tended, in most cases, to favour large purchasers; and little was done by the Constituent Assembly to sell land in small lots or to encourage the rural population to combine. So an important part of the agrarian problem remained unsolved, and peasant dissatisfaction continued.

As befitted an Assembly in which middle-class interests played so large a part, the Constituents were more consistent and thorough in their handling of commercial and industrial reforms. These, for reasons that we have noted, were omitted from the Declaration of Rights. Meanwhile, opinion had hardened against the anomalies and controls of the Old Régime, and the Assembly passed a number of laws that, in large measure, removed past restrictions on the nation's economy and introduced free trade in the internal market. A unitary system of weights and measures was introduced; local

tolls and *péages* were abolished and customs posts rolled back
to the national frontiers; and the guilds and controls on manu-
factured goods (a controversial issue in the *cahiers* of the
Third Estate) were finally suppressed in February 1791. In
matters relating to external trade, their policy was less decisive
and betrayed the pull of contending interests. Thus the India
Company lost its monopoly, trade beyond the Cape of Good
Hope was released from controls, and Marseilles lost its privileges in trade with the Levant. But freedom of trade was
another matter when it came to commercial relations with
other European countries: tariffs were maintained to protect
French industries, though manufacturers failed, for the present, to persuade the Assembly to repudiate the " Free Trade "
treaty of 1786 with England. However, all parties closed their
ranks when faced with the problems of labour. In June 1791,
the Constituents, for fear of the unemployed, closed down the
public workshops (*ateliers de charité*) set up to absorb and
employ the workless in 1789. The same month, they passed
the famous Le Chapelier law, by which combinations of
workers were declared illegal at a time when food prices, for
lack of controls, were liable to rise. The law followed strikes
of carpenters and other tradesmen in Paris and was passed in
response to the protesting petitions of manufacturers. No one
in the Assembly, not even Robespierre, objected. Trade unions
remained proscribed throughout the Revolution, and the law
was not finally repealed until 1884.

Most intractable of all the problems tackled by the Constituents, and most fateful in its consequences, was their settlement of the Catholic Church. The solution that they found
was by no means determined by philosophical contempt for
religion, by anti-Catholic bias, or even by particular considerations of class; and the deep divisions and hostility that the
settlement provoked were due, in part at least, to circumstances outside their control. It had been generally accepted—
and not least by bishops and parish clergy—that the Church
was in grave need of reform. As a corporative body, the
Church of the Old Régime had enjoyed immense wealth,

privileges and authority: the value of its properties, yielding an annual income of between 50 and 100 million livres, represented something between two-fifths and one-half of the landed wealth in every province of the realm; and it was exempt from all taxation other than what it voluntarily offered to the Treasury in the form of the *don gratuit*. A large part of these properties was held, not by the secular clergy, but by monasteries and chapters, which, as impropriators of tithe and other revenues, often paid a yearly stipend, known as the *portion congrue*, to the practising priest and chaplain, and whose own services to religion were being increasingly called in question by clergy and laymen alike. So little regard was, in fact, shown for the contemplative orders that, after an enquiry in 1768, no fewer than 1,000 communities had been disbanded and their properties transferred to secular uses. A social gulf separated the higher clergy of aristocratic bishops and abbots from the common run of parish priests: while a bishop of Strasbourg drew revenues of 400,000 livres and a wealthy abbot of Angers 50,000 livres, a humble *curé* might be expected to subsist on an income from tithe or *portion congrue* of 1,000 or 700 livres a year. Other divisions, too, had arisen: Gallican bishops, universities and *Parlements* had combined in 1762 to disband and expel the Jesuits; Jansenism, though a declining force after the mid-century, persisted to confuse preacher and parishioner on matters of doctrine; and—most significant of all—the parish priests, resentful of increasing episcopal pretensions, had become deeply infected with the Richerist claim that the Church should be governed, not merely by bishops and canons, but by the whole company of its pastors.

So the Church had been swept into the Revolution as a divided force, though by no means as a disinterested spectator. While bishops and abbots had supported the "aristocratic revolt" and called for the convocation of the States General, the parish clergy saw their own opportunity of settling old scores when the royal Council's instructions of January 1789 granted them the right to attend the electoral assemblies in person, while monks and canons might only send representatives. Taking full advantage of this dispensation, the parish clergy called in their separate *cahiers* for extensive reforms, for Church self-government on Richerist lines, and even for the right to elect their own bishops; they dominated the local assemblies of the clergy, and composed two in every three deputies of their order at Versailles. Here, as we have seen, it was the parish clergy who gave the warmest support to the claims of the Third Estate, and their defection from their ecclesiastical superiors played no small part in deciding the King, against his own inclinations, to order the two higher estates to join the self-styled National Assembly. So it was not altogether surprising that the Assembly should receive support, rather than discouragement, from the main body of the clergy when, in August 1789, it decreed the abolition of tithe, annates and plurality of offices, and ended the old corporative status of the Church and its right of self-taxation. Nor was the clergy unduly alarmed when, as proposed by Talleyrand (then Bishop of Autun) and Mirabeau, it was decided to nationalize Church properties and put them up for auction: the *curés* and their *vicaires,* at least, had little to lose (and possibly much to gain), and there was ample precedent for the view that such properties should only be held in return for services rendered. Again, when, in February 1790, the Assembly proceeded to dissolve, or regroup, the contemplative religious orders, few tears were shed except by those most immediately affected. It was not, in fact, any of these measures that brought Church and Revolution into serious conflict: this happened only after the adoption of the Civil Constitution of the Clergy in July 1790.

Even then, the collision was not immediate and might perhaps have been avoided. Several of the Constitution's provisions were acceptable enough to the main body of the clergy: neither bishops nor parish clergy had any particular objection to becoming salaried servants of the State: the priests, at least, were to be paid more generously than before; and the Constituents, though granting fuller freedom of worship to

Protestants (and later to Jews), had no intention of dis-
establishing the Catholic Church or of ending its privileged
status as the single State Church of France. Again, the clergy
was prepared to accept a long overdue re-drafting of diocesan
and parochial boundaries; but the drastic reduction of bishoprics from 135 to 83 (to accord with the new departments)
meant that several bishops—and many more parish priests—
would be deprived of their livings. More serious still was the
refusal of the Assembly to submit the Constitution, before it
became enforced, to a synod of the Church for its sanction:
thus both Richerist clergy and Gallican bishops might have
been appeased. But "corporations" had been abolished; and
to refer to an assembly of the Church what it was the sole duty
of the "nation" to decide would, it was objected (by Robespierre among others), be to subject the "general will", as
interpreted by the nation's representatives, to the overriding
veto of a single corporative body. On this point the Assembly,
apart from its clerical members, remained adamant. So
canonical sanction (if any) had to be sought from the Pope.
But Pius VI, although known to be hostile to the Revolution,
was engaged in delicate negotiations concerning the future
status of the old papal enclave of Avignon, and, fearing to
prejudice his temporal interests by an over-hasty decision on a
matter of doctrine, delayed his answer for several months.
The Assembly, however, was in a hurry: sees and livings were
falling vacant and, for lack of firm guidance and authority,
the clergy was becoming confused and divided. So, in November 1790, it burned its bridges, declared the Constitution to be
in force, and ordered clerics holding office to take an oath of
allegiance to the constitution of the kingdom (and, therefore,
by implication, to the Civil Constitution of the Clergy). The
lay deputies, firmly convinced that an agreement would be
reached, were appalled at the result: only two of the Assembly's 44 bishops and one-third of its clerical members
complied; and the clergy at large became divided into two
more or less evenly balanced opposing blocs of "jurors" and
"non-jurors"—a division that became all the more irrevoc-

able when Pius at last, in March and April 1791, slammed the
door on any compromise by condemning the Civil Constitution as a whole, suspending the conformist bishops (Talleyrand and Gobel of Lydda), and expressly instructing all clergy
to withhold, or to withdraw, their allegiance to the new
Church settlement. So, once the Pope had spoken in these
terms, those who acknowledged his authority or merely followed their own conscience in refusing the oath, became, by
inevitable stages, the declared opponents of not only the Civil
Constitution but of the Revolution itself and, as such, identi-
fied by "patriots" with aristocracy and counter-revolution.
From this followed, in turn, the tragic and fateful sequence
of emigration, proscription, and even the massacre, of "refractory" priests, the civil war in the Vendée, terror and
counter-terror. Another consequence was that, in time, the
new Constitutional Church itself, whose doctrine was the same
as that of the proscribed "fanatics", also lost credit, was
separated from the State, persecuted in the days of "de-
christianization", and followed by cults of Reason, of the
Supreme Being and Theophilanthropy—until the old Church
was re-established on new foundations by Bonaparte's Concordat of 1801.

But this is, of course, to anticipate events lying far beyond
the term of office of the Constituent Assembly; it is also a
reminder that the Constituents were not the only legislators of
the Revolution that played a part in reconstructing France
after the collapse of the Old Régime. The Revolution went
through many stages and by no means all their work survived.
The Constitution of 1791 was, in its main political provisions,
abandoned only a year after it had been adopted: in 1792,
the monarchy was overthrown and abolished and the Republic
proclaimed; the same year, the distinction between "active"
and "passive" citizens was removed and every adult male
(with some exceptions) was given the vote. The National
Convention, in 1793, created an exceptional court for dealing
with crimes against the State: so the Revolutionary Tribunal
came into being as an instrument of executive justice—a

creation that was, of course, entirely at variance with the Constituents' conception of an independent judiciary. The Jacobin Constitution of June 1793 was far more democratic and far more concerned with the needs of the poor than that of 1791; yet, under the impact of war and revolution, it was put into cold storage and a highly centralized "revolutionary government" emerged, based on the two powerful committees of Public Safety and General Security, whose members were drawn from the Assembly and which had at their service representatives "on mission" and "national agents", empowered to override the authority of departments and communes. Thus, the conception of the Republic "one and indivisible" came to replace that of the loosely-knit federative monarchy of 1791. Again, in its social legislation, the Convention went far beyond the limits drawn by the Constituents. Controls were placed on the price and supply of all the necessities of life; the peasants' outstanding debt to their landlords was (as we have seen) annulled; and some, admittedly hesitant, steps were taken to ensure that a part of the auctioned properties of Church and *émigré* nobility should find its way into the possession of landless or small peasants. Slavery in the colonies, which had been maintained by the Constituents, was abolished by the Jacobins in 1794; and the Convention, both before and after the fall of Robespierre in Thermidor (July 1794), laid the foundation of a national system of public education and a code of laws that eventually found expression in the Code Napoleon.

Yet a great deal of this legislation was ephemeral. Robespierre's Republic of Virtue gave way to the property-owners' Republic of Thermidor and the Directory; this, in turn, gave way to Napoleon's military dictatorship of the Consulate and Empire; and the Bourbon monarchy was restored in 1814. A second Chamber, or Senate, appeared under the Directory and was inherited, in substance though not in name, by Napoleon and the Restoration. The Republic of the Year II left enduring memories: its spirit lived again and some of its great moments were re-enacted in the later revolutions of 1830,

1848 and 1871; yet the greater part of its work—including price-controls, popular participation in local government, the freedom of negro slaves—was destroyed by one or other of its successors.

Nonetheless, with all these vagaries and constitutional expedients and experiments, a solid core of constructive legislation survived the revolutionary period and was carried on, beyond Napoleon's defeat and exile to St. Helena, into the Monarchies, Empire and Republics of the nineteenth century. Though " liberty " and democracy continued to have their ups and downs and though the wage-earner had gained little of permanent benefit from the Revolution, tax-exemption and privilege had gone; equality before the law and " the career open to talents " remained; France retained her economic and administrative unity; and the peasant kept such land as he had gained and his freedom from tithe and feudal obligations. In fact, a great deal of what was permanent in the legislation of the revolutionary years was that completed or begun by the Constituent Assembly; and it is no exaggeration to maintain that the legacy that the Revolution left was, in substance, that conceived in the decidedly bourgeois image of " the men of 1789 ".

Chapter VII

THE STRUGGLE FOR POWER

In proclaiming the Constitution on 28 September 1791 and in recommending it to Frenchmen with a stirring plea for national unity, Louis XVI solemnly declared: " The Revolution is over." It was a hope that was shared, far more sincerely, by the Assembly's majority and even by some of the democratic opposition. Yet, within a year, the Constitution had been brushed aside, the King had lost his throne, the leading constitutional monarchists were being proscribed or had emigrated, and the Revolution, far from being completed, was entering on a new and decisive phase.

There were a number of reasons why this should have come about, some of them arising from the circumstances and conflicts already described, others from events that were as yet only dimly discernible. The King, in the first place, had only accepted the Constitution with his tongue in his cheek: long before it had been signed he had made an unsuccessful bid to seek safety in flight and, having been returned ignominiously to his capital, continued to intrigue with the rulers of Sweden, Spain, Prussia and Austria for the restoration of his old authority by force of arms. So the King—and still more the Queen—could not be trusted, and their desertion and treachery made it impossible for the constitutional monarchists—the authors of the Constitution of 1791—to continue to govern or to achieve the sort of compromise that their Constitution had envisaged.

Again, only a minority of the nobility had willingly accepted the surrender of their old rights and privileges. Many had followed Artois and Breteuil into exile, or joined Condé's *émigré* army at Coblenz and Worms; yet these never accounted for more than one in twelve of the former noble families of

France. Another, smaller, minority actively opposed the Revolution from within and some 1,250 of these fell victim to the guillotine.[1] Some came to terms with the Revolution and numerous former aristocrats took part in the work of its assemblies, committees and tribunals even at the height of the Terror: in fact, the National Convention in 1793 included twenty-three ex-nobles, of whom seven were marquises and one a Prince of the Blood. But these were, of course, not typical and the great majority, though remaining in France and surviving the Terror, were never reconciled to the new order and, as a constant focal point of dissension, sullen resentment and suspicion, provoked the revolutionary authorities to take ever harsher and more vigorous measures to restrain their liberties and keep them in check. More serious perhaps were the effects of the division caused among the clergy by the new Church settlement, described in our last chapter. By alienating a large part of the parish priests, the revolutionaries of 1789 had embarked on a course that was to drive large numbers of not only the clergy but of their flocks among the devout and socially backward peasantry of the west and north-west, where traditional submission to both *seigneur* and priest remained strong, into the arms of counter-revolution. There followed the bitter civil and guerrilla warfare of the Vendée and parts of the south, which was to drain the future Republic of its manpower and resources and provoke ever harsher measures of repression.

These dissensions would, in themselves, have made it impossible to arrest the course of the Revolution and to stabilize its gains on the basis of the settlement of 1791. Yet it was not only the opposition of forces having more to lose than to gain by the Revolution that drove it onwards, but, even more, the intervention of classes that had looked to the outbreak of 1789 for a solution to their problems and whose

[1] See D. Greer, *The Incidence of the Emigration during the French Revolution* (Harvard Univ. Press, 1951) and *The Incidence of the Terror during the French Revolution* (Harvard Univ. Press, 1935).

hopes had, in the outcome, been disappointed or only partially realized. The peasants, as we have seen, had been freed from the tithe and the more oppressive taxes and feudal obligations; but few had satisfied their hunger for land, the burden of debt still remained, and small and landless peasants and share-croppers suffered, like townsmen, from rising food prices, and had received little or no protection from the encroachment on their old communal rights by enterprising farmers and land-owners. So the revolution in the village continued, though no longer with the explosive force of that of 1789, and served, in its own way, to stoke up the factional warfare of rival political groups. Again, among small urban proprietors and profes-sional men, there were many who had been debarred from voting—and many more from the right to sit in the Assembly —by the restrictions imposed, on Sieyes' suggestion, in October and December 1789; such men would play a leading part in the campaign to end the distinction between active and passive citizens and the qualification of the *marc d'argent*. Above all, there was the continued dissatisfaction of the great bulk of the urban *sans-culottes*—the small shopkeepers, workshop masters and wage-earners—particularly those in Paris, who had, by their intervention, ensured the success of the revolution of 1789 and had yet received no substantial reward—either in the form of political rights or of the material benefits of higher wages or of cheaper and more adequate supplies of food. Their particular grievances and aspirations were of long standing; but, in the context of revolution, they had been given a new content and a sharper definition by their own participation in events and by their acquisition of the new, infectious slogans and ideas of the "rights of man" and the "sovereignty of the people"—ideas borrowed in the first place from the bourgeois writers and journalists, but often adapted and transformed by the popular militants to serve their own purposes. Thus, by stages, the *sans-culottes* became a political force to be reckoned with and, by finding allies and champions among the political factions contending for power, served to deepen antagonism among the bourgeois groups and to drive the Revolution leftwards along courses neither intended nor desired by the "men of 1789".

Yet, had France remained at peace with the rest of Europe (as she was for nearly three years of revolution), it is possible that, in spite of these disruptive trends, the Revolution might have stopped in its tracks or, at least, not been carried far beyond the settlement of 1791. But, for reasons that will be outlined, war broke out in April 1792 and, by the violence of its impact, immeasurably sharpened all existing tensions and antagonisms. As Engels once wrote to Victor Adler: "The whole French Revolution is dominated by the War of Coalition, all its pulsations depend upon it." Inevitably, war gave a fresh encouragement to those seeking to destroy the Revolution from within and without and provoked, in turn, exceptional measures against counter-revolution, aristocracy and "fanaticism". It exposed the duplicity and treachery of the Court and brought about the fall of the monarchy. It led to inflation and rising food prices, and hence to vigorous resistance and agitation by the urban *sans-culottes*. Through inflation, treachery, defeat and social disturbance, it compelled the Assembly, contrary to its own cherished principles, to set up a strong "revolutionary" government, to institute the Terror, to control prices and to mobilize the nation for war. It was against this developing background of peace, war and social conflict that leaders and parties contended for power and the Revolution moved on through new phases and experiments. A part of the story will be told in the present chapter.

The year 1790 had been a year of comparative social calm. The price of bread had fallen temporarily to its normal, pre-revolutionary level; popular disturbance was in abeyance; and the Assembly had been able to proceed, almost undisturbed, with its programme of constitution-making. The opening months of 1791 witnessed a revival of agitation: the Parisian democrats of the Cordeliers Club had begun to interest themselves in the plight of the unemployed, whose workshops (*ateliers de charité*) were being closed down, and to give some support to striking workers; they had taken up the fight against the *marc d'argent* and the disfranchisement of passive citizens, and were enrolling wage-earners and small craftsmen in " fraternal " societies affiliated to the parent-club in the Rue Dauphine. This deliberate indoctrination of the *sans-culottes* by the democrats was to yield a rich harvest in the future, but it might have taken longer to show results had it not been for the King's attempt to escape across the Imperial border. To cover up his intentions Louis had instructed his minister, the Comte de Montmorin, to send out to foreign courts in April 1791 a letter extolling the virtues of the Revolution (described as " only the destruction of a multitude of abuses accumulated over centuries through the errors of the people or the power of the ministers "); but, both before and since, he had, in his secret correspondence with Spain, Sweden and Austria, repudiated all concessions made to the Third Estate and Constituents as having been extracted by force; and, since the end of 1790, the plan of escape that took place in June 1791 had been worked out with the Queen's devoted knight-errant, the Swedish Count Fersen. The plan was to leave Paris in disguise by night and join the Austrians at the eastern frontier-town of Montmédy, whence a call would be made to Europe's rulers to intervene against the Revolution. Owing to the bungling of the King and his associates and the vigilance of a village postmaster, the scheme miscarried and, on 25 June, the royal family was brought back from Varennes under heavy military and civilian escort to Paris. The episode had an electrifying effect and destroyed many illusions. For fear of an invasion, troops were mobilized at the frontiers; the Paris clubs intensified their agitation, and demonstrations called for Louis' abdication and the proclamation of a Republic. The Constituent Assembly was divided, but agreed on a compromise : the King was suspended from office but, having given a pledge to accept the pending Constitution, he was reinstated and the story was put out that he had been " kidnapped " by the enemies of the Revolution! The democrats and Republican journalists of the Cordeliers

Club, and even many of the more sedate sister-club of the Jacobins, refused to accept the verdict and organized a series of protesting petitions. The last of these, while not specifically demanding a Republic, called for Louis' abdication and was supported by a large crowd in the Champ de Mars in Paris. Some 6,000 had already signed the petition displayed on the *autel de la patrie*, when the Paris Commune, led by Bailly, decided to proscribe the demonstration, declared martial law, and sent Lafayette with 10,000 National Guards to disperse it. Meeting opposition, the Guards opened fire, killing and wounding some sixty petitioners; a further two hundred were arrested, while the Cordeliers Club leaders—including Danton—sought refuge in flight. It was a fateful episode, not so much because it won new recruits for a Republican movement (as yet in its infancy) as because from now on the old Third Estate of 1789 was irrevocably split. Already three weeks earlier, to mark their disapproval of the democrats' agitation to remove the King from office, the majority of constitutional monarchists, headed by Barnave and the brothers Lameth, had broken with the Jacobin Club, in which deputies of both Left and Centre had hitherto been united, to form their own society, the Club des Feuillants. Thus the Jacobins, among whom Robespierre was playing an increasingly important role, emerged as the acknowledged leaders of the Left within the Assembly and of the popular movement outside; and Jacobins, Cordeliers Club democrats and *sans-culottes* were drawn closer together in common opposition to the majority of Constituents, now held responsible not only for denying the humbler citizens the right to vote but for shedding their blood on the Champ de Mars.

The King's flight to Varennes, though its immediate effects were masked by the Assembly's attempts to forgive and forget and to unite the nation round the new Constitution, had other far-reaching consequences besides. It played its part in the series of developments leading up to the outbreak of war with Austria and Prussia on 20 April 1792. Though urged by Artois and the *émigrés* to intervene firmly against the Revolution, the "liberal" Austrian Emperor Leopold II, who had succeeded to the throne of his brother Joseph in 1790, had resolutely refused to take action. He no doubt regretted the indignities suffered by his sister, Marie Antoinette, but he had pressing enough problems to attend to within his own dominions and, like Pitt's government in England, he was inclined to welcome some measure of constitutional reform in France. The picture was changed by Louis' flight from Paris and his subsequent suspension from office; and, believing the French royal family to be in physical danger, Leopold issued the Padua Circular on 5 July, inviting Europe's rulers to concert "vigorous measures" in order to restore "the liberty and honour of the Most Christian King". This threat, however, was considerably toned down in the Declaration of Pillnitz issued jointly by Austria and Prussia on 27 August: by this time, Louis had been recalled to his duties, the Constitution was on its way, and besides, the response of the other powers to the Circular had been distinctly chilly or lukewarm. Consequently, the Declaration was more of a face-saver than an effective threat and merely invited the powers, *if* they could all agree, to prepare to unite to restore order in France: thus there was no suggestion of an immediate armed intervention. Yet, whatever its intentions, the Declaration was a provocation, which both served to unite the counter-revolution at home and abroad by giving it a programme, and provided the war party in France with a further pretext for banging the martial drums.

For, quite apart from the alleged crimes of the Revolution, the possibility of a rupture between France and Austria already existed. The Emperor's *protégé*, the Elector of Treves, had allowed Condé's army of *émigré* nobles to train and arm within his territories at Coblenz; and the German princes holding estates in Alsace had refused to accept the abolition or redemption of their feudal dues as decreed by the French Assembly in August 1789. Yet Treves had submitted to French coercion and agreed to disband the counter-revolutionary force at Coblenz; and negotiations on the princes' claims might, in spite of the support given to them by the Emperor and the Diet at Frankfort, have ended in agreed settlement if there had been a reasonable measure of goodwill on either side. But this proved impossible, both because of the growing belligerency of the Imperial Court (Leopold was succeeded in March 1792 by the more aggressive Francis II) and of the emergence of a strangely assorted war party in France. On the one hand, there was the Court itself which, encouraged by the Queen and her advisers, began to count on France's military defeat as the best means of restoring its own authority. Closely associated with the Court was the War Minister, Narbonne, current lover of Necker's daughter, Madame de Staël, whose plan was to provoke a limited war with a view to strengthening the power of the Crown by the way of a military dictatorship. But most effective of all in rousing the country to a state of warlike fervour was the new Left in the Legislative Assembly (which had succeeded the Constituents on 1 October 1791), led by Jacques-Pierre Brissot, deputy for Eure et Loir and closely associated with a group of deputies, several of them from the south-western department of the Gironde.[2] From October 1791 on, Brissot preached an armed crusade of the peoples against the crowned heads of Europe, in the course of which the peoples, liberated by their own endeavours or by the victory of French arms, would rally to the flag of revolution, while the King would be compelled to call on Brissot's supporters to take office. Brissot carried the argument from the floor of the Assembly to the Jacobin Club, where, in December, a heated debate took place on the theme between himself and Robespierre. Robespierre, alone of the Jacobin leaders at this time (if we except Marat, editor of the radical *L'Ami du Peuple*), opposed Brissot's plan for a

[2] At this time commonly called *Brissotins* and, after September 1792, Girondins. As Dr. M. J. Sydenham has argued (*The Girondins*, London, 1961), they had no clear-cut identity, and no distinctive policy other than one of fairly consistent opposition to the main body of Jacobins after October 1791. Yet this—and their eventual fate— gives them (like the Jacobins themselves) a certain identity, and I shall continue to call them by their traditional names in the following pages.

military crusade on the grounds that, far from promoting the cause of revolution abroad, it would play into the hands of its opponents and realize Narbonne's aim of military dictatorship at home. But Brissot won the day and the main body of Jacobins, the Parisian sections and clubs, and the great majority of the deputies to the Legislative Assembly, rallied to his view; and, after negotiations with the Emperor and the German princes had broken down in March, France declared war on Austria on 20 April and soon faced the combined armies of Austria and Prussia, led by Frederick II's old general, the Duke of Brunswick.

But Brissot's triumph was short-lived and it was Robespierre who, in the long run, was proved correct and whose party was to reap the harvest. At first things appeared to go Brissot's way: even before war broke out, the King was compelled to dismiss Narbonne and his Feuillant ministers and call to office men of the Brissotin connexion—Dumouriez, a professional soldier and spokesman for the anti-Austrian party; Clavière, a Swiss financier; and Roland, a civil servant and husband of a more famous wife. But the French forces, far from acting as " armed missionaries ", being quite unprepared for battle (still less for an offensive), fled in disorder from Brunswick's armies, and France lay open to the enemy. Armed counter-revolution broke out in the south. The *assignat* had fallen to 63 per cent of its face value in January and grain riots followed in the provinces. In Paris, as the result of civil war in the West Indian colonies, the price of sugar had trebled and provision shops in the *faubourgs* were broken into by angry citizens, who compelled grocers to sell their wares at the former price. Treachery in high places added further fuel to the flames: the Queen's intrigues with the Austrian Court were becoming widely suspected and the conviction grew, and was ably exploited, that an " Austrian Committee " was planning to restore the absolute monarchy by the aid of foreign arms. Brissot had boasted that such treasonable activities would redound to the advantage of his own party (" *il nous faut de grandes trahisons* ", he had claimed), and he and his associates did not hesitate to inflame popular passions against the Court. So much so that Louis felt obliged to dismiss the Brissotin ministers—an action that provoked a popular demonstration in Paris on 20 June, and in the course of which the petty shopkeepers and craftsmen of the two revolutionary *faubourgs* of St. Antoine and St. Marcel paraded in arms before the Assembly and broke into the Tuileries palace, where they obliged the reluctant Louis to don the Cap of Liberty and drink with them to the health of the nation.

This proved to be a dress-rehearsal for the greater and more violent insurrection of 10 August that captured the Tuileries and overthrew the monarchy. Yet the Brissotin party, though it had stoked up the flames and its ministers had been temporarily reinstated in office, derived no profit from it. In fact, by this time, they had surrendered the leadership of the popular movement to Robespierre and their Jacobin rivals. The truth is that, like the sorcerer's apprentice of legend and many other parties before and since, they were not prepared to face up to the consequences of the storm that they had themselves let loose. Having demagogically aroused the sections and *faubourgs* to demonstrate against the monarchy and having threatened to overthrow it, they now drew back in support of the King: they had not bargained for a Republic that would be at the mercy of the votes and weapons of the hitherto "passive" citizens, or *sans-culottes*. So the Jacobins, who had had little to do with the demonstration of 20 June, stepped into the breach. Pétion, who had succeeded Bailly as Mayor of Paris and was associated with Brissot and the Gironde, was still the hero of the day when the annual Festival of the Federation was celebrated on 14 July; but, by the end of the month, the mood had changed and forty-seven of the capital's forty-eight sections had declared for the King's abdication; and, by this time, Sieyes' old distinctions had broken down and passive citizens had been invited to attend the sectional assemblies. Yet, even now, Robespierre was arguing that the future of the monarchy, as of the Constitution itself, should be decided by a popularly elected Convention rather than by a resort to arms. But the genuine fears of a counter-revolutionary *coup* (the air was thick with rumours of plots and Lafayette had recently deserted the front to urge drastic measures against the democrats) and the pressure of the sections and clubs persuaded the Jacobin leaders to promote an armed insurrection. Preparations were already on foot when popular fears and hatreds were given a still sharper edge by the Duke of Brunswick's Manifesto of 1 August, which threatened the Parisian sections and National Guard with summary vengeance, should the invaders find them arms in hand. So, partly as the outcome of a premeditated design and partly as a measure of self-defence, Jacobins, visiting contingents of militiamen from Marseilles, Brest and other cities, and the Parisian sections and National Guard combined, under the direction of a newly formed "revolutionary" Commune, to capture the Tuileries by force of arms and drive the King to seek refuge in the Legislative Assembly. He was deposed six weeks later by the new National Convention, and the Republic was proclaimed.

In the wake of the revolution of 10 August 1792 followed the grisly episode known as the September Massacres, when the prisons of Paris were entered by armed bands, who set up hastily improvised "people's" tribunals and executed some 1,100 to 1,400 of their inmates—priests and political prisoners among them, but mainly common-law offenders : thieves, prostitutes, forgers and vagrants.[8] It was a mysterious episode, defying exact analysis; yet it seems to have been largely the product of a panic-fear engendered by the threat of counter-revolution and invasion : Verdun, a bare 200 miles from the capital, had just fallen to the Prussians; and able-bodied Parisians, responding to the summons of Danton, the new Minister of Justice, were flocking to enrol for service at the front, thus leaving the city more exposed. While the massacres were going on, and for some days after, there were persons in authority who were prepared to applaud them as a necessary act of popular justice, and even to recommend them as an

[8] P. Caron, *Les Massacres de septembre* (Paris, 1935).

example for others to follow. But once the crisis was past, there was no party or faction that would justify or claim credit for them; and the charge of having provoked or condoned them—or even of having failed to put a stop to them—became an accepted weapon in the struggle between parties, in which Jacobins sought to discredit Girondins and Girondins to blacken Jacobins, while royalists and moderates hurled the accusation at both parties without discrimination. And yet, whatever their origins and unsavoury as they were, the massacres were an event of some importance: they appeared to complete the destruction of the enemy within some weeks before the volunteers at Valmy, on 20 September, routed Brunswick's army and drove it back across the frontier. Thus the Republic, proclaimed that autumn, became established on what seemed at first a solid enough foundation—by the victory of the Revolution over its enemies at home and abroad.

The new Assembly, or National Convention, elected by male adult suffrage,[4] met on 20 September 1792. Of its 750 members, only 96 were former Constituents, while 190 others had sat in the Legislative Assembly. So there were many newcomers—among them the youthful Saint-Just, who was to become Robespierre's devoted supporter and lieutenant. Socially, they differed little from the members of the two preceding parliaments: there was a similar preponderance of former officials, lawyers, merchants and businessmen, though appreciably more provincial *avocats,* doctors and teachers; as before, there were no small peasants, and there were only two working men of their number—Noël Pointe, munition-worker of St.-Etienne, and Jean-Baptiste Armonville, wool-comber of Rheims. Politically, the Convention was composed of three main groups. The majority was formed by the great mass of independent deputies, not committed to any particular faction, known as the " Marsh " or " Plain "; to win the

---

[4] Yet workers and others living in furnished rooms or lodgings appear to have been debarred from voting until the further " revolution " of May-June 1793. Even after this, domestic servants remained disfranchised.

support of a large part of these would, of course, be a vital element in the struggle of the other parties for control of the Assembly. Of the latter, the larger group was that of the so-called "Girondins" (as the former Brissotins were now termed by their opponents), led by Vergniaud, Brissot, Gensonnet and Guadet, who, though not themselves in a majority, generally controlled the balance of voting and supplied most of the ministers. Against them were ranged the Jacobins or Mountain (so-called from the upper tiers of seats they occupied in the Chamber), who included all but one of the twenty-four deputies of Paris, headed by Robespierre, Marat and (on occasion) Danton. This first phase of the Convention's history was, in fact, marked by a prolonged and bitter duel between the Gironde and Mountain, which only came to an end when the leaders of the former were purged from the Assembly by another popular insurrection in June 1793. The Gironde had the advantage of numbers, of having at their service the greater part of the Paris press, and of enjoying considerable support in the provinces; at the same time, their equivocal behaviour in the August revolution had lost them their following among the Paris militants. The Mountain, on the other hand, while weak in the provinces, had, as the acknowledged victors of August, the solid backing of the clubs and sections of the capital. Thus the Jacobins now emerge as the consistent champions of Paris as the main bastion of revolution, while the Girondins are driven, partly from choice and partly from the circumstances of their election, and the tactics of their opponents, to advance "federalist" or national-provincial, policies in deliberate opposition to the pretensions of the capital but, in other respects, not greatly distinguishable from those promoted by the Constituents of 1789-91. Again, while all parties were committed, with varying degrees of enthusiasm, to the prosecution of the war to victory, the Girondins, as firm believers in economic liberalism and spokesmen for business interests, were far more consistent—and doctrinaire—than their opponents in clinging obstinately to *laissez-faire* solutions in all matters relating to the nation's economy, food-supplies and the general conduct of the war. The Jacobins, too, were predominantly *bons bourgeois* and showed little enthusiasm for a directed economy, still less for a division of properties; but they were closer to the people, more flexible in their attitudes, and more able and willing to yield gracefully to popular pressure and to adapt their views to meet the needs and exigencies of the moment. Thus the Girondins, on whom fell largely the task of government, by resisting exceptional measures and controls, fell increasingly foul of the sections and popular movement in Paris, and when a further round of treasons and defeats faced the Republic in the spring of 1793, they were held accountable and lost further credit. It was this and their growing tendency to promote the "federalist" claims of the provinces against the Jacobin conception of "the Republic one and indivisible" that finally provided their opponents with the means and the pretext for expelling them from the Assembly.

Meanwhile, the struggle for power was waged over more immediate issues. In the first round, the Gironde succeeded in persuading the Assembly to disband the "revolutionary" Commune that had usurped authority in Paris on the eve of the August revolution and had armed itself with exceptional powers. Once the crisis was over, their exercise was bound to be offensive to the nation's accredited representatives; so the Jacobins did little to justify the Commune's extra-legal activities and, after a few heated exchanges, gracefully consented to its liquidation. More stubborn and prolonged was the battle over the trial and execution of Louis XVI. After his surrender to the Legislative Assembly, Louis had been lodged with his family in the Temple prison to await his fate. Robespierre now proposed, on behalf of the Jacobins, that he be brought before the Convention and sentenced to death as a traitor to the nation. There should be no formal trial, he urged in a famous speech, as the King had already been judged by the people: "The right of punishing the tyrant and the right of dethroning him are the same things; they do not take different forms." The people having already passed judgment, the Convention had, therefore, merely to record a sentence of death. While accepting a part of this argument, the Assembly decided in favour of a trial, but one in which it should itself be both prosecutor and judge. Several of the Girondin deputies wished to spare the King's life; but such was the weight of evidence against Louis (an iron chest containing his secret correspondence had recently been unearthed in the Tuileries) that they chose to join in the unanimous verdict of guilty. Following this, they resorted to manœuvre: having failed to obtain a stay of execution, they demanded a referendum; but again they were outvoted, and Louis was executed on 21 January 1793.

But as long as victories could be recorded for French arms —and the troops of the Republic had, following the rout of the Prussians at Valmy and Jemappes, recently annexed Belgium and were preparing to occupy Holland—the Girondins retained the balance of power within the Assembly. In March, however, Dumouriez was driven back from the Netherlands and, failing to persuade his army to march on the Convention, disperse the Jacobins and restore the Constitution of 1791 with Louis XVII as King, he deserted to the enemy. Mutual recriminations followed in the Convention. The Girondins, as close associates of the general, were the more exposed; but, to defend themselves, they turned the attack against Danton, who had been sent to parley with Dumouriez on the eve of his desertion. The attempt failed: Danton, hitherto a mediator between the warring factions, was driven into closer partnership with the Jacobins, and the Gironde emerged further scathed from the encounter. Another result of this crisis was that the Assembly, under the compelling pressure of events, was persuaded to enact a number of exceptional measures that would prove of the greatest importance to the Revolutionary Government of the future: they included the creation of a Revolutionary Tribunal, a Committee of Public Safety and "revolutionary committees" in the sections or communes, and the despatch to the provinces of agents vested with the Convention's authority and soon to be known as "representatives on mission".

Meanwhile, the economic situation was also working to the advantage of the Mountain and to the detriment of their adversaries. The *assignat* had fallen to only half its nominal value in February, and the price of food, after remaining comparatively stable in the preceding summer and autumn, had taken another sharp upward turn in the spring. Once more, the prices of colonial products—coffee, sugar, candles, soap—had risen out of all proportion; but, this time, the rise covered a far wider range of consumers' goods than in February 1792. The riots that followed were, correspondingly, more intense and widespread than those of the year before; and, on 25 and 26 February, grocers' shops in almost every section in Paris were invaded by *sans-culottes*, who refused to pay more than they had for such products in 1790, or even helped themselves without paying anything at all. The City Council, the Jacobin Club and the parties in the Convention all joined in denouncing this infringement of the sacred rights of property: Barère (who was soon to desert the Plain for the Mountain) spoke darkly, though without a shred of supporting evidence, of "the perfidious incitement of aristocrats in disguise"; while Robespierre deplored that "patriots" should be so far misled as to riot, for what he termed *de chétives marchandises*. But, though none of the Assembly's spokesmen was prepared to condone such activities, it was once more the Girondins, as the governing party and that most thoroughly committed to upholding the freedom of the market, that reaped all the disadvantages, while their opponents correspondingly benefited. In March, the Paris Commune, led by Jacobin supporters, decided to fix the price of bread, by the aid of a subsidy to bakers, at 3 sous a pound—a mere 50 per cent above the normal pre-revolutionary level at a time when other prices had more than doubled; and, two months later, the Assembly followed suit by passing its first "Maximum" law, whereby local authorities all over the country were authorized to control the price and supply of bread and flour. Meanwhile, a movement had begun in the Paris sections, clubs and streets calling for a popular "insurrection" to purge the Assembly of the Girondin leaders. Such an uprising was, in fact, attempted on 10 March by the small group of extreme revolutionaries known as the Enragés, whose leaders were Jacques Roux, the "red" priest of the Gravilliers Section, Théophile Leclerc and Jean Varlet. The Enragés stood closer than any other group at this time to the *sans-culottes* in the streets and markets and, alone of the parties, actively supported the demand that a ceiling be placed on the prices of all consumers' goods; and Jacques Roux had been implicated (with what justice is uncertain) in the February riots. Varlet had been drawing large audiences to his open-air rostrum on the Terrasse des Feuillants, at the gates of the Assembly, where he demanded the death-penalty for hoarders and speculators, the impeachment of Roland, Minister of the Interior, and the removal of Brissot from the Convention; and considerable response would have been forthcoming for his and his associates' call for an uprising, had the Paris Commune, the Faubourg St-Antoine and the Jacobins been willing to give it their blessing.

But the Mountain and Jacobin leaders were in no immediate hurry. They had learned wisdom from experience; and while, unlike their Girondin opponents, they were quite willing to use the popular movement to promote their political ends, they had no intention of allowing its direction to pass into other hands—either to the Enragés or to Hébert, the editor of the popular *Père Duchesne*, whose influence was steadily increasing in the Cordeliers Club and the Paris Commune. Besides, they feared that a premature rising would entail a too drastic purge of the Convention, whose Rump would be powerless to resist the economic demands of the *sans-culottes*; that it would be accompanied by a new outbreak of prison massacres, and leave Paris isolated in the face of the combined hostility of the provinces. So they proceeded with caution; but by early April they were ready to formulate their programme, win the support of the sections, and wrest

the leadership of the popular movement from either group of
"extremists". Accordingly, on 5 April, in the Jacobin Club,
Robespierre's younger brother, Augustin, publicly invited the
sections to present themselves at the bar of the Convention
and "force us to arrest the disloyal deputies". The response
was immediate and, within a week, the sections had "named"
twenty-two deputies of the Gironde, whose removal from the
Assembly would both meet the popular demand for a purge of
the discredited Convention and assure the Mountain of a
working majority within it. By mid-April, three in four of
the sections had given their individual support—many of them
further stirred to action by the Girondins' folly in summoning the popular Marat before the Revolutionary Tribunal.
The Commune endorsed the demands and, a month later, at
its invitation, the great majority of the sections formed a
Central Revolutionary Committee at the former Archbishop's
Palace, which organized and directed the revolution of 31
May—2 June with almost military precision. The National
Guard was enlarged and its command given to Hanriot, son
of a domestic servant and a former customs clerk, in the place
of Santerre, the wealthy St. Antoine brewer. In addition, it
was decided to raise in the sections a revolutionary militia of
20,000 *sans-culottes* who should be compensated for their loss
of work by the payment of 40 sous for each day spent under
arms. The tocsin was sounded, workshops and *barrières* were
closed; and, after a couple of false starts, the Tuileries were
surrounded on 2 June by a combined force of National Guards
and armed *sans-culottes*. The deputies, after attempting an
heroic sortie from the Assembly and finding every exit
blocked, surrendered ignominiously to the insurgents' demands. Twenty-nine deputies and two ministers of the
defeated party were placed under house arrest. There was
nothing said for the moment about the most urgent of the
items on the popular programme—that food prices be controlled—but the Mountain had achieved its immediate aims.

From now on, the Jacobin leaders were assured of a working majority and they proceeded, with remarkable speed, to

celebrate and consolidate their victory by passing through the Convention and primary assemblies the Constitution of June 1793—a charter of the greatest historical significance in that, for the first time, a nation was provided (on paper at least) with a system of government both republican and democratic, under which all male citizens had the vote and a considerable measure of control over their representatives and governors. It certainly had its limitations : as Roux pointed out to an enraged Assembly, it failed, for example, to make adequate provision for the economic needs of the poor. Meanwhile, however, the Jacobins had other more pressing problems to attend to. Stirred by "federalist" agitation, the city of Lyons and parts of the south and south-west had overthrown their Jacobin authorities and risen in arms against the newly purged Convention; Toulon was preparing to surrender to the English (at war with France since 1 February 1793); and the revolt of the Vendée peasants in support of their priests and landlords—soon to be followed by that of the Breton and Norman *chouans*—had, since March, been sapping the country's military strength. Even in Paris, the moderates (among them the notorious ex-Marquis de Sade) were still in control of a dozen sections of the centre and west. The economic position continued to deteriorate. The *assignat,* having fallen to 36 per cent of its value in June, slumped further to 22 per cent in August. Food prices rose again in the summer and, though the price of bread had been fixed, there were shortages and queues at bakers' shops in June, August and September. In this atmosphere, it was impossible to continue to resist the insistent popular demand for a general control of prices, and the further demands for exceptional measures to restrain hoarders and speculators and to ensure the supply of food to Paris and other cities.

Matters were brought to a head by a further intervention of the Parisian *sans-culottes*. In July and August, the remaining strongholds of "moderation" had been purged of their bourgeois and conservative elements; and, during August and the first days of September, resolutions were pouring in to the

Convention calling for measures to place a ceiling (or " maximum ") on prices, to curb inflation and restrain speculation and hoarding. These demands of the small tradesmen and property-owners, who now dominated the sectional assemblies, were given a sharper edge by the massive street-demonstrations of the lower order of *sans-culottes*—the wage-earners and small craftsmen—that took place in the city on 4 and 5 September. The " insurrection " started in the early morning with meetings of building workers and workshop journeymen of the Temple and St. Denis districts, north of the City Hall. Another contingent set out from the boulevards, near the Ministry of War, whose secretary was Vincent, one of Hébert's lieutenants. Calling for bread, the demonstrators advanced on the Place de Grève and the City Hall. The Commune's leaders, Hébert and Chaumette, tried at first to fob them off with a display of oratory; but it was agreed, on Hébert's suggestion, that they should reassemble the next morning and march to the Convention and present demands for severe measures against hoarders and political suspects; the Jacobin Club also promised to join in. The same evening, the Commune, while giving orders to disperse building workers who were claiming higher wages, instructed workshops to close on the morrow so that masters and journeymen might attend the demonstration. In the flood of rhetoric that followed in the Assembly on the 5th, the questions of prices and supplies, though they had been the prime movers in the agitation on the 4th, were once more conveniently forgotten. Yet important decisions were taken : sections were to meet only twice a week, but needy *sans-culottes* were to be paid 40 sous per attendance; suspects were to be rounded up; and, after several months' delay, an *armée révolutionnaire,* recruited from city *sans-culottes,* was set on foot, which, as an instrument of the Terror (now put on the order of the day), was to ensure the adequate provision of supplies to Paris from the neighbouring countryside.[5] At last, having tried or debated every

[5] For a full study see R. C. Cobb, *Les Armées révolutionnaires* (2 vols., Paris, 1961-3).

other expedient, the Convention yielded to popular pressure and, on 29 September, passed the law of the *Maximum Général,* which pegged the price of not only bread but of a large range of essential goods and services at levels prevailing in the departments in June 1790 plus one-third, while raising wages by one-half. The measure was well received by the small shopkeepers, masters and journeymen of the capital, who had been its most eager and insistent promoters. "The people," wrote an agent of the Ministry of the Interior the next day, "has received with delight the decrees of the National Convention which fix the prices of essential goods." The measure raised new problems, too, but they were not immediately apparent.

Thus a new and distinctive phase of the Revolution had opened. Like their predecessors, the new ruling party, the Jacobins, owed their ascendancy largely to popular intervention but, unlike them, had quite deliberately courted the people and accepted them as their allies. In return for their support, the *sans-culottes* had received substantial benefits: they had won the right to vote and their demand for cheap food and the control of supplies. Not only that but, this time, there had emerged a certain division of authority between the governing party and their popular allies as well. While the Jacobins controlled the Assembly and organs of government, from which the *sans-culottes* were almost entirely excluded, the popular militants, for their part, held office in the Commune and dominated the sectional assemblies and clubs, the local "revolutionary" committees and battalions of the National Guard. Yet, being riddled with contradictions, the partnership could not last long: these had already become apparent on the morrow of the common victory and would become far sharper in the critical months ahead. Its bonds already loosened in October 1793, by the summer of 1794 the alliance lay in ruins and brought down both partners in its fall. How this happened will be told in the next chapter.

Chapter VIII

ROBESPIERRE

The new "revolutionary" Government did not begin to emerge until October 1793; yet the new phase of the Revolution really opened when Robespierre and his principal lieutenants joined the Committee of Public Safety in July. Up till now, the Committee had not done much more than fulfil its original function of acting as a watch-dog over the executive council of ministers; now it became the core of a strong government, the first that the Revolution had created.

The twelve men who composed the Committee until Robespierre's fall a year later were a remarkable team; "a stranger set of Cloud-Compellers," Carlyle wrote of them, "the Earth never saw." They by no means formed a closely-knit party group and it was only the compelling problems of the moment that forced on them cohesion and unity of purpose. The weakest and shortest-lived was Hérault de Séchelles, former *parlementaire* and aristocrat, who had achieved temporary distinction for the part he played as the Assembly's President in expelling the Girondins in June; he fell from the Committee in late December and, three months later, went to the scaffold with Danton. Two members had, since June, emerged from the Plain: Bertrand Barère, a "trimming" lawyer, and Robert Lindet, who took charge of food supplies. Four men were to concern themselves mainly with military matters and supplies to the armed forces: Prieur of the Marne, lawyer and emissary to the armies; Prieur of the Côte d'Or, an engineer officer who undertook the supply of munitions; Jeanbon Saint-André, a Protestant ex-pastor and specialist in naval affairs; and the great Lazare Carnot, a military genius whom even Napoleon termed "the organizer of victory". There were two strong-arm men of the Left recruited from the

Cordeliers Club after the September riots : Collot d'Herbois, a former actor, and Billaud-Varenne, lawyer and pamphleteer. They were matched in vigour and eloquence by Robespierre's two intimate associates : Georges Couthon, another lawyer, condemned by paralysis to perambulate in a wheel-chair; and Louis Antoine Saint-Just, a law graduate barely twenty-six years of age, visionary and man of action, proud and courageous and said by an opponent to "carry his head like the Holy Sacrament". And, lastly, there was Maximilien Robespierre, who, though holding no particular office, soon became accepted as the Committee's outstanding leader.

Historians have generally, until recent times, given Robespierre a rough handling : taking their cue from the men who overthrew him, they have tended to dismiss him as a prim and thin-lipped fanatic, a petty tyrant and "man of blood", dedicated to the cult of the guillotine and aspiring to personal dictatorship; even his reputation for "incorruptibility" has been thrown in his teeth; and Acton called him "the most hateful character in the forefront of history since Machiavelli reduced to a code the wickedness of public men". More recently, since Albert Mathiez took up the cudgels in his defence, he has been represented, if not as the incarnation of all the virtues, at least as the leading public figure of the Revolution, its most consistent democrat and the most persuasive of its spokesmen. Robespierre was born at Arras in 1758, the son and grandson of lawyers, and acquired a taste for the classics and a love for Rousseau from his Oratorian teachers at the College of Louis-le-Grand in Paris. It was from Rousseau that he drew his belief in the sovereignty of the people and in the social utility of a religion stripped of superstition, and his social ideal of a republic of small and middling property-owners, uncorrupted by either wealth or poverty : this conception lay at the back of much of his talk of "corruption" and "virtue". Already known as a poor man's advocate, he was elected to represent his native town in the States General of 1789. At Versailles and in the Constituent Assembly, he soon distinguished himself as a liberal and a democrat and as a consistent champion of the Rights of Man. After September 1791, being debarred, like other Constituents, from sitting in the Legislative Assembly by a " self-denying ordinance " that he had himself proposed, he devoted his energies to the Jacobin Club and the administration of the capital. In the winter and spring of 1791-2, his opposition to Brissot on the great issue of the " revolutionary " war lost him his popularity for a while among the Paris sections and clubs, but, by the summer, his reputation had been restored and he played a leading part (though behind the scenes) in the overthrow of the monarchy, joined the " revolutionary " Commune after the event, and became the Mountain's chief spokesman in its duel with the Gironde in the National Convention. He took no direct part in the May-June insurrection that expelled them, but, in many ways, his was the brain that inspired it. By this time, having long been an ardent defender of the inviolability of the Assembly and of the unrestricted freedom of speech and the press, he had been brought by his experience of war and revolution to shed his liberal beliefs. The Revolution, he now maintained, could only be saved and its external and internal enemies be defeated if, with the aid of the armed *sans-culottes*, a strong central government were set up to restrain both the remnants of aristocracy and the " egoism " of the rich. " What we need (he wrote at this time) is *a single will*. This rising must continue until the measures necessary for saving the Republic have been taken. The people must ally itself with the Convention, and the Convention must make use of the people." It was a programme that looked beyond the June " days " to the tasks facing the Committee of Public Safety in the autumn and winter of 1793.

Purged of its Dantonist members, who had vainly attempted to end foreign invasion by negotiation and the " federalist " revolt in the provinces by conciliation, the new Committee took firm measures to organize the nation's defences. The west-country rebellion was taken seriously in hand, and a properly equipped force despatched to the Vendée achieved early success. Caen, Bordeaux, Nantes, Marseilles and Lyons were wrested from the "federalists" and restored to revolutionary authority; and the siege of Toulon by an English fleet was raised, largely through the skill and initiative of a young artillery officer, Napoleon Bonaparte. On 23 August, the Convention agreed in principle to mobilize the nation for war by ordering a *levée en masse* of the whole French population : while the young should go to battle and married men forge arms, women stitch tents and uniforms and children make bandages, even the old men were to "repair to the public places, stimulate the courage of the warriors and preach the unity of the Republic and the hatred of Kings". State workshops were set up to manufacture arms; armies were recruited, trained and equipped by the organizing genius of Carnot; while representatives were sent on continuous missions to the front to strengthen the troops' morale and ensure their supplies. Thus the Republic, with nearly a million men under arms, began to clear its soil of the invaders : Jourdan defeated Coburg at Wattignies in October; Hoche pursued the enemy across the Vosges; Kellermann freed Savoy; the Spaniards were driven back over the Pyrenees; and finally, in June 1794, Jourdan's victory over Coburg at Fleurus drove the last Coalition soldier across the frontier.

Meanwhile, the "economic Terror" had at last brought currency speculation and inflation under control : the *assignat,* having fallen to 22 per cent of its value in August, rose to 33 per cent in November and to 48 per cent in December. During these months, too, in spite of war, the supply of food to the population of the cities was probably more regularly assured than at any other time since the autumn of 1791. Nor were more far-reaching social measures entirely neglected. The peasants' debt to their former landlords was finally written off in July 1793, thus completing the legislative destruction of feudalism; while some efforts were made (though admittedly half-hearted) to encourage small peasants to combine and purchase the lands of *émigrés,* now put up for auction in smaller lots. Possibly more radical in intention, though they came to nothing, were the Convention's later decrees, inspired by Robespierre and Saint-Just, to divide and distribute the confiscated properties of "suspects" among poor and needy "patriots" (the laws of Ventôse, February-March 1794). The Committee also looked to the future by laying before the Assembly a succession of drafts relating to education, industry, the civil code and public assistance. Some of them did not survive the fall of their promoters; others became part of the body of laws that eventually emerged from the Revolution. Little wonder that the great Committee has, on one score or another, won the applause of even some of its severest critics.

But, to realize their aims, the new rulers of France were compelled, far more by the logic and pressure of events than by the teachings of the *philosophes,* to abandon the haphazard methods of government accepted by their predecessors; and Robespierre's conception of a government of "a single will", hastily sketched in June, began to take shape in the autumn. Its basis had, as we noted, already been laid by the exceptional measures adopted as a result of the crisis of March 1793; and others had followed in August and September. But to call the nation to arms and institute the Terror against hoarders and speculators was one thing; to direct their operation was another. In fact, during the autumn months, something like administrative anarchy prevailed in a number of departments, as local committees, *armées révolutionnaires* (many raised without the Assembly's authority), and powerful "pro-consuls" like Fouché, Tallien and Carrier, armed with extraordinary powers, tended to interpret and apply the law after their own fashion.[1] So the needs of war, of civil peace and public order—quite apart from any personal considerations—combined to persuade Robespierre and his associates to take further steps to strengthen their control in Paris. Such measures, of course, to be effective, could hardly fail to flout the liberal-democratic provisions of the Constitution of June 1793. On 10 October, the Convention was persuaded to take the first step by declaring that "the provisional government of France is revolutionary until the peace". Thus, the excep-

[1] R. C. Cobb, *Les Armées révolutionnaires,* vol. II.

tional measures were given a greater degree of permanency and the democratic Constitution of 1793 was, for the time being at least, put into cold storage. But to conclude from this, as many have done, that this was intended all along and that "revolutionary" government corresponded to the long cherished ambitions of the Jacobin leaders is to misrepresent both their principles and the evolution of their policies. We have no means of knowing whether they ever sincerely hoped to restore the Constitution once the war was over; though we do know that it was not they but their successors who finally buried it and proscribed its advocates. Marat, it is true, had long since called for a one-man dictatorship on the Roman model; but Marat cared little for "philosophical" niceties and, anyway, he had been stabbed to death by Charlotte Corday in July 1793. Robespierre and the other leaders, however, were highly susceptible to the teachings of the "philosophers" and these prescribed not a dictatorship or "revolutionary" government, but a strong legislature, a weak executive and the "separation of powers".

Admittedly, Rousseau's writings on the State and on the "general will" might provide an argument: had he not suggested that it might be necessary to "force men to be free"? But no more in Rousseau than in Montesquieu could there be found a recipe for the system of government that took legislative shape in the law of 4 December 1793—a system, it should be noted, that, under the circumstances, was as readily accepted by the Plain as by the Mountain. While deriving their authority solely from the Convention, the two Committees of General Security and Public Safety were vested with full executive powers. The first was made responsible for police and internal security: thus the Revolutionary Tribunal and the work of the local vigilance and "revolutionary" committees were to be its special province. The second had far more extensive powers: to control ministers, appoint generals, conduct foreign policy, and to purge and direct local government. In fact, the transfer of authority and centralization of government were effected not so much at the expense of the Convention as of the departments and communes. Only in one respect was the authority of parliament ostensibly weakened: by curbing the independence of the " representatives on mission ", sent out since April by the Convention, and subjecting them to the rigorous control of the Committee of Public Safety. But the activities of local authorities were severely restricted: departments were left with purely routine functions, districts were made responsible for executing " revolutionary " decrees, and the old *procureurs* (proctors) of departments and communes were replaced by " national agents " answerable to the central government. The independence of Paris, long the mainstay of the Jacobins in their struggle for power, was further curbed by depriving the Commune of the right to send commissioners to the provinces, by limiting its control over the National Guard, and by subjecting the " revolutionary " committees of the sections to the direction of the Committee of General Security. The Terror remained, but it was to be institutionalized and directed from the centre. It was the end of anarchy, but it was the beginning of the end of popular initiative as well.

Thus, strong government had at length emerged and it is doubtful if the Republic's achievements could have been realized without it. Yet, by its very nature, it could hardly fail to provoke a chorus of protests from former supporters and injured parties. The opposition arose, in the first place, from within the Jacobins' own ranks and from their allies of the Cordeliers Club; but it was by no means united, and divided early into two mutually hostile factions. The opposition of the Right gathered round Danton and the so-called party of the Indulgents; and that of the Left round Hébert and the leaders of the Paris Commune and Cordeliers Club. Danton, dismissed from the Committee of Public Safety in the reshuffle of 10 July, retired at first with a new wife to his country estate at Arcis-sur-Aube and appeared to be nursing his wounds in silence. But encouraged by old friends—among them the journalist Camille Desmoulins—he returned to the capital in

November and began to lead what was alternatively a pressure-group and an organized opposition within the Assembly. In so far as the Dantonists had any precise political programme, it was to break up the "revolutionary" government, restore the freedom of action of local authorities, dismantle the machinery of the Terror, liberate the national economy from controls and to negotiate a peace—in the first place, by detaching England from the European coalition. They divided their activities: Danton himself was their spokesman on matters of administration and higher policy; Desmoulins founded a new journal, *Le Vieux Cordelier*, in which he campaigned for greater "clemency" and the release of "suspects"; while others, being perhaps of a more practical disposition, displayed their contempt for economic controls by dabbling in share-deals and engaging in shady financial ventures.

Unlike the Dantonists, the Left opposition had little following in the Convention: their main hunting-grounds were the Cordeliers Club, the Paris Commune, the *armées révolutionnaires* and the clubs and sections, among whose militants they continued to enjoy considerable support. The Jacobin leaders had already destroyed their main rivals for popular favour, the Enragés, and arrested their leaders: Jacques Roux had committed suicide in jail in October. Since then, Hébert had taken over Roux's programme and grafted it on to his own: in his popular and scurrilous organ, *Le Père Duchesne*, he called day in and day out for a more vigorous prosecution of the war and a more frequent use of the guillotine against hoarders and speculators, merchants and shopkeepers, whose activities, he claimed with considerable justice, were undermining the operation of the price-controls enacted by the Convention. Hébert and his lieutenant, Chaumette, also played, with Fouché, a leading part in stoking up the campaign against the Christian religion in both Paris and the provinces. While the Assembly had generally restricted its coercive measures to the "non-juring" or "refractory" clergy, the Constitutional Church now also came under fire;

and in the wave of "de-christianization" that spread from Paris and the department of the Nièvre (where Chaumette had a following), churches were closed wholesale, priests and bishops were compelled to give up their offices, and the Goddess of Reason was solemnly enthroned, to the accompaniment of civic incantations, in the Cathedral of Notre Dame. It is probable that the earlier agitation of the "Hébertists" was intended to spur the Jacobins and the Convention to greater energy rather than to usurp their authority; but the law of 4 December, by extending the power of the Committees at the expense of the Commune, the denunciations of the Dantonists and the growing hostility of Robespierre gradually drove them into more open opposition.

The *sans-culottes*, too, had their reasons for objecting to the new governmental measures; they were, in fact, partly directed against themselves. They had, as we have seen, become a force to be reckoned with by those in authority, whether as allies or as opponents. Gradually, through a series of purges, the Paris sections and the Commune had been recast in their social image: during this period of the Revolution, nearly three in four of the members of local "revolutionary" committees were small manufacturers, tradesmen and craftsmen; and similar elements accounted for 93 of the 132 general councillors of the Commune.[2] In many provincial centres, the proportion of *sans-culottes* on local governing committees may have been even higher.[3] This created a problem of divided counsels, as it is hardly surprising that the political ideas and social aspirations of such men, though sharing much in common with them, should differ in important respects from those of the proprietors, lawyers, doctors, teachers and businessmen who sat in the Convention or even from those of the smaller lawyers, tradesmen and civil servants who pre-

[2] See A. Soboul, *Les Sans-culottes parisiens en l'an II* (Paris, 1958), pp. 444-45; and P. Sainte-Claire Deville, *La Commune de l'an II* (Paris, 1946), pp. 42-76.

[3] See N. Hampson, *A Social History of the French Revolution* (1963), pp. 209-13.

dominated in the provincial Jacobin clubs and societies.[4] While both Plain and Mountain now favoured strong government to destroy the Revolution's enemies and win the war, the *sans-culottes* clung to the discarded Constitution of 1793; they passionately believed that popular sovereignty was essentially vested in the primary assemblies, and therefore in the Paris sections; and they demanded the frequent recall and constant accountability of deputies to their constituents. Such being their views, they could hardly fail to challenge the Jacobins' claim that, "for the duration", the Convention and its committees should be the sole custodians and executors of the "general will". Again, while the Jacobins and the Convention—even the Robespierrists among them—were prepared to tolerate controls and State-direction of the nation's economy merely as exceptional and temporary measures, to the *sans-culottes* they appeared to ensure a more permanent degree of security and social justice: in September, a Paris section had even called for a ceiling on incomes and limits to be placed on the size of farms and businesses. And while the Jacobins, as employers and as members of parliament and government committees, were interested in checking the upward movement of wages, the wage-earners among the *sans-culottes* (particularly numerous in Paris) had every motive and, owing to the shortage of labour in time of war, every opportunity for pushing up earnings as high as employers would be willing to pay. So, in one way or another, by the end of 1793 the old alliance between Jacobins and people was beginning to wear thin.[5]

At first, it was the "Hébertist" challenge that faced the Jacobins with the greatest danger. The activities of the "dechristianizers", both in Paris and the provinces, filled them with particular concern: they had enough difficulty already in checking the spread of the peasant rebellion in the west without gratuitously throwing into the arms of counter-revolution

[4] C. Crane Brinton, *The Jacobins* (new edition, New York, 1961), pp. 46-72, appendix II.

[5] For a full treatment, see Soboul, *Les Sans-culottes parisiens en l'an II*, and (for the provinces) Cobb, *Les Armées révolutionnaires*, vol. II.

great numbers of Frenchmen whose religious beliefs persisted, and who could not fail to be outraged by the violent attacks on priests and the closure of churches. So when, in November, the Commune closed down every place of worship in Paris, Robespierre riposted by denouncing Fouché, Chaumette and their associates as atheists and diversionists, and called for a return to the Convention's agreed policy of the right to worship. Danton, summoned from Arcis and seeing an opportunity for driving a wedge between Robespierre and his two former "Hébertist" colleagues, Collot d'Herbois and Billaud-Varenne, joined in the fray. So a complicated three-cornered fight ensued, variously fought out in the Jacobin Club, the Convention and the two Committees, in the course of which the government's spokesmen, led by Robespierre, alternately sought allies in one faction or the other, but more frequently leaned towards Danton and the Indulgents in order to weaken and destroy the Left. Thus encouraged, the Indulgents stepped up their own campaign; and the growing violence of their denunciations, particularly those of Desmoulins in *Le Vieux Cordelier*, compelled Robespierre to break with the Dantonists and engage both factions at once; besides, a lieutenant of Danton's, Fabre d'Eglantine, had, in pursuit of financial gain, been found guilty of falsifying a decree of the Assembly relating to the East India Company; and Danton's own efforts to end the war were endangering the government's military operations. So the outcome was the almost simultaneous destruction of both groups. In early March, Hébert and his Cordeliers Club allies, Vincent and Ronsin, tried to force the pace by threatening another insurrection on the model of that of June or September 1793; but it was a gesture of despair rather than of strength, as, by this time, their hold on the Commune and the sections had been weakened. The conspirators were arrested and guillotined on 25 March; Chaumette followed them to the scaffold three weeks later. This equally sealed the fate of Danton and Desmoulins, whose survival, after the destruction of Hébert, would have led to a move to the Right and the overthrow of the Committees. Robespierre's personal affection for Des-moulins made him hesitate to sign their death-warrant; but his scruples were overruled by Saint-Just, Collot and Billaud and, after a hurried and embarrassing trial, the Dantonists were executed on 5 April.

Danton's fate, though distasteful to former associates in the Convention, caused not a ripple of protest in the sections or among the *sans-culottes*. Hébert's execution, too, was taken calmly; the prevailing mood was one of apathy rather than anger. But the very silence was ominous : Hébert, though not loved like Marat, had been a familiar mouthpiece for popular passions and prejudices and his removal snapped the links that had bound the *sans-culottes* to the Commune, now purged and converted into a Robespierrist stronghold. Besides, Hébert's fall had inevitably been accompanied by an attack on those popular institutions in which his influence had been strongest : thus, the Parisian *armée révolutionnaire* (following its offshoots in the provinces) was disbanded; the committees for tracking down hoarders were dissolved, soon to be fol-lowed by the majority of the " popular " societies in the sec-tions which, unlike the original *sociétés populaires,* lay out-side the close guidance and scrutiny of the Jacobin Club. As the " revolutionary committees " had already been firmly tied to the Committee of General Security, the sections themselves soon ceased to reflect the independent views and activities of the *sans-culottes* and tended to become mere rubber-stamps for Jacobin directives and government decisions. Saint-Just noted the change and summed it up in a phrase : " *la Révolu-tion est glacée* ".

The *sans-culottes,* thus politically silenced, were further estranged by the government's economic measures. The *Maximum* laws, after rousing early enthusiasm, had proved a disappointment. For a while, prices remained stable; but the laws could only be enforced in a country of predominantly small producers and distributors by further measures of coercion and repression; and these the government, anxious to retain the support of peasants, merchants and manufacturers, was quite unwilling to take. So producers, large and small, began to resort to wholesale evasions of the law; and shopkeepers, in turn, passed on the higher prices that ensued to their customers. The *sans-culottes,* as small consumers, reacted violently, demonstrated against butchers and grocers, and demanded more vigorous measures of control. By January, the authorities were faced with the choice of either intensifying the Terror against the law-breaking merchants and producers or of officially relaxing the regulations at the expense of the protesting consumers. Urged by Barère, they decided on the second course: in late March, an amended *Maximum* was published providing for higher prices and profit margins; currency speculators were allowed to show their faces once more; and the *assignat* had, by July, slipped back to 36 per cent of its nominal value. Consequently the agitation in the markets revived and the Jacobin leaders had their share of the epithets hurled at merchants, speculators, and shopkeepers. And more was to come. The *Maximum* law of September 1793 provided, as we saw, for the control of wages as well as of prices; under existing circumstances, this meant that local authorities were required to *reduce* wages to a level fifty per cent above that of 1790. This had been done in many districts where workers' resistance was not likely to be strong; but not in Paris, where wages had risen two or three times above their pre-revolutionary level and where the Commune, as long as the " Hébertists " were in charge, had had little intention of enforcing this part of the law. The government itself, however, was responsible for wages in its own workshops and had introduced new scales (tempered somewhat by expedience) for its arms-workers and others. Meanwhile, to prevent wages in private industry from getting out of hand, it had on more than one occasion invoked the Le Chapelier Law against workers' " combinations " and had even sent strikers before the Revolutionary Tribunal. Yet the greater problems remained and, even after the fall of Hébert, the Commune hesitated for many weeks before taking so dangerous a step as to reduce the current earnings of a large part of the Parisian population by one half, or even more. When they took the plunge and published the new scales on 23 July, it was at an unfortunate time; and the hostility of the wage-earners no doubt played its part in Robespierre's fall from power a few days later.

Meanwhile, for some weeks past, Robespierre and his group had been losing their hold on the Convention and the governing Committees. Though the Convention had accepted, without much demur, the successive purges of Girondins and Dantonists, their elimination had left fears and resentments that another crisis would bring into the open. These had been stirred afresh by the law of the 22nd Prairial (10 June 1794) and the speed with which it had been rushed through the Assembly. The law, drafted by Robespierre and Couthon following an attempt on Robespierre's and Collot's lives, speeded the process of justice within the Revolutionary Tribunal and deprived the prisoner of the aid of defending counsel; but it also appeared to many deputies to threaten their parliamentary immunity. From this law, too, sprang the "Great Terror" which, in Paris, accounted for nearly 1,300 of the guillotine's 2,600 victims. But more important, perhaps, in weakening the links that had hitherto bound Robespierre and the deputies of the Plain was the victory won at Fleurus on 26 June, as a result of which the Republic was cleared of foreign troops and the road to Belgium lay once more open. So why, it began to be whispered, continue to support a policy of Terror and tightened belts, reluctantly accepted at a moment of crisis, when that crisis was now past? Besides, the danger from the Left was over: the "wild men" of the Commune had been silenced and the *sans-culottes* had had their wings clipped and their leaders arrested. So the alliance, having lost its purpose, began to disintegrate and the cordiality of allies to give way to resentment and suspicion—all the more so as it was rumoured by Robespierre's enemies that he and his group, far from preparing to relax the rigours of "revolutionary" government, were drafting further proscription lists and were aiming at setting up a personal dictatorship or "triumvirate".

Meanwhile, deeper divisions had arisen in the two governing Committees, both within the Committee of Public Safety and in the relations between the two. Since the law of December 1793 that prescribed their respective duties, there had always been a certain overlap in their operations: the Committee of General Security was nominally responsible for all matters relating to police and security, but the other Committee had its own right of access to the Revolutionary Tribunal. More recently, the overlap had become more serious when the Committee of Public Safety, in April, created its own police department for prosecuting erring and dishonest public officials; and this inevitably tended to draw the anger of the rival Committee's members on to the heads of Robespierre and Saint-Just, who had made the new department their special concern. The law of 22nd Prairial was, as we saw, drafted by Robespierre and Couthon and, being in a hurry to present it to the Assembly, they had omitted to consult those who considered themselves most intimately concerned with its operation. The Security Committee had its revenge: by stacking the tumbrils with victims in June and July, they contributed to that *nausée de l'échafaud,* or revulsion against the guillotine, that rebounded on the heads of the government's best-known leaders. Again, Robespierre's enthusiasm for a civic religion on a Rousseauesque model had led him to persuade the Assembly to adopt his own creation, the Cult of the Supreme Being (7 May 1794)—a measure calculated to discomfort both "atheists" and "fanatics", but to cater for the beliefs of the great bulk of religious-minded revolutionaries, whether Christian or other. Whatever might have been its ultimate reception (the Cult perished with its author two months later), its immediate result was to draw the fire of "de-christianizers" and Voltairian deists, who feared a revival of Catholic "fanaticism" and suspected Robespierre of aspiring to be the "pontiff " of a new religion. Among such critics were Amar and Vadier, members of the Committee of General Security.

Within the major Committee a conflict of principles and personalities had been waged since May. Bitter disputes had broken out between Carnot and Saint-Just on the conduct of military operations : Carnot accused Saint-Just, who had been a successful emissary to the armies in Alsace and in the North and played a distinguished part at Fleurus, of meddling with matters beyond his competence. The " practical " men, Carnot and Lindet, who tended also to be moderates, clashed increasingly with the " ideologues ", Robespierre, Couthon and Saint-Just, whom they accused of being over-indulgent towards the *sans-culottes* : Lindet, for one, objected on this score to the laws of Ventôse. Robespierre, in turn, found himself increasingly at variance with the views of the " terrorists ", Billaud and Collot, who continued to parade " Hébertist " sympathies. Collot had been Fouché's partner in the savage pacification of Lyons and was closely associated with a group of other " terrorists " who had been similarly employed—Barras and Fréron at Toulon, Tallien at Bordeaux, and Carrier at Nantes. As the crisis within the Committees developed, such men, fearing the hostility of Robespierre, who had had several of them recalled by the Assembly to account for their excesses, tended to rally round Billaud and Collot and stand together in common defence against their accuser.

By the end of June, the atmosphere within the Committee of Public Safety had become so charged with suspicion and mutual recrimination that Robespierre withdrew in disgust from its meetings and confined his activities to his private office in the Rue Saint-Honoré and the forum of the Jacobin Club. In the long run, the gesture could not fail to rouse further suspicion against him. This became the greater when, refusing Barère's offer of mediation, and apparently ignorant of his dwindling support within the Plain, he decided to appeal to the Convention against his dissentient colleagues. So, in a long speech on 8th Thermidor (26 July 1794), he passionately defended his conduct against his critics and pleaded that the Revolution could once more be saved and the reign of "virtue" finally triumph if only one last surgical operation were performed—the removal of a small group of "impure" men, at whose identity he hinted but whom he obstinately refused to name. It was a fatal miscalculation—or a deliberate courting of martyrdom—of which Saint-Just, who was aiming at a compromise, appears to have heartily disapproved. Robespierre was heard in silence and the Convention declined to allow him the usual courtesy of sending his speech to be printed; while Barère, ever susceptible to changing winds, rallied to the new majority. The same evening, the identical speech was enthusiastically applauded by the Jacobins. But the alliance of moderate Jacobins, Plain and "terrorists", temporarily united by a common fear, proved to be the stronger. During the night, the confederates concerted their plan of action for the Convention's session on the morrow. Saint-Just, who had prepared a speech for the occasion and rose to defend his colleague, was shouted down; Robespierre was greeted with cries of "Down with the tyrant!" and refused a hearing. Saint-Just, the two Robespierres, and their brother-in-law Lebas were placed under arrest, and sent under close escort to the Committee of General Security.

Yet, even now, the day might not have been lost if the Paris sections and their armed battalions had rallied in support of the Jacobin leaders, as in August 1792 and June 1793. Not only the Jacobin Club but the Commune continued to voice support for the arrested men; Hanriot, Robespierrist chief of the National Guard, escaped from the squad sent to arrest him; and the turnkey of the prison to which Robespierre and his group were directed refused to acknowledge their escort's mandate, so that they were free to seek refuge among their friends of the Commune. But, despite the dilatoriness of their opponents, the leaders were unable to recover their lost fortunes, partly because they themselves lacked the will or the desire to lead an insurrection, but, far more, because, when it came to the point, the *sans-culottes*, estranged by their policies, showed little inclination to take up arms for a cause that they no longer believed in. It was certainly not for lack of time or opportunity to make their minds up. All through the afternoon and evening, the two contending parties, based respectively on the Commune and the Convention, sent mutually conflicting orders, threats, pleas and declarations to the sections and battalions of the National Guard, appealing to their loyalties. At one time, in response to the Commune's summons, over 3,000 armed men, supported by thirty-two pieces of artillery, were drawn up outside the City Hall. But they lacked both leadership and purpose and, as the tide of debate in the sectional assemblies and " revolutionary committees " turned against the Robespierrists, the whole of this force melted gradually away. Meanwhile, the Convention had declared the " conspirators " to be outlaws; and Barras, armed with the Convention's mandate, encountered no resistance when, in the early hours of 10th Thermidor (28 July), he appeared at the City Hall with 6,000 men and carried off his prisoners for formal identification by the Revolutionary Tribunal. A few hours later, they were hustled to the Place de la Révolution for execution. Among twenty-two victims, Robespierre was the last but one to mount the scaffold. It was perhaps typical of his austere probity that, after a year of high office, he should have left an estate of little more than £100. The next day, 71 councillors of the Commune, also implicated in the " Robespierrist conspiracy ", followed him to the guillotine : it was the largest, and the last, of the great holocausts of the Revolution in Paris. With them perished not only a man or a group but a system. And what followed Thermidor was hardly what the most active of Robespierre's opponents—and still less the passive bystanders, the Parisian *sans-culottes*—had expected or bargained for.

Chapter IX

THE BOURGEOIS REPUBLIC

The fall of Robespierre led to something of an anti-climax. The Revolution continued, though at a slackened pace; and the Republic—a new " republic of proprietors "—lingered on through a series of crises, until Bonaparte's grenadiers swept it aside in the *coup d'état* of Brumaire (9-10 November 1799).

Barère, like his colleagues, had hoped that once Robespierre had been removed business might go on as usual. Reporting to the Convention on 28 July, he described the events of 9th Thermidor as " a partial commotion that left the government intact ". But he failed completely to grasp the nature of the forces he had helped to unleash. The Revolution, far from continuing on its course, took a sharp swing to the Right (some have even argued that it stopped altogether). Within a month, the apparatus of " revolutionary " government had been scrapped or recast; within a year, he and his " terrorist " colleagues, denounced as *la queue de Robespierre,* were on their way to Devil's Island; the *sans-culottes* were once more disarmed and disfranchised; and the rulers of 1795, after a period of hesitation, tried to revert to the " principles of 1789 ".

It was not the Jacobin remnants but the Plain that proved to be Robespierre's successors. New men came forward : Boissy d'Anglas, consistent advocate of a return to government by " proprietors "; strong-arm men and converted " terrorists " like Barras, Tallien and Fréron; and two lawyers, Merlin of Douai and Merlin of Thionville. Sieyes re-emerged from the Plain, having " existed " (as he said) during the months of Jacobin Terror; and, for a short while, Cambon, financial expert of the Jacobin Convention, and Lindet carried influence as opponents of Robespierre, but soon, like many others, los† favour owing to their old associations. Later, these groups were reinforced by a return to the Assembly of 75 former Girondins, saved from the guillotine by Robespierre, and a handful of royalists : these tended to form a Right wing within the Convention. Meanwhile, the Mountain, depleted by the purge of 9th Thermidor and desertions to the Plain, formed a dwindling and silent group on the Left.

The Plain, then, emerged as the victors of Thermidor. There were idealists and " ideologues " among them; but, on the whole, they were hard-headed men, to whom the Revolution had been a profitable business : it had given them authority and status; many had been enriched by the purchase of " national properties ", others by lucrative government contracts—a process that would be carried further by the annexation of neighbouring provinces. As regicides, they were inclined to Republicanism and were fearful of a restoration—even of a constitutional monarchy. Their complaint against the Robespierrists had been not so much that they had mobilized the nation for war and instituted the Terror, as that they had preached social democracy, given too free a rein to the *sans-culottes*, and meddled with private property and the freedom of the market. Robespierre having fallen, their objects were, therefore, to dismantle the machinery of Jacobin dictatorship, end the Terror (now obsolete), put the *sans-culottes* back in their proper places, return to a more liberal economy, and carry the war to a victorious conclusion. Along with this, they hoped that the new régime might be stabilized with the firm and voluntary support of the " patriots of 1789 ".

But the last of these expectations proved over-sanguine, owing both to the divisions among " patriots " and the intrusion of a new and embarrassing " ally " outside the Assembly. After Thermidor, a triangular political struggle ensued in the Paris sections, now divided between moderates, neo-" Hébertists " and Jacobins. The moderates (the majority) generally reflected the aims of the Plain. The neo-" Hébertists ", whose hostility to Robespierre had thrown them into the arms of his Thermidorian opponents, had formed an Electoral Club from which they attacked "revolutionary" government and called for the application of the Constitution of 1793; at this time, their spokesmen included Jean Varlet, the former Enragé, and Gracchus Babeuf, editor of the *Tribun du Peuple*. Meanwhile, the Jacobins, though renouncing their former devotion to Robespierre, continued to advocate the "revolutionary" principles and methods of 1793-4. The Jacobins held control of some eight or ten sections and succeeded, two months after Thermidor, in getting Marat's remains transferred to the Pantheon for re-burial. But their success was short-lived. Encouraged by the divisions among "patriots", a new element entered the fray in the form of the *jeunesse dorée*, the "gilded youth" (or *muscadins*, as they were often called), led by the renegade "terrorist", Fréron. The *jeunesse* was recruited from middle-class youth, bankers' and lawyers' clerks, shop assistants, army deserters and sons of "suspects" and of guillotine-victims. Organized in bands, they made sallies into the popular districts, beat up Jacobin workmen, shouted anti-"terrorist" slogans and drowned the strains of the *Marseillaise* in those of their own song, the *Réveil du Peuple*. Under this impetus, a veritable "witch-hunt" was instigated in the sections against Jacobins and "terrorists", both real and alleged. Purges followed in rapid succession; the moderates regained control of the sections; and the Convention was compelled by the weight of opinion thus aroused to close down the Jacobin Club in November. By this time, the neo-"Hébertists"—and Babeuf in particular—had begun to regret their faith in the Thermidorian leaders; but it was too late, and the Electoral Club was closed in its turn and Babeuf was arrested soon after.

Meanwhile, the Convention had proceeded with its own reforms. The day after Robespierre's execution, it had been agreed, at Tallien's suggestion, to renew the membership of the government Committees a quarter at a time every month: thus power should no longer be concentrated in the hands of a few men. It was only a first step. On 24 August, sixteen committees were set up, twelve of them with executive powers, to carry out the work previously done by the two Committees of Public Safety and General Security. Both these Committees were reduced in powers and independence. The latter, it is true, regained its undisputed control over police and security, though these functions became progressively reduced; while the former, the mainstay of Robespierrist ascendancy, lost all control over local government and the armed forces, now placed under a specially constituted Military Committee responsible to the Convention. Thus, while government remained strong, the Assembly resumed some of its old authority. Similar considerations underlay the changes made in local government, though here the purge of elements considered socially undesirable was the more evident motive. The old vigilance and "revolutionary" committees were swept away wholesale or brought under central control. In Paris, the Commune was abolished and the forty-eight "revolutionary" committees were grouped together in twelve *comités d'arrondissement*, from which all Jacobin militants were excluded and in which the predominant social element was no longer the small shopkeeper and craftsman, but the merchant, civil servant or professional man. Similarly, the civil committees of the sections were purged, put under the direct control of the Convention, and their numbers made up by persons selected by its Committee of Legislation; here again, the *sans-culottes* and Jacobins of the Year II gave way to the substantial property-owners and moderates who had wielded authority before June 1793. Finally, in the sectional assemblies, now to meet only once every ten days, the influence of the *sans-culottes* was further reduced by withdrawing the old compensation of 40 sous for attendance.

The Terror, too, was officially brought to an end and, after the final blood-letting of 28-29 July and a few more scattered victims, the guillotine as a political instrument virtually ceased its work. The law of 22nd Prairial was repealed, the prisons were opened and "suspects" (500 in Paris in one week alone) were released. A few public trials were staged —including those of Carrier, held responsible for the mass-drowning of his victims at Nantes, and Fouquier-Tinville, notorious as the public prosecutor of the "Great Terror"; after which the Revolutionary Tribunal was quietly put aside. Yet at unofficial Terror-in-reverse continued. As "suspects" were released and some *émigrés* returned, the numbers of those wishing to settle old scores with Jacobins, "terrorists" and former members of committees were proportionately increased. In Paris, the unofficial White Terror was limited to the activities of the *muscadins*: there were beatings, denunciations and intimidation, but there was little bloodshed. In the provinces, however, it assumed a far more violent and vicious form: in the Lyonnais, the Company of Jesus flung the bodies of their victims, men and women, into the Rhone, and prisoners were massacred wholesale in jail and on their way to prison; while in other southern cities, bands of the so-called Companies of Jehu and the Sun indiscriminately murdered "terrorists", "patriots of 1789" and—most eagerly of all—purchasers of former Church properties. Such massacres were deplored in Paris; but the Convention and its Committees, which had unleashed these forces, were quite powerless to keep them under control.

The economic situation also got out of hand; but here the new rulers, determined to liberate the economy from the controls of their predecessors, bore the direct responsibility. As a first step, in October 1794, the *Maximum* legislation was so amended as to allow prices to rise to a level two-thirds above that of 1790; soon after, penalties for infringing the law were reduced and, to encourage foreign trade, controls on imports were abandoned. On 23 December, the *Maximum* laws were virtually abolished and free trade in grain was restored within the Republic. In Paris, the price of rationed bread was still maintained at 3 sous a pound—though bread could now, in addition, be sold on an open market; the basic meat ration was also retained at a new price of 21 (formerly 14) sous a pound; otherwise, prices were free to find their "natural" level. The consequences were disastrous: though producers were temporarily appeased, inflation embarked on a rapid upward spiral and prices soared beyond the means of all but the large consumer. The *assignat,* which had already fallen to 28 per cent of its old value in October and to 24 per cent in November, fell further to 20 per cent in December, 17 per cent in February, and to 7½ per cent in May 1795. In the provinces, where controls had been all but completely abandoned, the winter and spring brought near-famine conditions: at Verdun, for example, the workers' daily bread ration was reduced to half-a-pound and its price rose to 20 sous a pound. In Paris, rationed meat was often unobtainable; and the bread ration, though fixed at 1-1½ pounds per head in March 1795, fell in subsequent months to 8, 6, 4, or even 2 ounces; so that small consumers were compelled to supplement their ration by buying in the open market at a price that rose from 25 sous a pound on 25 March to 16 livres (over twelve times the amount) seven weeks later. Meanwhile, wages, though freed from the restrictions of the ill-fated *Maximum* of July 1794, had not the slightest chance of catching up; and it seems likely that the real wages of Parisian workers in April and May 1795 were not only far lower than in 1793-4 but had fallen back to the catastrophic level of the early months of 1789.

Such was the background to the great popular insurrections of Germinal and Prairial (March and May 1795). Political motives, too, played a part: many of the *sans-culottes* had been won for the "Hébertist" demand for the Constitution of 1793. But it was above all the government's economic measures and their consequences that stirred them from their apathy. In January, when the prices of many goods had already doubled since the repeal of the *Maximum,* the old familiar threats against merchants and shopkeepers were heard again; but threats passed to action only when the bread ration began to fail in the last two weeks of March. On 12th Germinal (1 April), it failed completely in some sections; women stormed bakers' shops; building workers met to protest against a decree debarring them as lodgers from buying rationed bread; and sections on both sides of the river joined forces to march on the Assembly. As Boissy d'Anglas was addressing the Convention, the insurgents—men and women —burst into shouts of "Bread, bread!"; some wore in their caps the slogan "Bread and the Constitution of 1793". But they lacked leaders and, having no settled plans, put conflicting demands before the Assembly. They received little support from the deputies of the Mountain; and when Merlin of Thionville appeared at the head of a mixed band of loyal National Guards and *jeunesse,* they dispersed without offering any resistance.

As the insurrection petered out, the Convention took police measures to restore order, settle old scores and prevent a further outbreak. Paris was declared to be in a state of siege and its armed forces were placed under the supreme command of a regular army officer, General Pichegru; more ex-"terrorists" were arrested or disarmed in the sections; a dozen deputies of the Mountain (including Robespierre's old enemies, Amar and Cambon) were arrested; and the unfortunate trio, Barère, Billaud and Collot, together with Vadier (of the former Committee of General Security), were sentenced to deportation. But as the Convention did virtually nothing to remove the basic cause of these disorders, both the hardship and the agitation continued. In Normandy, food-convoys were pillaged along the Seine. Robespierre's name began once more to be invoked with veneration. On 16 May, when the Paris bread ration fell again to two ounces, police agents gave warning of another imminent rising, a prospect that became all the more certain when, three days later, calls to armed insurrection were widely distributed around the city and suburbs— among them a printed manifesto entitled *Insurrection du Peuple pour obtenir du Pain et reconquérir ses Droits,* which precisely outlined the plan to be followed and gave the movement its central slogan: "Bread and the Constitution of 1793".

The popular revolt that followed, one of the most stubborn and remarkable of the Revolution, was essentially a social protest, inspired by hunger and hatred of the new rich; yet it was accompanied by the political demands learned and absorbed since Thermidor: the release of the "patriot" prisoners, a freely elected Commune and the Constitution of 1793. It lasted four days and opened on 1st Prairial (20 May) with a massive invasion of the Assembly by housewives and women of the markets, followed by whole armed battalions of the central districts and *faubourgs*. The programme of the insurgents was read to the Assembly which, prompted by the deputies of the Mountain, had little choice but to accept them. But once more, as in Germinal, for lack of leaders and a clear purpose, the intruders, having gained their first objective, spent hours in noisy chatter before being ejected by the loyal battalions of the western sections called in during the evening. This time, however, the insurrection continued in the Faubourg St. Antoine; the City Hall was captured; the gunners of the loyal sections deserted; and the Convention was surrounded, besieged, and threatened, as in June 1793. But the rebels were bought off with promises and, having retired to their homes for the night, left the field to their opponents. The *faubourg* was invested by a force of 20,000 regular troops under the command of General Menou and, deserted by its allies, surrendered without a shot. This time, the repression was thorough and ruthless. Fourteen deputies of the Mountain were arrested, of whom six were executed. A Military Commission tried 149 persons, and sentenced 36 to death and 37 to prison and deportation. In the sections there followed a massive toll of proscriptions, in which the settling of old scores and concern for future security played a far larger part than tracking down and punishing the actual culprits of May 1795. 1,200 were arrested and 1,700 disarmed in a single week, and more arrests followed later.[1] It was an important turning-point. With the proscription and removal of its leaders (both actual and potential), the Parisian *sans-culottes* ceased to exist as a political and military force. The "popular" phase of the Revolution was over. From now on, the bourgeoisie, the

[1] For a detailed account, see K. D. Tönnesson, *La Défaite des sans-culottes* (Oslo-Paris, 1959).

"notables" and *honnêtes gens* could proceed with their work without the embarrassing intervention of their one-time allies.

Meanwhile, the Thermidorians, though they had renounced and destroyed the Jacobins' programme at home, had been content to follow their lead in the conduct of war and to reap its material benefits. The victors of Fleurus had become the Army of the Sambre-et-Meuse; in October 1794, under Jourdan, they forced the Ruhr and threw back the Austrians across the Rhine. Meanwhile, the armies of the Moselle and the Rhine occupied the Palatinate, and the army of the North, under Pichegru (soon to be won over by royalist agents), seized Maestricht, crossed the Meuse and the lower reaches of the Rhine, and occupied Holland. In January 1795, the Batavian Republic was proclaimed. On the Spanish front, Moncey had taken San Sebastian and pushed on to occupy Bilbao and Vittoria. Meanwhile, Prussia, defeated in France and anxious to get its full share of partitioned Poland, had begun to withdraw its armies from the west. In April 1795, she left the coalition and signed the Treaty of Basel with France, leaving the Republic in possession of the left bank of the Rhine. The Dutch now also formally withdrew from the war and, by the Treaty of The Hague (May 1795), became France's ally, surrendered to her Dutch Flanders, Venloo and Maestricht, and agreed to support an occupation force of 25,000 men and to pay an indemnity of 100 million florins. Spain followed suit and, at Basel in July 1795, ceded Spanish San Domingo and, a year later, signed a treaty of alliance with the victors. Meanwhile, after prolonged debate, the Convention had decided to annex Belgium. Austria and Britain remained in the war, soon to be joined by Russia; but its nature had changed. The Jacobins' war of revolutionary defence had passed, by almost imperceptible stages, into one of annexation and conquest.[2]

The Thermidorians now faced the task of giving France a constitution that accorded with their own political beliefs and aspirations. The democratic Constitution of 1793, with its

[2] See Chapter XI.

deceptive promises and calls to "anarchy" and insurrection, had to be finally buried; and that of 1791, though dear to some, could of course not be restored : the Republic (it was hoped) had come to stay; the uni-cameral system had revealed its weaknesses; and further safeguards would have to be found against popular and royalist pressure. The new constitution—known as the Constitution of the Year III—was, suitably enough, introduced, and largely inspired, by Boissy d'Anglas, champion of the new propertied classes. Its accompanying Declaration of Rights and Duties was conceived, broadly speaking, in the spirit of the liberal "principles of 1789", but with significant departures from it : equality became essentially equality before the law and not in civil rights; the right of insurrection was withdrawn; property-rights were more clearly defined and safeguarded; and a citizen's duties, as well as his rights, were elaborately set out. The male adult suffrage of 1793 was abandoned and a return made to the restricted franchise and system of indirect election of 1791; but electoral qualifications were more generous : "active" citizens now included all Frenchmen aged 21 and paying taxes—other than priests, returned *émigrés,* and imprisoned "patriots". But to serve as a brake on legislative experiment, the Assembly was divided into two Chambers : a Council of Five Hundred, aged 30 and above, with powers to initiate legislation; and a Council of Ancients, consisting of 250 members of 40 or above, empowered to transform the "resolutions" of the lower Chamber into laws. Executive authority was vested in five Directors, each holding office for five years; but the "separation of powers" was restored and the Directors, though appointed by the Councils, could neither sit in them nor initiate their laws. Local government regained a part of its autonomy, but held far less than in 1791. Finally, to counteract the danger of a royalist upsurge, the Convention decreed that, in the coming elections, two-thirds of the deputies to the new legislature must be elected from its own ranks.

The primary assemblies, summoned for the dual purpose of

approving the "two-thirds" decrees and ratifying the Constitution, met in September 1795. The new constitutional provisions were accepted readily enough; but, in Paris, the "two-thirds" decrees had a very different sort of reception; and before the Convention dispersed in late October, it had a royalist rising on its hands that came near to overthrowing it. Royalist and counter-revolutionary agitation had, in one form or another, been a matter of concern since 1789; but, until war broke out, it had achieved little success. After the King's execution, royalist activity from both without and within had played its part in fostering rebellion in the Vendée and the "federalist" departments of the south, west and north. Yet, as long as the Jacobins remained in power, these dangers had been held in check and had barely affected the capital. The royalists had, however, taken fresh heart from the more liberal policies of their successors. By now, they were divided into two main groups—the "ultras", who demanded a return to 1787 and the total restoration of the Old Régime; and the constitutional monarchists who, broadly speaking, favoured a restoration of the Constitution of 1791. Unfortunately for the "constitutionalists", the Count of Provence, who "succeeded" Louis XVI first as Regent for the young Louis XVII and later as Louis XVIII, was a determined "ultra". This confusion of divided counsels was reflected in the disastrous expedition which, equipped and financed by Britain, landed at Quiberon Bay in July 1795; bungled from the start, it was easily crushed by General Hoche. This was a serious set-back for both groups; but, in Paris, soon after, the "constitutionalists" were able to exploit with great skill the widespread dissatisfaction roused in the sections by the Convention's decrees of the "two-thirds". In fact only one section—that of Lepeletier, in the financial quarter of the city—was directly controlled by royalists; but the worthy bourgeois and civil servants, who now dominated the great bulk of the sections, were easily persuaded that the Assembly's decrees were a dangerous infringement of the rights of electors; and when the Convention, anticipating trouble, drafted troops into the capital and allowed former "terrorists" to arm and attend the assemblies, "property" appeared to be endangered as well. Every single section except that of the Quinze Vingts, in the Faubourg St. Antoine, rejected the decrees; and, having completed their lawful business, they refused to disperse. Open rebellion broke out on 13th Vendémiaire (5 October 1795), when 25,000 Parisians sprang to arms and a dozen sections, led by Lepeletier, marched on the Convention. But Barras, who had been given command of the Paris forces (General Menou had openly proclaimed his royalist sympathies), called to his assistance General Bonaparte and a number of other young generals; the advancing sections were met by withering artillery-fire (Bonaparte's famous "whiff of grapeshot"); and the rebellion was crushed. Reprisals were strikingly mild : there were only two executions and most of the ring-leaders got away. A remarkable feature of the whole affair was the behaviour of the *sans-culottes* who, though starved and oppressed by the Thermidorian Convention, refused to give any support to the royalist rebels.

The new constitution now came into force and the men of 1795, having warded off rebellion from both Right and Left, appeared to be firmly in the saddle; and yet the period of the Directory proved to be one of confusion and intense political instability. In part, this was due to the nature of the constitution itself : by providing for annual elections (of one-third of the Councils and one in five of the Directors) it offered a constant invitation to ferment and disorder; and its failure to provide adequate machinery for legally settling disputes between the executive and legislature led to continuous appeals to force. More seriously, it soon became evident that the new rulers lacked the support within the country that would assure them of steady majorities and stable government. By their policies and electoral provisions, they had estranged not only royalists and Jacobins, but the moderate bourgeois and property-owners of the capital as well. From this false start they never recovered; and, compelled to manœuvre and manipulate in order to maintain themselves in power, they followed a see-saw policy of playing off one political faction against another—of alternately encouraging the royalist Right against the Jacobin Left and leaning on the Left to get the better of the Right. When this failed, as it inevitably must, the only solution was to call upon the army, already installed in Paris before Vendémiaire, to redress the balance. Thus, behind the façade of a liberal constitution, the generals tended more and more to become the ultimate arbiters of political disputes and the ground was prepared, long before the final *coup d'état* of Brumaire, for the military dictatorship of Bonaparte.

Vendémiaire had swung the pendulum once more to the Left, and the new Assembly met to the accompaniment of stirring appeals for Republican unity and concord; there was a revival of Jacobin activity; the clubs reopened; and Babeuf's paper, the *Tribun du Peuple*, appeared again on the streets. But the spirit of harmony was short-lived: the onslaught of their "patriot" critics alarmed the authorities, all the more so because the economic situation was going from bad to worse. By the end of 1795, the *assignat* of 100 livres was worth only 15 sous and, in February, the *assignat* collapsed altogether; within six months, its successor, the *mandat territorial*, had suffered the same fate. Prices rocketed further and, in the spring of 1796, bread was selling in the open market for 80 livres a pound and meat for 100. While the new rich displayed their wealth with arrogant unconcern, poverty was (in the words of a police observer) "at its lowest depths", while hospitals and almshouses were overcrowded with the sick and destitute. Nor was it only the *sans-culottes* that suffered: small *rentiers* and public servants, their pensions and earnings dwindling under the impact of inflation, shared their misfortunes. It was against this background that Babeuf launched his "Conspiracy of the Equals", the first attempt in history to establish a communist society by political means—and yet a minor episode in the Revolution, as it commanded little support and was quickly crushed. Babeuf had, since 1789, been attracted by the "agrarian law", or sharing of goods in common, as a means of achieving economic equality. By the time of Robespierre's fall, he had abandoned this as an impracticable scheme and was moving towards a more complex plan of collective ownership and production. This, in essence, was still his ultimate aim when, in the winter of 1795-6, he conspired with a group of former Jacobins, club-men and " terrorists " to overthrow the Directory by force. The movement was organized in a series of concentric circles : there was an inner insurrectionary committee, composed of a small body of intimates who alone were fully informed of the " conspiracy's " aims; beyond it, a group of sympathizers, ex-Jacobins and others, including Robespierre's old opponents, Amar and Lindet; and, finally, on the fringe, the Paris militants that had to be won, computed by Babeuf at some 17,000 men. The plan was original and grievance was rampant; but the *sans-culottes*, cowed and silenced since Prairial, failed to respond. The conspirators were betrayed by a police spy to Carnot, now a Director and moving fast towards the Right. 131 were arrested and thirty shot out of hand; while Babeuf and some of his principal associates were brought to trial and guillotined a year later.

Once more, the pendulum swung to the right, this time supported by a massive influx of royalists into the Assembly. In the partial elections of April 1797, only eleven former deputies to the Convention were returned out of a total of 216; the rest were mainly constitutional monarchists who now gave the Assembly its first royalist majority. Pichegru was elected president of the Five Hundred and Barbe-Marbois, another royalist, of the Ancients. To make matters even worse, the near-royalist Carnot was joined in office by Barthélémy, a convinced monarchist; and it seemed as if the monarchy might be voted back by constitutional means. While Barras hesitated, the other two Republican Directors—Reubell and Larevellière-Lepaux—favoured strong action to preserve the Republic. But how? An appeal to the people conjured up all the horrors of 1793; and the Jacobins were too weak to tilt the balance. The generals remained as the only choice, both as Republicans and as interested parties in a war that the royalists were anxious to end. Bonaparte, fresh from his victories in Italy, and Hoche, newly appointed commander of the Army of the Sambre-et-Meuse, promised their support; and soon Bonaparte's lieutenant, Augereau, and a part of Hoche's forces were marching on the capital. Barras decided to support his more determined colleagues and, on 18th Fructidor (4 September 1797), they struck at the royalist majority. Barthélémy and Pichegru were arrested and imprisoned, while Carnot escaped; the Councils were purged of 214 deputies; and 65 persons were deported to the "dry guillotine" of Guiana. Returned *émigrés* had, once more, to leave the country, while hundreds of priests were deported and others compelled to take new oaths of loyalty. The victorious Directors armed themselves with new powers; but the liberal Constitution had already proved itself to be unworkable.

From now on, the fate of the Republic lay less in the hands of the politicians than in those of the generals—particularly of the young and ambitious General Bonaparte, whose part in the *coup d'état* of Fructidor had won him official recognition for his daring, but unauthorized, settlement of Italy.[8] So he was already determining the foreign policy of the Republic. At Campo Formio, having settled and signed the terms of peace with Austria (October 1797), he boasted of France's imperial mission in the Mediterranean; and, the next spring, he wrecked all chances of an early settlement with England by persuading the Directors to send him to Egypt to open up an Empire in the East. He was to return eighteen months later to become master of France.

Yet, once Bonaparte was safely in Egypt, there was no immediate reason for the government to contemplate such a prospect. It had emerged from its victory in Fructidor with an enlarged Republican majority in the Chambers; royalist activity was temporarily at a low ebb; and the severe measures taken against returned priests and *émigrés* met with little open opposition. Once more, it could turn its attention to the

[8] See Chapter XI.

danger from the Left; and when the Jacobin challenge revived in the elections of May 1798, the Assembly passed a law (the law of 22nd Floréal) which excluded 106 deputies from sitting in the Chambers. So, secure once more, the Directory was able to settle down to some useful—though limited—reforms. Steps were taken to stabilize the currency by withdrawing the discredited paper-money from circulation and declaring a moratorium on all outstanding debts—thus paving the way for the financial reforms of the Consulate. The system of taxation was overhauled, brought up to date and put on something like its modern footing. Following good harvests in 1796-8, the price of grain fell—a source of irritation to the producer, but a much-needed relief to the long-suffering consumer. Yet the government remained at the mercy of contractors, speculators and financiers and the budget, despite contributions from the annexed and occupied countries, remained unbalanced; industry, too, continued to stagnate; and the maritime war with England—not to mention Bonaparte's Egyptian adventure—played havoc with foreign trade.

A solution to such long-term problems could, of course, be found only by a stable government and one either willing to revert to the draconian measures of the Year II or (failing that) having at its command ample resources from satellite or conquered territories. The Directors were naturally inclined to the latter solution; but their aggressive ambitions brought on their heads a second Coalition, this time embracing Britain, Austria, Russia, Turkey and Sweden. The war opened badly, for France and her armies, though supported by freshly conscripted levies (raised by Jourdan's law of 5 September 1798), were defeated by the Austrian Archduke Charles in Germany and Switzerland and driven from Italy by the Russian general, Suvorov. Meanwhile, the Belgian provinces were in revolt and the peasant *chouans* were up in arms once more in the west. The Directors repeated their old denunciation of the double-headed monster, royalism and " anarchy "; but in the elections of 1799 two-thirds of the government candidates were defeated and the Jacobin minority was strengthened. Sieyes, known as a critic of the Constitution, took office in the place of Reubell and, with the support of the Assembly, carried through a parliamentary *coup d'état* (the 30th Prairial) against his colleagues. The ministerial reshuffle that followed actually brought a Jacobin—Robert Lindet, Robespierre's old associate on the Committee of Public Safety—to the Ministry of Finance. Once more, the needs of a defensive war compelled the Republic to resort to measures of "public safety" and to condone a Jacobin revival. The Jacobin press reappeared, the clubs revived—among them the important Club du Manège, directed by Drouet, former postmaster-hero of Varennes and associate of Babeuf. Conscription was universally applied, forced loans were raised, and relatives of *émigrés* and royalist agitators were rounded up as hostages. When the reverses of the spring were followed in the summer by the landing of an Anglo-Russian force in Holland, Jourdan even invited the Five Hundred to repeat the old declaration of *la patrie en danger*. He was sharply opposed by Lucien Bonaparte, Napoleon's youngest brother, who pleaded that executive powers be extended rather than that they should be "carried away by a revolutionary tide". Jourdan's proposal was defeated. It was the old dilemma: should they appeal to the masses or strengthen the authority of the few?

The issue was decided, as after Fleurus, not by the defeat but by the victory of Republican arms. In September, Masséna defeated Suvorov in Italy and drove him out of Switzerland; and the Anglo-Russian force under the Duke of York came to grief in Holland. The danger of invasion had been removed and "the great nation" lived again. Meanwhile, General Bonaparte, though victorious against the English at Aboukir, had been thwarted in Syria and decided to return home to seek fresh laurels in Europe. Leaving his army in Egypt and dodging Nelson's patrols, he landed secretly at Fréjus on 9 October 1799. His recent failures were ignored or forgotten and he was greeted by an ecstatic press and public as the great victor of Italy, the peace-maker of Campo Formio, the one man able to impose on Europe a peace honourable to

French arms. Meanwhile, the royalist danger continued; property-owners, alarmed by the measures of " public safety " and the Jacobin revival, spoke darkly of " anarchy " and the return to 1793; there was further talk of the need to revise the Constitution and to provide stable government by strengthening the executive. It was in this atmosphere that Sieyes (that " mole of the Revolution " Robespierre had termed him) planned a further, more decisive, *coup d'état*. Once more, as in Fructidor, the army must be called in to force the hands of the Assembly—but, this time, an Assembly with a Republican majority. So, having tried Joubert and Moreau in turn (the former was killed soon after and the latter declined), Sieyes and his fellow-conspirators, Fouché and Talleyrand, turned to Napoleon, the man of the hour and one well suited by his popularity, his military record, his ambition and his Jacobin past to play the part assigned to him. By playing on the fears of a " terrorist " plot, they persuaded the Councils to meet on 10 November (19th Brumaire) outside Paris at Saint-Cloud under the protection of Napoleon's grenadiers. The Ancients were soon won over, but the Five Hundred proved obstinate and, when Bonaparte entered uninvited to address them, there were shouts of " Outlaw him! Down with the dictator! " The general lost his head, but his brother Lucien, who (conveniently) was in the chair, saved the situation by calling in the guards. The Five Hundred were driven out, the Directory was dissolved, and full authority was vested in a provisional Consulate of three—Sieyes, Roger-Ducos and Bonaparte. Though not generally realized at the time, it was the end of the bourgeois Republic and power passed into the hands of a military dictator.

Three weeks later, a new Cæsarean constitution was drafted and offered to the assemblies. It was accompanied by a proclamation of the Consuls that rang down the curtain on ten years of history: " The Revolution is established upon the principles which began it: it is ended."

PART THREE

Revolutionary Europe

Chapter X

EUROPE AND THE FRENCH REVOLUTION

We saw in an earlier chapter that, even before the revolution in France, political movements were taking place in a number of European countries whose purpose was to challenge, in one form or another, the accepted traditions, institutions and loyalties of the old aristocratic society. Such movements we noted in the Austrian Netherlands (Belgium), the United Provinces (Holland), England, Ireland, Switzerland, and even in Austria and Poland. In none of these countries, however—with the possible exception of England—did these movements, whether promoted by "enlightened" monarchs, middle-class "patriots", or (more rarely) by the common people themselves, achieve any substantial results. In France, and in France alone, did a revolution take place in 1789 that was not only to overthrow governments and political institutions but to uproot and radically transform the social order itself.

Yet it is hardly surprising that the events taking place in France during the next ten years should have given a fresh edge and stimulus to the earlier movements and, in some cases, given them a new revolutionary content. This happened sometimes by the propagation of the French revolutionary ideas; sometimes by the impact or occupation of France's crusading armies; and, to a greater or a lesser extent, by the action taken against their rulers by the people of the countries concerned. The eventual outcome was so to transform the Europe of the

Old Régime that, at the close of the revolutionary and Napoleonic era in 1815, there was hardly a country west of Russia
and Turkey and north of the Pyrenees whose society and
political institutions had not been profoundly affected. From
this result and the events that preceded it some historians have
concluded that the French Revolution was not so much a
unique and particular phenomenon as merely one " phase " of
a far wider convulsion that they have variously termed a
" western ", " Atlantic ", or " world " revolution.[1] This is an
important question to which we shall return in the next
chapter.

One early result of the French Revolution was to divide
European society into two distinct and mutually hostile
groups—its supporters or " patriots " on the one hand, and its
opponents or " counter-revolutionaries " on the other. But
this was not immediately apparent, as the fall of the Bastille
and other early episodes were generally well received. There
were, of course, exceptions : the Empress Catherine of Russia,
the Kings of Spain and Sweden, and Edmund Burke in England were resolutely hostile almost from the start. Yet the
more usual and immediate reaction was one of enthusiasm,
relief, benevolent neutrality, or even a sort of malicious glee.
" Liberal " Emperors like Joseph II and his successor, Leopold
II, of Austria, though brothers of the Queen of France and
as such anxious for her future, were not at first unduly disturbed. English dissenters, liberal Polish noblemen, and reformers everywhere, whether aristocratic or plebeian, drew
hope and courage from the successful challenge to " despot-

---

[1] The case has been argued by R. R. Palmer in " The Revolution
of the West, 1763-1801 ", *Political Science Quarterly*, March 1954,
and in *The Age of the Democratic Revolution*, vol. 1, *The Challenge*,
pp. 4-6; by J. Godechot in *La Grande Nation* (2 vols. Paris, 1956), 1,
7-37 and *Les Révolutions* (1770-1799) (Paris, 1963); and by
Godechot and Palmer in a joint contribution to the 10th Congress of
Historical Sciences (Rome, 1955) entitled " Le Problème de l'Atlan-
tique du XVIIIe au XXe siècle ", *Relazioni del X Congresso Inter-
nazionale di Scienze Storiche* (Florence, n.d.), 172-239. See also P.
Amann, ed., *The Eighteenth-Century Revolution: French or Western?*
(Boston, 1963).

ism" in France. More remarkable still was the chorus of enthusiasm voiced in intellectual and artistic circles from Madrid to St. Petersburg: by English poets and scientists (Blake, Burns, Coleridge, Southey, Wordsworth, Priestley and Telford); by German poets and philosophers (Wieland, Klopstock, Fichte, Kant, Hegel and Herder); by Italian *illuminati*, rationalists and Free Masons; by Beethoven in Germany and Pestalozzi in Switzerland. Many of them changed sides later; but, at this stage, they might have applauded Wordsworth's poetic raptures and echoed Samuel Romilly's opinion (shared by Charles Fox) that the revolution in France was "the most glorious event, and the happiest for mankind, that has ever taken place since human affairs have been recorded". In some countries, as in England, there were other reasons for the general satisfaction expressed at the turn of events in France. France was the traditional enemy and her present convulsions would, it was supposed, weaken her for years to come as a commercial rival and active belligerent. Many thoughtful Frenchmen recognized this possibility and some told Arthur Young, even before the fall of the Bastille, that "the English must be well contented at our confusion". This was certainly the view of Pitt's government; and Lord Grenville, then Home Secretary, wrote in September that the French would not "for many years be in a situation to molest the invaluable peace which we now enjoy". Pitt himself was expressing similar opinions until 1792.

So, for one reason or another, the French Revolution got off to a good start and, during 1789 and the greater part of 1790, there was a general readiness to let it take its course and comparatively little was said about the dangerous explosive consequences it might have for France's neighbours. But subsequent events and the construction put on them abroad were soon after to change this mood, among the privileged and propertied classes in particular, into one of apprehension and concern. The French Revolution, it now appeared, was very different from the American: the drastic land reforms, the expropriation of the estates of the Church, the emigration of nobles and moderates and the tales that they told, all served to alarm conservative opinion. Meanwhile, democrats and reformers from other countries—large numbers of Belgians, Dutchmen and Germans; fewer English, Scots and Irish; and occasional Italians, Spaniards and Russians—had arrived in Paris, imbibed the new revolutionary ideas and, returning to or corresponding with their homelands, started clubs and newspapers in the image of the French; while the French press itself, like the paper edited by Camille Desmoulins, began to concern itself increasingly with the problems of France's fellow-" patriots " abroad. All this alarmed respectable society even more; so that when Edmund Burke, in November 1790, published his *Reflections on the Revolution in France*, he found a ready audience that bought up 30,000 copies and eleven editions of his work in little over a year. Unlike the majority of the intellectuals of his day, Burke condemned the Revolution from the start and as a whole. Far from welcoming it as a necessary means of curing France of age-old ills, he deplored the uprooting of the past, preached the sanctity of property and tradition and the virtues of gradual change, and even extolled the merits of the French higher clergy and Queen Marie Antoinette. With the " rights of man ", he argued, the French were preparing to tear down the whole social fabric, not only in France but elsewhere, and to rush blindly along a path of total renovation. " It is with infinite caution," he asserted, " that any man should venture upon pulling down an edifice, which has answered in any tolerable degree for ages the common purposes of society, or on building it up again without having models and patterns of approved utility before his eyes." The author was congratulated on his work by the Empress Catherine; he found a host of admirers and imitators abroad—among them, Friedrich von Gentz in Germany and Mallet du Pan in Switzerland; and the *Reflections* became the almost unchallenged Bible of counter-revolution in every European country.

But naturally Burke met with hostility as well as support; and, in England, none of his critics challenged his defence of

the Old Régime in France and his championship of conservative gradualism with greater vigour and success than Thomas
Paine, already distinguished as a radical pamphleteer of the
American Revolution. In his *Rights of Man* (1791), Paine
replied to Burke's apologia of the French Court in a memor-
able phrase: "He pities the plumage, but forgets the dying
bird"; and, striking at the core of his opponent's argument, he
claimed that "the vanity and presumption of governing beyond the grave is the most ridiculous and insolent of tyrannies". The book was badly received by the English propertied classes, particularly as Paine went on, in a second
volume, to make a frontal assault on the British monarchy and
established Church; but it was eagerly read by reformers,
Protestant dissenters, democrats, London craftsmen and the
skilled factory-hands of the new industrial north: its sales
were prodigious and may have reached a million copies. So
now the great "debate" on the French Revolution had
started, and political opinion everywhere tended to divide into
supporters and admirers of the French—generally to be found
(though by no means universally) among the professional and
manufacturing or trading middle class and urban craftsmen—
and those who, fearing that property or religion or monarchy
was everywhere endangered, became their most resolute opponents. The counter-revolution, thus launched, took a variety
of guises differing from country to country. It might confine
itself (as for long in England) to harrying and persecuting
local "patriots" and democrats and blocking reform; to
inciting "King and Church" riots among peasants and urban
workers against the Revolution's supporters, as in Birmingham, Manchester, Brussels, Naples and Madrid; or it might
engage in open intervention against the Revolution in France
itself, either by subsidizing the activities of French *émigrés*
and their agents, or by joining military coalitions to restore the
old order in France. In all countries outside France and her
neighbours, it tended to promote a religious revival, to discredit Enlightenment and discourage reform. We shall return
to some of these aspects later; here we are more immediately

concerned with the impact of the French Revolution on the democratic and revolutionary movements in Europe.

It is hardly surprising that this impact should have varied greatly from one country to another. Some countries, like Russia and Turkey, were far removed from France's borders, and their traditions and social development made them almost totally immune to the penetration of revolutionary ideas. Others, like Bavaria and parts of Belgium, were protected from contagion by a pious peasantry and clerical domination. Spain, though sharing a common frontier with France, was similarly placed and had, moreover, but a small educated middle class to act as the main channel for the new ideas. England's evolution had been very different, but she was made the more resistant by her relatively high standard of living, her island-position and her traditional enmity to France. There were countries, on the other hand, whose geographical position, cultural traditions and social evolution made them susceptible to French revolutionary ideas and to the penetration of her armies. Such countries were Holland, Belgium, the Rhineland, Switzerland and Italy; and, although all countries felt the impact of the events in France, it was in these alone that revolutions modelled on the French took place; yet even in these, as we shall see, no revolutionary government survived once French military protection had been withdrawn.

We have already seen that England was one of those countries in which the French Revolution, at its outbreak, evoked an enthusiastic response. There were various reasons for this: she had a free press; her rulers were delighted rather than outraged by the French challenge to "despotism"; religious dissenters, parliamentary reformers and Whig opposition Lords all saw some political advantage to be gained from events across the Channel; and, not least, she was going through the first throes and disturbances of an Industrial Revolution. Burke's onslaught naturally took its toll of early admirers; but even after opinion had begun to harden against the French, they found their supporters among a combination of social elements including middle-class radicals and reformers, Whig aristocrats, and spokesmen for the London craftsmen and industrial workers of the north. They engaged in varied activities. In London, Dr. Richard Price used the platform of the Revolution Society (founded to commemorate the " Glorious Revolution " of 1688) to extol the virtues of the French, and the Society sent a congratulatory address to the Constituent Assembly in Paris. Under the stimulus of French events, old reform societies revived and new ones came into being. Major Cartwright's Society for Promoting Constitutional Information, founded in 1780 and long since moribund, gained a new lease of life in 1791 and came under the more radical influence of John Horne Tooke and Thomas Paine. Constitutional and Reform Societies sprang up in Manchester, Sheffield, Norwich, Leeds, Nottingham and other cities, corresponded with France and collected boots and comforts for the French armies. The Foxite Whigs founded a more moderate Society of the Friends of the People and engaged in lengthy duels with Pitt and Grenville in the Houses of Parliament. And, most significant of all, a London Corresponding Society was started by Thomas Hardy in January 1792, which not only corresponded with the French and with its numerous affiliates at home, but acted as a centre for radical agitation in England : composed of craftsmen and small tradesmen, it was the first political association of workingmen to be formed in any country. Thus in England, more than in any other country outside France, the Revolution left its mark on the industrial workers. Yet it was not deep enough at this stage to survive persecution and war. After 1792, Pitt's government took active steps to suppress the " Jacobins " and reform societies in both England and Scotland : the severest punishment was that meted out to the Scottish " martyrs "—Muir, Palmer, Margarot and others—who were transported to Botany Bay for their part in convening a British Convention in 1793. London juries were less harsh than the Scottish Courts of Judiciary, but the radical movement gradually subsided and lay dormant for nearly fifteen years. A final flicker appeared, however, in the mutinies of Spithead and the Nore in 1797. Primarily, these were seamen's revolts against low wages, brutal discipline and filthy food; but Parker, leader at the Nore, was a member of the United Irishmen, and the central committee formed on Parker's ship proposed to sail to the Texel and petition the French National Convention for protection. But it is equally significant that not a single ship obeyed the signal to sail and that the Spithead mutineers actually demanded to be sent against the French once their grievances had been met. For, by this time, the first phase of popular " Jacobinism " in England was all but spent.

Strangely enough, " Jacobinism " stood a greater chance of success in Ireland than it ever did in England or Scotland. It might be supposed that the Irish, being predominantly peasants and Catholics like the Spanish and Bavarians, would have been less likely to become infected with the ideas of the Enlightenment and the French Revolution than the English or the Scots. This would have been true enough had it not been for the fact that the Irish rebellion, temporarily appeased by the concessions of 1782-4, broke out again, under cover of the European war, in 1794. It took two forms : the national independence movement of the United Irishmen, led by the Catholic Lord Edward Fitzgerald and the Protestant Wolfe Tone; and the massive agrarian revolt of the land-hungry Irish peasantry. The aristocratic and middle-class leaders were undoubtedly men of the Enlightenment : they had read Rousseau, they preached the " rights of man " and religious toleration, and Tone and Fitzgerald came to France to discuss their plans with the National Convention. The Catholic peasants, too—such was their hatred for the traditional enemy across St. George's Channel—burned candles for the victory of French arms and prepared to welcome a French invasion. Hoche's first attempt to land in the winter of 1796-7 was premature and proved abortive. A second attempt was planned for the spring of 1798; but the British government got wind of the plans and arrested the rebel leaders as they were about to sail for France. The peasant rebellion, intended to coincide with a landing that failed to take place, broke out in June and was pitilessly repressed. When General Humbert's fleet at last arrived in September 1798, it was already too late. It was the last attempt, and England escaped (perhaps less miraculously than it appeared at the time) from the greatest danger she had to face before Napoleon's invasion-threat of 1805.

Poland, too, though her social structure quite unfitted her to follow in the path of the French Revolution, was profoundly affected by the events taking place in France. France had long been allied to Poland and of all countries was the one to which Poles concerned for their country's survival looked with the greatest expectancy for aid to resist the predatory ambitions of her Russian, Prussian and Austrian neighbours. The outbreak of revolution in France was greeted with varying degrees of enthusiasm by Polish intellectuals, liberal members of the *szlachta* (nobility) and even by their King, Catherine's one-time lover and *protégé*, Stanislas Poniatowski. As with the Irish, it was the fear of foreign domination that brought them into the French revolutionary camp; but the Poles went further. They formed a "philosophical" club at Prince Radziwill's home, which earned them Catherine's irate epithet of "Jacobin", and, by a political *coup d'état*, compelled the diet in May 1791 to adopt a constitution in many respects similar to that adopted the same year by the French. It introduced important innovations: the diet was declared representative of "the nation as a whole"; the *liberum veto*, which had long obstructed all legislative and executive initiative, was abolished; the throne was made hereditary and judges elective. Yet the constitution, the creation of liberal nobles, remained essentially aristocratic. No more than a handful of bourgeois were admitted to the diet and, more important, the social order remained as little altered by these reforms as that of Russia and Prussia had been by those of their respective "enlightened despots": the peasants, it is true, were placed under the protection of the law, but serfdom remained. Yet even these minor reforms were too much for

the more conservative magnates, who invited Catherine to
send in a Russian army to compel Stanislas to withdraw the
constitution; the second partition of Poland by her three
powerful neighbours followed soon after. It was this second
national humiliation that prompted the patriot Kosciusko to
launch an insurrection in the spring of 1794. This time,
something like a national-popular movement developed and
Kosciusko was supported by the craftsmen and working
people of Warsaw. But the French were both unable and
unwilling to lend support (they had, by now, lost all sympathy
with the liberal aristocrats of Poland), a third partition followed, and Poland for some years disappeared from the map.

A country whose society and institutions were similar to
those of Poland was Hungary. She, too, had her " national "
troubles : we have noted her disputes with Maria Theresa and,
above all, with the Emperor Joseph II. But Hungarian nationalism, in so far as it existed at all, was skin-deep : the great
noble families normally spoke German and only paraded their
attachment to the Magyar tongue and traditions in order to win
popular sympathy for their private vendettas with the Habsburg monarchy, which had encroached on their " liberties ".
The leaders of the aristocratic revolt against Joseph quoted
from Rousseau and Voltaire but, when Leopold succeeded
Joseph, they insisted that serfdom be restored on their estates
as the price of their allegiance. The Hungarian nobility,
however, continued to parade revolutionary sentiments and,
in 1793, the diet drew up a constitutional act and a Declaration of the Rights of Man in imitation of the French; yet they
were meekly withdrawn when the new Emperor, Francis II,
who had turned his back on the liberal experiments of his predecessors, opposed them. In fact, in Hungary as in Austria,
the only genuine " Jacobins ", who not only believed in democracy but had a social as well as a political programme, were
small groups of middle-class officers, writers, lawyers, professors and civil servants—men like Lacskovicz, a former
officer, and Condorcet's friend Martinovicz—who had been
trained as much in the school of " Josephism " as of the

Enlightenment and the French Revolution. Martinovicz and his six fellow-"conspirators" were executed in May 1795, a few months after two of his Austrian counter-parts had been hanged in Vienna. They failed because they were divorced from the people and were unable to turn to political account the land-hunger and war-weariness of the peasantry; but their ideas survived and it is they rather than the rebellious noblemen of 1788-90 that were the real forerunners of Hungary's first national revolution in 1848.

Of the countries bordering France, none was so little affected by her example as Spain. We have seen in an earlier chapter that Spanish institutions and society in the eighteenth century were, in some respects, similar to the French. But her middle class was weaker and less mature; her peasantry was poorer, less literate and more closely subjected to the domination of priest and *señor*; her nobility had, in consequence, less inducement than the French to compete for control of the central government; and, above all, the country was sharply divided between a relatively prosperous north and east and a poverty-stricken centre and south. For these and other reasons, the Enlightenment had made little headway outside the main urban centres, there had been no "aristocratic revolt", and the French Revolution had, even at its inception, roused little sympathy and support. In addition, the Spanish government and Church resorted from the start to a systematic repression of "patriots" and imposed a blanket of silence on all news from France: even Burke's *Reflections* were suspect for the problems that they raised and were for long condemned by the Inquisition! In consequence, there was little that Spanish democrats could do other than to emigrate across the border, and small groups of "Jacobins" gathered on French soil, at Bayonne and elsewhere. Even when French armies began, in 1793, to occupy Spanish towns and provinces, they met with a remarkable ideological resistance. A veritable crusade for "Religion, King and Country" was preached against the godless French and won popular support even in large cities like Barcelona and Madrid. In 1797 and 1798, there were popular revolts against rising food prices in Guadalajara, Seville and Asturias; but, by then, Spain was France's ally against England. The significant point to note is that war with Britain was more unpopular than war with France and that Spain provides an early example of that militant "Church and King" conservatism that, in Catholic peasant communities in particular, proved to be an important auxiliary to the armies of France's enemies.

"Jacobinism" made little headway (though it existed) in Russia, the Balkans or the Scandinavian countries—still less in such distant outposts as Constantinople, Aleppo and Smyrna—and it only remains to consider here the early impact of the Revolution on the peoples adjacent to France's eastern and south-eastern borders. Of these, as we saw, the Dutch, the Belgians and Genevans had already become involved, before July 1789, in political disputes with their rulers. The Dutch Patriots, when abandoned by their French allies before the Orangist victory of 1787, had closed down their clubs and societies; but these reappeared two years later with the news of the outbreak of revolution in France. However, the Dutch Patriots were cautious and relatively inactive; and, in January 1793, after Belgium had been invaded by French armies, the French representative in Amsterdam reported to the Ministry of Foreign Affairs in Paris that the Patriot party was non-existent at The Hague and weak in Rotterdam and Amsterdam. Besides, unlike the Jacobins in France, it was largely composed of rich merchants and manufacturers who, though dissatisfied with both Stadholder and city regents, had retained a healthy respect for property and feared for their businesses and fortunes. Consequently, the Patriots showed little inclination to support the French armies when they occupied Dutch Brabant for a while in February 1793. In the following weeks, as Dumouriez withdrew through Belgium before deserting to the Austrians, Patriot activity revived. But two of the seven provinces—Zeeland and Guelderland—remained obstinately attached to the Stadholder's cause; and, even elsewhere, the majority of simple townsmen and country-dwellers appeared to see the French as the mere allies of the bourgeoisie. So, contrary to the early hopes of the French, the long-awaited Dutch Patriot revolution held fire and only broke out when the French occupied the country in January 1795.

In Belgium, as we noted in our second chapter, something like a national revolt against Joseph II's innovations had begun in 1787. In its opening stages, it took the form of an " aristocratic revolt" led by the Estates party of Van der Noot; but soon a rival leadership appeared in the moderate democratic party of J.-F. Vonck. As in England and the United Provinces, the outbreak of revolution in France was received with great enthusiasm throughout the country; but here it also acted as a stimulus to open rebellion. Vonck entered immediately into contact with the new authorities in Paris; " patriot " volunteers were enrolled in Brabant and in the neighbouring independent bishopric of Liège; the people rose in Liège and drove out their bishop; a " patriot " army under General Vandermersch expelled the Austrians from Ghent and Brussels; and, in December, the Austrians, having offered little resistance, withdrew from the Belgian provinces. Thus the Belgians, having attained their national independence, looked like following in the footsteps of the French; and the Vonckists prepared to reorganize their institutions on more democratic lines. But events in France, while momentarily strengthening the democrats at the expense of their rivals, also had the effect of driving a deeper wedge between the Belgian parties and of dividing the country in two. The Estates party had the solid backing of the Catholic Church and the merchant guilds; with their support they managed, in January, to proclaim a United States of Belgium, based on the more conservative American model and not on the French, as desired by their rivals. A " witch-hunt " was launched against the Vonckists, whose moderate reformist aims were represented as part of a sinister plot to destroy Belgium's traditions and fundamental " liberties ". In Brussels, which in December had hailed the " patriots " and volunteers, a popular insurrection broke out against them in March. The houses of wealthy Vonckists were pillaged and destroyed; the volunteers were stoned and disarmed; and one " patriot " leader was forced to his knees and made to declare : " I recognize, by order of the Brussels people, that the Patriotic Society of which I am a member is nothing but a band of rogues." Many of the democrats were arrested, others sought refuge in France. Thus an " aristocratic revolt ", when faced with the consequences of a national revolutionary uprising, had turned to counter-revolution. Profiting by these divisions, the Austrian armies returned in December 1790, re-installed the prince-bishop of Liège and restored the *status quo* in the Belgian provinces. With their patrician rivals removed from office, many of the democrats returned from exile to await their own and their country's " liberation " at the hands of the French.

The Swiss cantons and their associated territories were composed of rural areas, some of which enjoyed a sort of primitive democracy, and city-states governed by bishops and merchant aristocracies. This oligarchic form of rule had already, as we have seen, been challenged in the 1760's, with temporary success, in the city of Geneva. The revolution in France helped to develop the democratic movement and to spread it to other cantons. In 1790, a Helvetian Club was formed in Paris among the Swiss refugees and democrats resident in the capital; they ran their own newspaper, disseminated revolutionary propaganda in the cantons, and invited their countrymen at home to follow their example. The Swiss Germans also caught the contagion from the neighbouring French—but German-speaking—province of Alsace. In Basel the " patriots ", led by Peter Ochs and Gobel (later Constitutional Bishop of Paris), stirred up such an agitation among the peasants that the bishop took fright and called in Austrian troops to restore order; but after the first French victories in this region, the democrats voted for union with France, and a part of the bishop's territories became the new French department of Mont-Terrible (March 1793). Peasant insurrections also occurred in the rural districts of Vaud and Valais, but were sternly repressed and their leaders hanged. In Geneva, the democrats, robbed of their earlier partial victory by French intervention (1782), took power again in December 1792 and extended full rights of citizenship to all, including both Burghers and Natives. A revolutionary committee was set up to govern the city, Jacobin clubs were formed (there were fifty in 1793), a Revolutionary Tribunal was installed, and a " reign of terror " followed, in the course of which patricians were imprisoned and executed, or merely heavily taxed. But while this was the most advanced stage that the revolution ever reached in Switzerland, it was probably in German-speaking Zürich that the French Revolution had its largest following: among them were such distinguished local notables as the painter Fuseli, the educational reformer Pestalozzi, and the Rolands' friend, the Protestant pastor Lavater. They formed a revolutionary club which, in 1794, launched a comprehensive programme of political and social reform. The " conspirators " were rounded up and 260 persons were imprisoned or exiled. But the agitation continued and spread to the neighbouring rural districts of Glarus and St. Gall; and, in September 1798, the peasants of St. Gall compelled their abbot to agree to commute a part of their feudal obligations for a small monetary payment. It was, in fact, a strength of the Swiss revolutionary movement that, in several cantons, in contrast with that in the Dutch and Belgian provinces, it was compounded of both middle-class urban and peasant elements.

German reactions to the French Revolution were, at the outset, similar to the English, but they were more varied and the results proved more lasting. Apart from a small number of large sovereign states like Prussia, Bavaria and Saxony, Germany was composed of a congeries of Free Cities and petty principalities, both lay and ecclesiastical, virtually sovereign but still owing some allegiance to the moribund Holy Roman Empire : the Rhineland states alone, with a population of 1,300,000, had no fewer than 97 separate rulers—dukes, margraves, landgraves, Imperial knights and ecclesiastical electors and princes. The confusion and multiplicity of political institutions were almost matched by those of social rank, the middle classes were generally excluded from public affairs, and serfdom was prevalent outside the western regions and the single state of Baden in the south. Yet in sharp contrast with these tenacious survivals from the medieval past was the vigour of Germany's intellectual life and institutions. No other country had more and better universities; none had so thriving a press (1,225 journals were launched in the 1780's alone); and few countries, if any, had produced so rich a crop of literary and scholarly talent as Germany in the past thirty years. It was the age of the *Aufklärung* (Enlightenment), Goethe's and Schiller's romantic period of *Sturm und Drang* ("Storm and Stress"), and of a profound literary and cultural revival. Among "enlightened" ideas, those of Montesquieu and Rousseau had taken root and, particularly since the American Revolution, had been eagerly discussed in the press, the universities, Masonic lodges, literary clubs and groups of *illuminati*. In such circles the Revolution met with an almost unanimous response. The fall of the Bastille was hailed by Johannes von Müller, Swiss historian and secretary to the Archbishop of Mainz, as the happiest occasion since the fall of the Roman Empire and by the historian Herder as the most momentous since the Reformation. Among poets acclaiming the event were the venerable Klopstock, Wieland, Bürger, Hölderlin, Tieck and Wackenroder; Goethe and Schiller, however, though not outspokenly hostile, remained comparatively unmoved. Other supporters included, among philosophers, Kant, Hegel, Fichte and Schlegel; and, among political journalists, Schlözer at Göttingen and Archenholz and Nicolai at Berlin. Hamburg, Klopstock's city, celebrated with odes and banquets; and even rulers like the Duke of Brunswick, the Duke and Duchess of Gotha and Prince Henry of Prussia joined in the chorus of praise.

Already, there were a few dissentient voices, including old-style Whigs like Rehberg and Brandes at Göttingen. These

were inevitably joined by others as the Revolution developed:
as the end of "despotism" and "privilege" was followed by
the sale of Church lands, emigration, the fall and execution of
the King, Terror, Jacobin dictatorship and democratic experiment; and as Burke's *Reflections* began to exercise its spell
over more conservative minds. An early convert was Schlözer
who, after the October "days" at Versailles, began to lament
the "mindless tyranny of the mob". Johannes von Müller, so
enthusiastic at the start, was wavering in 1790 and, by 1793,
was declaiming against "those madmen and monsters in
France". Even more thorough was the conversion of Friedrich
von Gentz who, having been an admirer of Rousseau and Mirabeau, was won over by Burke and, next to Burke himself,
became the leading oracle of the counter-revolutionary crusade
against France. To others, more radical, it was the Terror or
the execution of Louis that brought disillusionment—among
them, Wieland, Jean-Paul Richter, Schleiermacher, Klopstock
and Hegel; while Goethe and Schiller, though by no means
indifferent, maintained their Olympian detachment. Some,
however, never fully lost their enthusiasm—the poets Bürger,
Tieck and Wackenroder; the philosophers Herder, Fichte and
(more hesitantly) Kant; and Georg Forster, librarian of the
University of Mainz, who not only condoned the execution of
the King and welcomed the Republic, but became a leading
figure in the revolution at Mainz that followed its occupation
by General Custine's troops in the autumn of 1792.

In the long run, the attitude of the intellectuals was, no
doubt, of considerable importance for Germany's future. But
of more immediate significance was the impact of the Revolution in other quarters—on the bourgeoisie, politicians and
peasants in a number of cities and states. Of these, none were
more exposed to the French "contagion" than those in the
Rhineland provinces, adjoining France's eastern border. The
dominions of the Electors of Cologne, Treves and Mainz and
of the rulers of Baden and the Bavarian Palatinate were caught,
as it were, in pincers between the revolutions in Alsace and

Liège. In Baden, peasant-disturbance was minor and quickly suppressed; in the Palatinate, there were mutinies at Landau and Zweibrücken, and peasants revolted against the hunting rights of the nobility and refused to pay their dues. The ecclesiastical principalities of Cologne, Treves and Mainz were more deeply affected, partly through the influence of Elogius Schneider, ex-Franciscan and former professor at Bonn, who, expelled by the Elector of Treves, took a university post across the border at Strasbourg, where he became a leading political figure. In Cologne, the Third Estate, taking their cue from the French, demanded an end of fiscal inequality; at Bonn, the "patriots" formed a revolutionary club; while in Mainz, whose Elector made himself doubly unpopular by following Austria and Prussia into war with France (April 1792), townsmen rioted against rising prices and peasants against their landlords' exactions. So here, as in the Swiss cantons, the victorious French armies of 1792 and 1794 were to find a situation that favoured their political and military aims.

Beyond the Rhine, the French impact was less direct and was only fully felt in Napoleon's time. In Saxony, peasants protested against the *corvée* and feudal dues; but Saxony, like Mecklenburg in the north, was among those areas that emerged relatively unscathed from the whole Revolutionary and Napoleonic experience. Bavaria was hardly affected until the Directory, when Munich was for a while occupied by the French, and the *illuminati* and their leader, Montgelas, began to exercise considerable influence at Court. Hamburg, as we saw, greeted the Revolution with banquets; and, a year later, the liberal Hamburg merchants, inspired by Georg Sieveking, a wealthy merchant-prince and patron of letters, celebrated the Feast of the Federation and continued to do so for some years to come. But the French connection was valued as much for commercial as for political reasons; and once Hamburg found herself (at the Empire's bidding) at war with France alongside the English, enthusiasm for England began to eclipse that for France; and later, having been annexed by Napoleon, Hamburg was one of the few German states to revolt against his rule. In Prussia, the impact of the Revolution went deeper and was more lasting. Frederick the Great's successor, Frederick William II, was a weak and indolent ruler and his reign saw an aristocratic and clerical revival. Yet the French found allies at Court : Prince Henry and Hertzberg, Frederick's old foreign minister, who led a peace-party that helped to shorten the war that broke out with France in 1792. The liberal bourgeoisie, though wavering, was never entirely hostile to the Revolution; the younger officers were said to be infected with French ideas; and, in Silesia, between 1794 and 1796, secret societies were formed by a group including a business man, an army captain and two government officials. Silesia was also the scene of considerable popular disturbance : in the winter of 1792, peasants refused to pay dues to the Junkers; soon after, weavers rioted over wages and called on the French to come to their aid. In 1793, there were riots in Breslau and a bloody revolt among Silesian Poles; and, in 1796, a general "spirit of revolt" among Silesian peasants was attributed to the agitation carried on by troops demobilized after the war with France. In the long run, the greater part of Germany emerged radically transformed from the Revolutionary and Napoleonic period; but, in these earlier years, it was not the south, the north or the centre but these peripheral frontier regions—the Rhenish and Silesian provinces—that were the most deeply affected.

In Italy, too, there were factors that favoured the progress of French revolutionary ideas : a large educated, and mainly anti-clerical, middle class, already steeped in the teachings of the Enlightenment; widespread resentment at the alien domination of Austrians in the north and centre and Spaniards in the south; a nobility that, in many respects, shared the advanced views and political aspirations of the educated middle class; and a seething mass of peasant discontent. After the initial enthusiasm, the weaknesses, however, became equally evident. There was the difficulty, in a country so divided, of concerting the scattered efforts of the various groups which, in response to the revolutionary doctrines of the

French, began to think in terms of national unity and liberation. There was, too, the even greater problem of how to find
a common political meeting-ground between the wealthy
middle-class or aristocratic " Jacobins " and the impoverished
peasants and urban masses. The first of these difficulties
would begin to be overcome when Bonaparte himself pointed
the way by imposing something like a unified system of administration over the greater part of the Italian peninsula; the
second would prove a more intractable problem in the poor
and Catholic south than in the more prosperous and anti-
clerical north. The northern Kingdom of Piedmont and
Sardinia had, moreover, the additional advantage, from the
point of view of would-be revolutionaries, of lying close to the
French border and of enclosing the province of Savoy, where
a movement for union with France had already long been in
existence. Savoy was the first Italian province to rebel and, in
1789, peasants who had won freedom from manorial dues
refused to pay their landlords any compensation. Soon after,
in neighbouring Piedmont, peasants rioting for land-reform
declared themselves to be citizens of France; while, in Turin,
its capital, there was a " Jacobin " attempt to overthrow the
government in 1794. Francophile sympathies also united the
educated classes and the common people at Bologna and in
other parts of the north; but, further south, free-thinking
bourgeois, *illuminati* and middle-class " Jacobins " tended to
stand alone, or even to be the object of deep popular hatred
and suspicion. In Naples, the Masonic lodges and " patriot "
societies were probably stronger and more numerous than
anywhere else in Italy; but when the local " Jacobins " attempted to lead an insurrection against their rulers in 1794,
the common people remained obstinately aloof. Not surprisingly, the Church and governing circles were able, as in Spain
and Belgium, to exploit these antipathies and turn them to
their own advantage. In January 1793, we find a French
envoy, Hugo de Bassville, being massacred in the course of a
popular riot; and, in Naples, the city poor, if hostile to
" Jacobinism ", which they associated with the middle-class

rich, were all the more responsive to the call of " Church and King ".[2]

The reaction of Europe to the first years of the revolution in France was, then, an extremely varied one. Leaving aside for the moment the counter-revolution and the attitudes of governments, how can we briefly summarize the impact of the Revolution on the countries of Europe on the eve of France's military expansion and conquests? On the one hand, there were countries like Turkey, Russia, Spain, the Balkans, Austria, and Hungary, and the Scandinavian states which, in spite of local pockets of " Jacobinism ", remained, at this stage at least, largely untouched by the revolution in France. There were countries like England and Scotland where the initial support for French revolutionary ideas had, by 1795, died a natural death, or had been stamped out or driven underground by repression and the impact of war. There were others like Poland and Ireland where, for quite exceptional reasons, the French Revolution had met with a remarkable degree of support; but, lying beyond the range of French military assistance, their rebellions were easily crushed. Among France's closer neighbours, Holland's abortive Patriot " revolution " of 1787 had been given a new shot in the arm by the events in France, but showed little sign of developing into open revolt by the spring of 1793. In Belgium alone, a revolutionary situation was already present by the summer of 1789, and, in Liège and Brabant in particular, was brought to a head by the impact of the revolution in France; but, subsequently, the democratic movement had been weakened by internal counter-revolution and the restoration of Austrian authority. Finally, the impact of the French Revolution had been considerable in parts of Germany and Switzerland and most of Italy; but, as in Holland, enthusiasm for French ideas had been largely confined to the urban middle class and educated circles and it was only in a handful of Swiss cantons, in the German Rhineland and Prussian Silesia and in the Italian provinces of Piedmont

[2] See E. J. Hobsbawm, *Primitive Rebels* (Manchester, 1954), pp. 112-13; and *The Age of Revolution* (London, 1962), pp. 82-3.

and Savoy that anything like a popular revolutionary movement had, by 1793, sprung up in the wake of the events in France.

In the next chapter, we shall see how these various movements were affected by France's entry into the war, her victories and military expansion.

Chapter XI

REVOLUTIONARY WAR

It has been suggested in an earlier chapter that the war that broke out in 1792 was by no means due to any single and particular cause. For example, it was not, and it never became, a straightforward crusade of the crowned heads of Europe against revolutionary France. This element, however, certainly played a part. Burke had preached such a crusade after 1790 and Pope Pius had, by his general condemnation of the Revolution in April 1791, given it his moral support. The idea was attractive to a number of Europe's rulers: it appealed to Catherine of Russia, Gustavus of Sweden, Charles of Spain and Frederick William of Prussia; and the Austrian Emperor Leopold, though his inclinations were liberal, had good reason to give it careful consideration, as he felt obligations to his sister and, besides, was constantly reminded of his responsibilities by the persistent, though unwelcome, advice of the *émigré* Comte d'Artois and his secret correspondence with the French Court. But, whatever their personal feelings in the matter, Europe's rulers had other preoccupations: Spain and Sweden were militarily too weak to take any initiative against their old ally; Sweden was also diverted by her claims on Finland; Russia and Prussia were both concerned with Poland; and Leopold, besides his own interest in Poland and Turkey, had the even more compelling urge to restore his authority in Belgium and Hungary. And England, as we have seen, was, despite Burke's promptings, prepared to let the Revolution take its course and, in addition, was anxiously watching Russian moves in the East. Under these conditions, a general coalition of old Europe against the Revolution was hard to bring about and, even when it appeared (as in 1793-5) to have been achieved, it was factors other than the purely ideological that played the major role and, by their very nature, constantly threatened to pull it apart.

It is unnecessary to repeat here in any detail the reasons that brought Austria and Prussia into war with France in April 1792 : the new Emperor Francis II's hostility to the Revolution, the dispute over the German princes' claims in Alsace, and Brissot's agitation for a peoples' crusade against " despotism " all played their part;[1] besides, the Courts of Berlin and Vienna counted on a short war, believing that France would collapse without a fight.[2] Meanwhile, Catherine offered 15,000 men—but only after Poland had been pacified; Hesse and Mainz, alone of the German states, supplied a contingent; and after the August revolution in Paris, England, Russia, Spain, Holland and Venice showed their disapproval by breaking off relations with France. But Russia, while happy to egg on the Austro-Prussians, continued to find Poland a more profitable field of operations; and Spain, England and Holland only entered the coalition in the spring of 1793 for their own particular reasons. Holland was brought in by the threat of a French invasion, while for the others Louis' execution on 21 January and the diplomatic protests that followed provided the immediate pretext. But whereas Spain, despite her counter-revolutionary pretensions, was dragged in against her will (for months there had been a *Brissotin* campaign in France to dethrone all the Bourbons), England's case was quite different. It was certainly neither Burke's preaching nor the anti-Jacobin fury of George III that forced Pitt to abandon his neutrality, but the conviction that Britain's own vital and traditional interests were being endangered. France had been the national enemy since Louis XIV's day and, during the past century, the two countries had been ranged on opposing sides in nearly every dispute affecting Europe and its overseas possessions. The issues then disputed remained unsolved and would be raised again in the course of a twenty-year conflict. Yet it was

[1] See pages 126-9 above.
[2] See G. Lefebvre, *The French Revolution from its Origins in 1793* (London and New York, 1962), pp. 220-3.

not these general causes, any more than the believed threat to established property and authority, that brought England into war, but the particular dangers that she felt from France's occupation of Belgium, her opening of the River Scheldt to navigation (in defiance of the Treaty of Utrecht), and her imminent invasion of her ally, Holland. Thus, to England's rulers, the French, irrespective of their system of government, were repeating the earlier threats of Philip II and Louis XIV to her island security.

The entry of England, Spain and Holland into the first co-alition against France was followed by that of Naples, Rome, Venice and Sardinia; and so, in the spring of 1793, France found herself faced with an almost universally hostile Europe. But it was a Europe that had by no means composed its differences and continued to be divided within itself. Consequently, as the war went on and French military skill and morale improved, coalition followed coalition and each in turn broke down, disrupted both by French victories and by its own internal weaknesses and contradictions. Thus, after defeats by France in 1794-5, Spain and Holland changed sides and Prussia, hostile to Austria in Germany and anxious to steal a march on her in Poland, signed a separate peace and withdrew from the war. Austria and her remaining continental allies were compelled by Bonaparte's victories in Italy to make peace at Campo Formio; and England, left to fight alone, enlarged her commercial and colonial empire at the expense of her rivals, built up her sea-power in the Mediterranean, and showed little concern for the land-fighting in Europe. The Tsar Paul, who had succeeded Catherine in Russia, provoked by Bonaparte's occupation of Malta, joined Britain, Turkey and Austria in a second coalition against France and her allies in 1798. This, in turn, fell apart when Russia, at loggerheads with Austria over Italy and defeated by Masséna in Switzerland, withdrew her armies a year later; and it collapsed when Bonaparte, returning from Egypt, defeated the Austrians at Marengo (1800) and imposed on her the treaty of Lunéville (1801). So England was left once more to face France alone;

but, this time, her maritime pretensions had stirred up against her an Armed Neutrality of former allies; she faced economic difficulties and political crisis at home; and she agreed to sign peace at Amiens in May 1802. This provided a temporary respite but settled nothing. France retained her new régime and her continental conquests from Holland to Naples; while England, though surrendering a part of her new colonial acquisitions, remained mistress of the seas. When war broke out again, new coalitions followed the same pattern of alternating defeat and desertion; and it would take Europe many years to achieve a unity of purpose that would redress the balance in her favour.

But, of course, it needed more than the divisions among her enemies to ensure France's military success. The French army that, in April 1792, was called upon to meet the combined forces of Austria and Prussia was quite unprepared for war, let alone for an offensive. It was not that it lacked the knowledge of scientific warfare or of the use of modern weapons. Gribeauval, the great Inspector-General of the seventeen-sixties and seventies, had introduced an improved flintlock musket and lighter and more efficient field-guns; and the French staff had, since the Seven Years' War, studied the principles of the new offensive warfare that the improvement in weapons had made possible. Bourcet, director of the Staff College at Grenoble, had written a treatise on mountain-war, in which he had taught the superiority of offensive over defensive strategy and the importance of combining dispersion with concentration, thus breaking with the rigid linear formation prescribed by even the best captains of the day. Guibert, in his *Essai général de tactique* of 1772, had carried the argument further: he had stressed the virtues of the simple battalion column against the prevailing line of battle; he had urged that an army must live on the country within its field of operations, thus dispensing with the costly and cumbrous baggage-train; and, being also a "philosopher", he had advised that armies be recruited from citizens, devoted to their country and capable of initiative, rather than from mercenaries, vagrants, or criminals, pressed into service by hunger or press-gang, or fear of the gallows. Finally, Du Teil, in an essay of 1778, had worked out the tactics of the new field-artillery, insisting on the concentration of fire-power on the decisive point and the combined use of artillery and infantry. And such ideas, which involved a revolution in the strategy and tactics of warfare, no longer remained in the realm of speculation : a great part of them had passed into the army drill-book drafted in 1788 and issued to the troops in 1791. They were to be the guiding principles in which a whole new generation of revolutionary officers and engineers were to be moulded and trained; and, in fact, the Revolution alone, with its destruction of privilege and its evocation of the nation-at-arms, could provide the conditions under which they might operate.

But, at present, the army was hardly equipped to turn them to good account : it had numbers and enthusiasm, but it lacked co-ordination, discipline, supplies and leaders. The old aristocratic officers had been weeded out in their hundreds by the troops themselves, civil war and mutiny had disrupted whole regiments, and of a former officer corps of 9,000 only 3,000 retained their commands. To fill the gaps in the regular army and in response to new ideals, battalions of volunteers (some 100,000 in all) had been recruited from the National Guards enrolled since July 1789. These citizen-soldiers were full of patriotic devotion, were comparatively well paid and elected their officers; but they had more enthusiasm than discipline or training, the generals treated them with contempt, and their privileged conditions of service enraged the " regulars " and caused endless friction. Such an army was no match for the 70,000 trained and seasoned troops that Brunswick assembled at the frontier; and Brissot's gamble, as we have seen, ended in disaster. An invading force, sent across the frontier towards Tournai and Liège, fled in panic after its first encounter with the enemy and fell back, with the bulk of the French army, towards Lille. France was only saved from further catastrophe by the cautious and traditional generalship of Brunswick, who failed to follow up his advantage.

It was, in fact, the weakness and divided counsels of her enemies rather than her own internal strength that gave France an initial breathing-space and the opportunity to snatch victory from defeat. By the time of her first successes at Valmy and Jemappes in September 1792, the " Austrian Committee " had been removed, the monarchy had been overthrown, Brissot and his band of garrulous enthusiasts had lost much of their influence, a few treacherous generals (among them Lafayette) had been cashiered or had deserted to the enemy, the artillery had been improved, and greater numbers of volunteers had been recruited, trained and equipped. But the major problems still remained : to merge the new citizen-soldiers with the old regulars in a single national army; to extract the maximum military advantage from the mass of citizens whom the Revolution made available for service; to find and train an efficient and trustworthy corps of officers; and to equip the army with a steady flow of the latest weapons by harnessing industry to the needs of war. These varying tasks were tackled with considerable success by the combined efforts of the National Convention, of the great Committee of Public Safety and of men like Carnot and the Jacobin military expert, Dubois-Crancé. The *national* army, based on universal and compulsory conscription, did not finally emerge until Jourdan's law of September 1798; but a series of intermediate measures— the *amalgame* of February 1793 and the *levée en masse* of the following August—served to break down the distinction between " blues " and regulars and raised armies whose numbers far exceeded those of the Old Régime : 300,000 in February and 650,000 in August 1793, and over three-quarters of a million in 1794. Such numbers could, of course, have been more of a hindrance than an asset, and many of the generals reared in the traditions of the past were appalled, rather than delighted, by the influx of recruits; but the genius of Carnot turned them to good account by finding instructors, weapons and supplies, and by adapting the teachings of

Bourcet and Guibert to the needs of the new mass armies that the Revolution had conjured up. Besides, as the old generals deserted or were cashiered or guillotined, new commanders were found to take their place, many of them in their twenties or early thirties when the Revolution broke out—men like Bonaparte, Hoche, Augereau, Jourdan, Murat, Masséna and several others. It was such armies and generals as these that, after the initial defeats of 1792 and the Belgian disaster of February-March 1793, won an almost unbroken succession of victories from June 1794, carried the war into the enemy's territory and broke up a succession of coalitions. The greatest of the new commanders, Bonaparte, had studied the teachings of Bourcet, Guibert and Du Teil in college at Valence and Auxonne and read the account of Maillebois' campaign in Piedmont of fifty years before.

These writings served, almost literally, as the blue-prints for the Italian campaign of 1796-7; and yet it needed more than the mere ability to read blue-prints and to learn from precedent to put them into such brilliant execution. The French had certainly no numerical superiority : at the outset, they had 38,000 troops and their Austrian and Sardinian opponents a combined force of 47,000. Nor had they the better equipment : in fact, six weeks after hostilities opened, the young general could tell his soldiers (and with a tolerable degree of accuracy): "You have won battles without guns, crossed rivers without bridges, made forced marches without boots, encamped often without food "; it was even said that two of his lieutenants had been compelled to share a single pair of breeches! And yet, within a month of his arrival on the scene, the new commander had won four great victories, driven a fatal wedge between the Austrian and Sardinian armies, and forced King Victor Amadeus, ignoring Austrian protests, to sue for a separate peace.[8] And Bonaparte went on, in similar style, to clear the Austrians from the centre and north of Italy and to bring his army (now substantially reinforced) within

[8] For a full account, see Spenser Wilkinson, *The Rise of General Bonaparte* (Oxford, 1930).

eighty miles of Vienna before signing the preliminaries to a general peace. At every stage of this remarkable campaign he closely followed the precepts of his teachers; and the speed of his marches, his flexibility of manœuvre, the heavy concentration of his artillery and his ability to make the maximum thrust, at every turn, at the enemy's weakest point showed that he had learned their lessons well.

But "revolutionary" wars, even more than others, cannot be fought by military means alone. The French political leaders, far more than the generals, were always conscious of this fact and consistently treated the war as a political almost as much as a military operation. One early step taken in the war of propaganda was the attempt to identify with France's cause distinguished foreigners—"patriots", reformers and men of letters—by conferring on them honorary titles of citizenship; and, in the last days of the Legislative Assembly, such titles were conferred on the Englishmen Joseph Priestley, Jeremy Bentham, Thomas Paine and William Wilberforce; the German poets Klopstock and Schiller; the Polish Kosciusko; the Americans Washington and Hamilton; and several others. The results were not striking, and some were embarrassed rather than delighted by the honour. More important were the successive declarations made by the Assemblies on the war, its conduct, its aims, its scope and the possibilities that it offered—declarations whose nature changed not only as new leaders took the place of old but as new political situations arose. In its first major statement on war and peace the Constituent Assembly had declared in May 1790: "The French nation renounces the undertaking of any war with a view to making conquests, and it will never use its forces against the liberty of any people." This famous "no-conquests" formula found its place in the Constitution of 1791 and was repeated by the Legislative Assembly in a statement of foreign policy on 14 April 1792, a few days before it declared war on Austria. Perhaps not surprisingly in the light of later events, it has been suggested that the deputies spoke with their tongues in their cheeks and never had any intention of abiding by these pious intentions. But this is to be wise after the event and to attribute to them a cunning and a foresight that they clearly did not possess. To members of all parties it was almost an article of faith that conquest and territorial expansion, while inseparable from the dynastic wars of the past (and those still waged by their opponents), were incompatible with the new ideas of Fraternity and the Rights of Man; and when war broke out, the majority, persuaded by Brissot, believed that the Belgian, Dutch and Rhenish " patriots " were waiting to receive them with open arms and that their " liberation " would be swift and painless. At this stage, apart from those working secretly for the Court, it was only Robespierre and the small group of his supporters who raised two pertinent objections: first, that the army was not ready for the task to which it was being assigned; and, secondly, that peoples are inclined to resist rather than to welcome " armed missionaries ".

The first of these propositions was put to the test, and with results that we have seen, two months after war began; but the second could only be tested when the French armies, having won their first victories in the autumn of 1792, were ready to march into Belgium and Holland and when the Assembly was faced with requests by the " patriots " of Savoy, Nice and the Rhineland to annex their territories to France. That the Assembly would consent to do so was by no means a foregone conclusion any more than it had been in September 1791, when, after long delay, it consented, in response to the wishes of the local population, to take over the papal enclave of Avignon. But Avignon lay a hundred miles within French national territory and it hardly seemed compatible with " popular sovereignty " to leave the Avignonnais, against their own expressed wishes, under alien rule. The same arguments were used to justify the rejection of the claims of the German princes to their feudal immunities in Alsace. But Nice and Savoy lay beyond the existing frontiers of France and were parts of the Kingdom of Sardinia. Even so, the precedent of Avignon was quoted in support of the Savoyards' request for union with France. The question was hotly debated in September 1792, when so ardent an internationalist as Camille Desmoulins warned that to annex Savoy, even in response to popular demand, would be to embark on a policy of conquest such as the Assembly had expressly abjured. So the request was at first rejected; but, soon after, the combined efforts of Danton, Girondin deputies, and internationally-minded foreign " patriots " like the Prussian Anacharsis Cloots persuaded the Convention to find a new formula to justify such measures. This was the famous doctrine of France's " natural frontiers " which, as Carnot was the first to define them, lay along the Rhine, the Alps and the Pyrenees. Such arguments prevailed and, on 27 November 1792, the Convention decided, with only two dissentients, to annex Savoy.

The problem arose even more acutely over the Low Countries and the Rhineland. France had, for the moment, been cleared of her enemies; the Austrians had been driven out of Belgium, the German princes from the Rhenish provinces and the Sardinians from Nice; and the Convention issued its declaration of 19 November that it would " grant fraternity and aid to all peoples who wish to recover their liberty ". This was, of course, a direct and deliberate provocation to the rulers of Europe, including the English; but it also raised further questions: who should speak for the " peoples ", who should define " liberty ", and what should happen to those who rejected it? In the case of Nice, there was no great problem, as the Niçois, like the Savoyards, were eager for union with France; and this was accepted. But the Convention had decided on 15 December that the new revolutionary authorities and assemblies to be formed in the occupied territories should be elected only by citizens taking an oath " to be faithful to liberty and equality and to renounce privilege ". So " patriots " alone had the vote; but the " patriots " of Belgium and the Rhineland, who welcomed " liberation " and voted for annexation, proved to be a minority. Thus the Convention, far from acceding to the spontaneous and enthusiastic wishes of the " liberated " peoples, had been led by the persuasive oratory of Dantonists and Girondins, the lobbying of foreign "patriots", the logic of France's "natural frontiers" and by the exigencies of war to take the first steps along the road of conquest and annexation.

The Gironde and the "patriot" groups in Paris had other expansionist aims as well—in particular, to set up "sister republics" in those countries beyond France's "natural frontiers" where she might be assured of a reasonable measure of support. This had the further advantage that such republics would, like the annexed territories, be expected to put the *assignat* into circulation, place their gold and silver at France's disposal and contribute, by subsidies and taxes, to her war expenditure. Such plans were already well advanced in January 1793, when the occupation of Holland was on the order of the day. But the Dutch and English joined the anti-French coalition in February; by April, the French had been compelled to withdraw from the Low Countries and the Rhineland; and the Gironde fell soon after. Thus a new situation had arisen and new men came into power. Robespierre, their leader, had been opposed all along to the war of "liberation", to the conquest of France's "natural frontiers" and the formation of "sister republics". Against these notions he now urged the need to respect existing treaties, and the rights of small nations and neutrals: the most that France should promise would be to assist a revolution that was already under way. Accordingly, foreign "patriots" in Paris fell under suspicion; and Cloots, implicated in an alleged *complot de l'étranger*, went to the guillotine. Yet, though rejecting a proposal to annex Catalonia (which the French armies entered in April 1794), the Committee of Public Safety favoured a plan for turning her into an independent republic under French "protection".[4] But, in general, not only principles but circumstances and opportunities had changed: from April 1793 to June 1794, the Republic, far from being in a position to expand, once more faced foreign invasion and was fighting

[4] R. Herr, *The Eighteenth-Century Revolution in Spain* (Princeton, 1958), pp. 286-96.

for its existence. Robespierre, as we know, fell from power a month after the victory of Fleurus; and it was only after Fleurus that these professions of faith could have been put more fully to the test.

Robespierre's successors, at least, reverted to the expansionist aims of the Girondin Convention. Certainly, in their case the temptation was greater than in his. By the autumn of 1794, Belgium and the Rhenish provinces were once more under French military occupation; Republican troops entered Amsterdam and The Hague, and the Stadholder fled to England. What should be done with the occupied territories? Carnot had, by this time, given up his support for the " natural frontiers " and (whether prompted by his memories of Robespierre or by his growing royalist sympathies) opposed annexation. He was supported by a few generals and army-commissars—among them Joubert and Kléber—who argued that the policy of annexation would lead to endless war. The royalists, wanting peace at any price, added their voices to theirs. They were opposed by a powerful expansionist group, including Sieyes and Merlin of Douai, the new advocates of a network of " sister republics "; the Alsatian Reubell, champion of the Rhine frontier and of outright annexation; Barras and Larevellière-Lépaux, both Directors; and a medley of Dutch " patriots ", generals, journalists, army contractors and industrialists. Some, like Barras, were concerned with little more than their own self-interest; others, like Reubell and the generals, argued in terms of military security; others again stressed the advantages that might accrue from a " common market " with Belgium and the Rhineland. Carnot and the peace-party were eventually eliminated by the *coup d'état* of 18th Fructidor (4 September 1797); but, long before that, expansionist views had once more prevailed. To satisfy them, Belgium was annexed as a French province in October 1795; while the Rhineland, before being annexed outright, was placed under French military government: it never became a separate republic as local " patriots " had hoped. Beyond the " natural frontiers ", however, this became the usual pattern;

and, in response to the repeated requests of Dutch and Swiss "patriots", Holland was declared a Batavian Republic in 1795 and Switzerland, after long delay, a Helvetic Republic in 1798.

Meanwhile, Bonaparte's victorious Italian campaign, his restless ambition and personal initiative had opened up even wider vistas beyond the Alps. The Sardinians had been forced to accept the accomplished fact of the cession of Nice and Savoy. At the peace of Campo Formio, Austria agreed to cede Belgium (another accomplished fact), to recognize the German princes' surrender of their Rhineland provinces, and to acknowledge France's title to the Ionian Islands; in return (in defiance of every revolutionary precedent), Venice, liberated from its local aristocracy by the French, was handed to the Emperor. But the rest of Italy had also to be disposed of. The Directors, whose eyes were on Germany rather than Italy, were willing enough to exact tribute but preferred to leave the direction of Italian affairs to the present rulers. But Bonaparte had other ideas and was in a strong position to dictate his own terms—particularly after an offer to surrender his command had met with an expected refusal. Piedmont, in spite of local Jacobin protest, was formally annexed to France; and Genoa, pending similar treatment, earned a temporary respite as a nominally independent republic. Many Italian "patriots" entertained similar hopes and the liberated cities of Parma, Modena, Ferrara and Bologna quickly declared themselves to be republics. Bonaparte, however, nipped this move in the bud, and summoned an assembly at Milan, from which emerged the short-lived Cispadane Republic—soon to be merged, by the addition of Lombardy and bits of former Venetian and Papal territory, within a larger Cisalpine Republic. Soon after, the Ligurian Republic was formed, based on Genoa, along the north-western coast. With Napoleon's return to France and his departure for Egypt, these republics became models for his successors to follow. In 1798, the Pope was removed to Siena and a Roman Republic, under French military protection, was proclaimed in the centre; and early in 1799, Championnet occupied Naples, whose King had joined Austria in an assault on Rome, and, flouting the Directors' orders, proclaimed a Parthenopean Republic in the south. These "sister republics" (or such as survived) were to assume new forms under the Consulate and Empire; but, for the present, they responded reasonably well to the revolutionary-expansionist aims of the Directors and flattered the ambitions of their generals.

During the first occupation of Belgium, the Convention's decree of 15 December 1792 had already formulated the principle that the "liberated" peoples must raise levies and contribute to the upkeep of France's armies; and, by such means, 64 million livres had, after six weeks, been paid into the French Treasury. Later, Belgium, with its rich wheatlands and pastures and stocks of Austrian *thalers,* was looked on as a sort of milch-cow that might save France from the near-famine conditions of 1795 and 1796. But the government's agents overreached themselves, they battened on the annexed provinces like locusts, and their extortions and requisitions went on at such a pace that whole areas were stripped of their resources and both Belgium and Holland shared in France's crisis and in her crop of popular disturbance. Holland had, on becoming a Batavian Republic, agreed to support an occupation army of 25,000 men and pay an indemnity of 100 million florins in silver coin or in bills of exchange on foreign banks. Such exactions became the greater as the war continued and the Directory was faced with increasing financial obligations. It worked to Bonaparte's advantage, as he soon found that the surest way of persuading the Directors to condone his Cæsarean methods in Italy was to replenish the Republic's coffers with loot and treasure from the occupied provinces. So the tax-collector followed hot on the heels of his conquering army and, in July 1796, Salicetti, commissar to the Army of Italy, estimated that the first three months' campaigning had already brought in a tribute of 60 million francs. But Bonaparte carried his exactions even further. In a message carried by Joubert to the Directors in November 1797, he presented a startling balance-sheet of victories in terms of prisoners, captured field-guns, treaties and negotiations, and "liberated" peoples; and to all this he added the remarkable boast: "Sent to Paris all the masterpieces of Michelangelo, Guercini, Titian, Paolo Veronese, Correggio, Albano, the Carracci, Raphael, and Leonardo da Vinci."

Bonaparte's Egyptian campaign was more blatantly imperialistic: it established no new institutions of any permanence, slavery was left untouched, and it neither attempted nor realized any "revolutionary" objects. The same cannot be said, of course, for the record of the French Republic in Europe during the period of its military expansion from the autumn of 1792 onwards. On Napoleon's "victory-banner" of 1797 the sentence just quoted was preceded by the following: "Liberty bestowed upon the people of Bologna, Ferrara, Modena, Massa-Carrara, Romagna, Lombardy, Brescia, Bergamo, Mantua, Cremona, part of Veronese, Chiavenna, Bormio, the Valtelline, the people of Genoa, the Imperial Fiefs, the people of the Departments of Corcyra, of the Aegean Sea, and of Ithaca." And this was by no means a mere empty boast or rhetorical flourish; nor did it simply mean that France's enemies or the former local rulers had been driven from their estates or ejected from their offices. The Republic's armies in Italy, as in Belgium, Holland, Switzerland, the Rhineland and Savoy, did not confine their activities to military operations, to plunder or raising subsidies even under the Directory. With the support, wherever possible, of local "Jacobins", they introduced new laws and political institutions based on the French, and even transformed the old social system. Princes, stadholders and foreign governors were deposed; new revolutionary authorities were installed; national armies were recruited; French laws and constitutions were imposed; and this process continued—in Poland, Naples and Germany, for instance—even under the Empire. Of course, the nature of these measures, and the degree to which they were "revolutionary" or "democratic", tended to reflect what was going on in France herself. The French democratic constitution of 1793, though widely acclaimed by " Jacobins " in other countries, found few imitators; but this was because France was at that time in no position to impose her institutions outside her own borders and the foreign " patriots " who admired them were, in most cases, powerless to do so without French support. There was, however, one exception : in the small city-state of Geneva, the democrats, having won a majority in the newly-formed National Assembly, in February 1794 carried through a constitution that, in most respects, was closely similar to that adopted by the Jacobin Convention—and then put into cold storage—a few months before. But it only survived two years, and with Robespierre's overthrow in France the ideas and institutions of the Year II ceased to be fashionable among her neighbours; so that a new Genevan constitution, more liberal than the French of 1795 but nevertheless modelled on it, took its place. In fact, it was the bourgeois constitution of the Year III, and not that of 1793, that became the general model for the succession of constitutions—ten in all—that were introduced in the " sister republics " between 1796 and 1799.[5] These varied considerably in detail and some were more freely discussed, and less peremptorily imposed by France's agents, than others. In the Batavian Republic, for example, the constitution that emerged in 1798 had been hotly debated for nearly three years : the Dutch democrats had long demanded male adult suffrage and a single-chamber Assembly and only agreed to a compromise on the insistence of the French agent at The Hague. Elsewhere, constitutions might be imposed or adopted, with the minimum of local discussion, from blueprints brought from Paris or issued by Napoleon's staff headquarters. But, whatever the method of consultation, the final results were almost uniformly the same : a more or less restricted suffrage (though often more liberal than in France), elections in two stages, a bi-cameral Assembly, and civil rights for Jews and religious toleration.

These constitutions were mainly short-lived : as the bourgeois Republic in France made way for the Consulate and

[5] See J. Godechot. *La Grande nation*. II, 418-49.

Empire, the political institutions of her satellites tended to be adapted to meet new needs. Yet, in one form or another, the new revolutionary authorities carried through measures that often proved to be lasting. The ghettoes in Rome and Venice, as previously at Bonn, were closed down; slaves were freed in Genoa, Malta and Sicily; feudal dues, tithe and the surviving remnants of serfdom (as in the Rhineland, Sardinia and Switzerland) were abolished; the privileged orders were dissolved; and the lands of the Church were confiscated and put up for auction. So a settlement broadly similar to the French of 1789-91 took place in all these territories. Yet the social revolution, like the political, was carried through in the spirit of 1795, not in that of 1793. The distribution of estates that followed their confiscation was less widespread than in France, and only wealthy bourgeois and the richer peasants benefited. The south of Italy, in particular, was a land of small and landless peasants, impoverished but not enserfed, and these gained nothing from the new régime and never expected to do so—a fact that helps to explain both their hostility to the French and something of the later history of the Italian Risorgimento with its long survival of southern peasant-hatred for landowner and urban bourgeois. In the Swiss cantons, tithe and seigneurial obligations were only redeemed at a heavy price; while, in Belgium and parts of Italy, new measures of public assistance failed to compensate the poor for the loss of religious charity. And, everywhere, those who had gained from the liberation of the land from tithe and feudal dues saw those gains wiped out by rising prices and the exactions of the tax-collector. So the French "liberators", instead of being met with gratitude, encountered a long series of hostile demonstrations by peasants or small urban consumers—as in Belgium and Switzerland in 1798-9 and in every part of Italy from those of 1796-7 in Pavia and Verona in the north to the great popular insurrections in Tuscany, Rome and Naples in 1798 and 1799. Often, such protests took place under the banner of the Catholic Church, and Roman citizens, Tuscan peasants and Neapolitan *lazzaroni* rioted and looted to cries of "Viva Maria!" There were, of course, exceptions: Protestant Dutch and Genevans were hardly likely to take part in such disturbances; and the Catholic Rhinelanders, who benefited more than others from the suppression of feudal obligations, remained comparatively calm. Most remarkable of all was the insurrection that took place in Piedmont in 1799 after its annexation by the French. Far from clamouring for the Old Régime and for the burial of the new, the insurgents, led by local Jacobins and formed of peasant bands from Asti, Alba and Mondovi, protested against the French violation of the sacred right of "popular sovereignty"; they carried portraits of the revolutionary martyrs, Marat and Lepeletier, and demanded a united Italian Republic. The incident is significant—it provided a first example of the new revolutionary idea of "nationalism" being hurled back in the teeth of the conquering French; and it also showed that the Piedmontese, alone of the Italians of the 1790's, were ready to follow the French along the path of a broader popular revolution than those who had turned their backs on the "democratic" revolution in France were now prepared to tolerate.

Piedmont's example, though exceptional, raises an important general question: how far were local "patriots" independent agents able to lead revolutions in their countries on their own account; and how far were they merely auxiliaries of the French who accepted French solutions? In all countries occupied by France or falling under her political influence there were, as we have seen, groups of "patriots" or "Jacobins" sympathetic to French ideas and more or less willing to attempt to apply them at home. The label "Jacobin" is here slightly misleading as it was attached indiscriminately by contemporaries, particularly by those hostile to the French Revolution, to all "patriots" regardless of their political affiliations. Thus, Catherine II angrily denounced as "Jacobins" the reforming Polish nobles of 1791; and Thomas Paine, though a "Jacobin" in England, in France in 1793 was considered a moderate and, as a Girondin member of the French Convention, narrowly escaped arrest and, possibly, execution. More accurately, the term was applied by the French authorities after 1795 to the more advanced democrats in countries that they occupied. In fact, there were important differences in the political complexion of the various national " patriot " groups : most of the Belgians, Swiss and Germans were moderates; the Dutch, after 1792, were divided in their allegiance between the Gironde and the Mountain; while the Italians more than any others—probably through the influence of Buonarotti—inclined towards the more advanced ideas of Babeuf. But whether moderates, Girondins, Montagnards or " Babouvists ", the influence that they were able to exercise would depend far less on the particular brand of their opinions than on their country's social development, its recent history, the part played in its national life by the Church, and its proximity or accessibility to France. It is factors such as these, far more than the aims and efforts of the local " Jacobins ", that explain why countries such as England, Spain and the greater part of Germany went through no revolution; and the example of Spain, in particular, shows that not even the French, whose armies occupied Catalonia in early 1794, could export a revolution against the solid resistance of a country's people or its history. Of the countries actually " revolutionized " by the French and local " Jacobins ", some were far more ripe for revolution and therefore far more accessible to French ideas than others; and these tended also to be those in which the " patriots " were more capable than elsewhere of acting as independent agents and of making a bid for power on their own account. We have noted examples of this in Liège and Brussels before 1789, in Savoy and parts of Switzerland and the Rhineland before 1795, and in northern Italy since. But, in other areas of France's military occupation, particularly in Italy south of Piedmont, the local " Jacobins " were quite incapable of leading a popular revolution or of taking power without the support of a French army. The Roman, Tuscan and Neapolitan " Jacobins " were zealous and active propagandists, they helped to prepare the way for French military occupation, and they served as deputies and administrators under the new revolutionary authorities. But they were lawyers and intellectuals, merchants and noblemen, cut off from the masses to whom they had little to offer; and, even under French protection, they were constantly exposed to the hostility of the people. Here, then, the revolution could in no sense be seen as a local product: there were pockets, both social and geographical, favourable to its internal development; but it was essentially imposed from outside and by French military intervention. And even where the "patriots", far from being mere tools of the French, had their own ideas about their country's political future—we have seen examples in Holland, Geneva and Piedmont—the settlement that finally emerged was that of post-Thermidorian France rather than of the "patriot" groups. It is also of some significance that in no single case did any one of these new régimes survive for a moment a French defeat or the withdrawal of French troops.

So we return to the wider question posed at the beginning of the last chapter. Are we dealing here with an essentially *French* revolution with its offshoots in other western countries; or are Professors Godechot and Palmer correct in suggesting that all these revolutions, the French and the American included, are merely "phases" of a more general "democratic" revolution of the West? There might perhaps be some point in attaching a general label of this kind to all the revolutions taking place in Europe and America from, say, 1550 to 1850—covering not only the American and the French, but the Dutch of the sixteenth, the English of the seventeenth, and various South American and European revolutions of the early nineteenth century. All of these raise, in one form or another, common problems relating to feudalism and capitalism, democracy and national sovereignty. In this wider context, the American Revolution of the 1760's and seventies may appear to be as closely linked with the English Revolution of 120 years before as with the French of twenty years after; and the German and Italian revolutions are seen in full flood rather than at their earliest beginnings. But if one chooses merely to consider the revolutions of the eighteenth century, one is struck rather by differences than similarities and by the small number that can claim to be revolutions in their own right. In Europe, the only " democratic " (or, more accurately, " liberal") revolutions taking place at this time in any way independent of the French were those in Liège, Brussels and Geneva; but the first two of these had been defeated by 1790 and only revived as the result of French military occupation. Revolutionary movements were also germinating, inspired by the French example, in the Rhineland, Piedmont and parts of Switzerland; but they only came to a head on the approach of France's armies. Elsewhere in Western Europe, revolutions, though owing something to local " patriots " and local conditions, were largely imposed by the French. In fact, of 29 constitutions adopted in European countries other than France between 1791 and 1802, all except three (two Genevan and one Polish) were the outcome of French intervention.[6] So strictly speaking, outside America, and perhaps the tiny state of Geneva, the only revolution in its own right was the French.

Even more important perhaps is the fact that the revolution in France went much further than elsewhere—not only in the sense that it was more violent, more radical, more democratic and more protracted, but that it posed problems and aroused classes that other European revolutions (and the American, for that matter) left largely untouched. This was partly due to a different historical development in these countries from that in France and partly to the fact that the French after July 1794 (when they began to impose their ideas on their neighbours) were no longer interested in promoting the democratic ideals of 1793—and ruthlessly crushed the Piedmontese when they attempted to do so. If we are only concerned with the spread of the ideas of the Enlightenment, the permanent legislation of the revolutionary assemblies and the liberal " principles of 1789 ", then the similarities between the revolutions in France and in these other countries are strikingly close : all went, with greater or lesser thoroughness, through a common bourgeois

[6] H. B. Hill, " The Constitutions of Continental Europe, 1789-1813, *"Journal of Modern History,* VIII (1936), 82.

revolution, which destroyed the old feudal institutions and obligations, expropriated the estates of the Church, abolished serfdom, legal inequalities and the privileged orders, and declared careers to be " open to talent "; and this process continued, though in a muted form, in Germany and Poland under the Empire. Important as this is, it leaves out an essential element of the French Revolution : the active participation of the common people from 1789 onwards and all the consequences that flowed from it. John Adams, it may be remembered, criticized the Dutch Patriots of 1787 for having been " too inattentive to the sense of the common people "; and they continued to be so. And this was by no means a failure peculiar to the Dutch : Belgian, Roman and Neapolitan " Jacobins " were equally divorced from the people and made little serious effort to bridge the gap. In some of these countries, it is true, there were temporary movements in which both " patriots " and peasants or urban poor took part and in which the latter classes voiced the slogans and ideas of their bourgeois allies; but these were exceptional and short-lived. In France alone, owing to the particular circumstances in which the revolution developed and broke out (and certainly not to any innate Gallic quality!), the " Fourth Estate " became the indispensable ally of the Third, exacted its reward, and even built up a distinctive political movement of its own. So in France we have such phenomena as the peasant " revolution ", the *sans-culotte* movement of 1793, the Jacobin Dictatorship, the *levée en masse* and *armées révolutionnaires,* and the social experiments and Republic of the Year II. These factors reappeared, often in more advanced forms, in the European revolutions of the nineteenth century; but, with minor exceptions, they did not in those of the 1790's—and still less so under the Consulate and Empire. In this sense, the revolution in France, though casting its shadow all over Europe, remained quite peculiar and unique.

PART FOUR

The Napoleonic Era

Chapter XII

NAPOLEON AND FRANCE

In summoning Napoleon Bonaparte to their aid in Brumaire, Sieyes and his fellow-conspirators had hoped, like Barère in Thermidor, to keep the political controls firmly in their own hands. Their object had been to install a military dictator who should, on their own terms, defend the threatened " natural frontiers " of France and keep the Jacobins and *sans-culottes* at bay. Such a resort to authoritarian government was nothing new in the Revolution: the Plain had, in the emergency of 1793, given its blessing to the dictatorship of the Committee of Public Safety; the " liberal " Convention of 1795 had denied the electors their constitutional rights by their decree of the " two-thirds "; and their successors under the Directory had, on more than one occasion, brushed the Constitution aside to cope with the alternative threats of royalism and Jacobinism. But, this time, the man selected for the job was of a different stamp and temperament from any other called upon to fill the role; and, far from retaining control of the situation, the Brumairians were soon to find that their would-be auxiliary was fully determined to impose his own pattern on events: he would, in fact, by an unusual combination of will, intellect and physical vigour, leave his mark for years to come on France and Europe.

Yet, in so far as it is possible to separate reality from myth in so remarkable a phenomenon, he was a man of strange paradoxes and contradictions: a modern romantic hero cast in the mould of a Cæsar or an Alexander; a man of action and rapid decision, yet a poet and dreamer of world conquest; a supreme political realist, yet a vulgar adventurer who gambled for high stakes; the enemy of privilege who boasted of his " uncle " Louis XVI and aspired to found new dynasties of Kings; an organizer and statesman of genius, and yet as much concerned to feather the nests of the Bonaparte clan as to promote the fortunes or greater glory of France; a product of the Enlightenment who distrusted ideas and despised intellectuals and " systems "; a lucid intellect with a vast thirst and capacity for knowledge, yet strangely impervious to forces that he had himself helped to unleash. And greatest paradox of all : the upstart " soldier of the Revolution " who carried the " principles of 1789 " to half the countries of Europe, and who yet was driven by personal ambition and contempt for his fellow-men to build a new despotism and a new aristocracy on the ashes of the old. The picture is obscured by the legend of Napoleon that grew from his monologues at St. Helena, where he was anxious to present himself as a man of peace eager to unite Europe in a confederation of self-governing nation-states. While this hardly corresponds to reality, it was that part of his aims and actions that he glossed over at St. Helena—his dream of world conquest, his restless aggression, his personal despotism and progressive denial of the egalitarian principles of the Revolution—that has stood up least well to the test of time. In a sense, therefore, myth and reality have joined hands; for it is the work of the " soldier of the Revolution ", far more than that of the despot, the conqueror, or creator of new aristocracies and dynasties, that has survived.

Napoleon himself, even in his wildest moments of renunciation, always acknowledged his debt to the Revolution; and certainly no career illustrates better than his own the justice of the revolutionaries' claim to have opened careers to talent. He was born at Ajaccio in Corsica in 1769, the son of a petty nobleman who, though of Genovese birth, had become French by the French conquest of the island a year before. Between 1779 and 1785, young Napoleon attended military college at Autun, Brienne and Paris; after which, he served as a lieutenant of artillery at Auxonne and Valence : at Auxonne, under Du Teil, brother of the expert on mountain-warfare. Like many young officers of the day, particularly those as penniless as himself, he welcomed the Revolution; he eagerly read Rousseau and flung himself into "patriot" politics in Corsica as a supporter of Paoli, the Liberator. But even before his final breach with Paoli and his expulsion from Corsica, he came to Paris and, in June 1792, witnessed the humiliation of Louis XVI in the Tuileries at the hands of the Paris "mob" : the experience made a lasting impression on him. Yet, in the struggle between the parties, he declared for the Mountain against the Gironde and distinguished himself, as a captain in charge of the artillery, at the relief of Toulon in September 1793. He was promoted brigadier and won the esteem and friendship of Augustin Robespierre, who was on mission to the Army of Italy. The friendship nearly ended his career : after Thermidor, he was jailed as a Robespierrist in the Fort Carré at Antibes; and, released a month later, he spent some months in search of suitable employment. He refused the post of commander of artillery in the Army of the West in 1795; but, luckily for his future advancement, he found himself in Paris in September, caught Barras' eye and, having crushed the royalist rebels in Vendémiaire, was rewarded with the rank of general. Through Barras again, he met Joséphine de Beauharnais, the widow of a revolutionary general, and married her on 9 October 1796. A week earlier, he had been given the command of the Army of Italy—an appointment that was not entirely unexpected, as he had powerful supporters and had, for long, been advocating the plan of campaign which he was now given the opportunity of putting into operation.

As we have noted, it was Bonaparte's remarkable success in Italy, his popularity with the public, and the aura of fame that clung to him throughout his Egyptian campaign, that prompted Sieyes and his associates to select him for the part he played in Brumaire. Yet, in retrospect, it seems surprising that the conspirators should have expected a man with such a record to submit tamely to their direction. At all events, they were soon disabused as, before a year was out, he had created a political system of his own and, thereafter, proceeded to consolidate his personal authority as opportunity offered. His first brush with Sieyes came over the new constitution that followed Brumaire. As the past-master of constitutional manipulation, Sieyes proposed an elaborate system of checks and balances based, as he put it, on the principle of " authority from above" and " confidence from below". Male adult suffrage was to be restored, but voters in the primary assemblies would only be empowered to elect one-tenth of their number to department assemblies which, in turn, would elect one-tenth of their number to compose a " national list ". From this list a centrally co-opted Senate would select a Tribunate to propose laws and a Legislature to pass them. Central and local government officials would be picked out by the Consuls from the national and departmental lists. The executive would be composed of a Grand Elector, appointed and subject to recall by the Senate, and two Consuls, one for foreign and one for internal affairs, nominated by him. Thus effective political authority would remain in the hands of the " notables" who, by their control of the Senate, could terminate at pleasure the rule of their appointed dictator.

Napoleon had no objection to Sieyes' plans for restricting the powers of the voters, but he had entirely other ideas about the part that he was himself to play in the constitution. Aiming at sole executive authority, he adroitly played off one group against another and ended up with a solution which looked like a compromise, but which, in essentials, met his immediate objections. Sieyes' list of " notabilities", his Senate and Tribunate were retained (the last with reduced legislative initiative); but, above all, there emerged a First Consul elected for ten years, with powers overriding those of his colleagues, answerable to none and solely responsible for the appointment of ministers and officials, and with the authority to initiate legislation after consulting a Council of State appointed by himself. The Constitution, put to a plebiscite in February 1800, was adopted by three million votes to fifteen hundred.

The Senate, however, and the Tribunate and Legislature that it appointed, retained considerable authority; and Sieyes and his colleagues still believed that, by their control of these, they could at least compel the First Consul to take them into partnership. Napoleon, however, had no such intentions. The Constitution allowed him to supplement the work of the Legislature by issuing decrees known as *senatus-consulta* : these he used freely and to good effect; moreover, quite illegally, he permitted the Council of State to interpret laws passed by the Assembly. It was the Council, in fact, which, selected by the First Consul from some of the most experienced legislators of the Revolution, co-operated with him in framing many of the most enlightened laws of the Consulate. Much of this legislation was, of course, concerned to centralize administration and strengthen the authority of government. An early priority was the police. The Ministry of Police, created by the Directory, was enlarged and given extended powers, and entrusted to Fouché, well qualified for the post both by his " terrorist " past and the part he had played in Brumaire. Under Fouché served Dubois, prefect of police in Paris, and similar prefects in every department. This was but one instance of Bonaparte's reversal of the principle of local election and the re-transfer of control from local authority to the capital : in this he followed the practice of the Old Régime and the Committee of Public Safety far more than that of the Constituent Assembly and Directory. Thus, while the communes and departments created in 1790 were retained—and have survived to the present day—a law of February 1800 placed the departments in the charge of prefects, responsible to the Minister of the Interior and modelled on the Intendants and " representatives on mission " of the past; and now even mayors were to be nominated by the government. In finance and justice, too, the First Consul abandoned practices adopted in 1790 and reverted to the methods of the Old Régime. The collection of taxes was taken out of the hands of local authorities and entrusted to a central body : this completed a process already begun by the Directory. Again, criminal courts were set up in the departments, with judges appointed by the First Consul himself, to try common law offences; further exceptional courts were created to deal with royalist subversion; juries were suspended in several departments, and recourse was even had to the notorious *lettres de cachet* of the Bourbon monarchy.

Exceptional measures such as these were sternly criticized by the liberal opposition in the Tribunate and Legislature and led to Napoleon's final breach with his old allies of Brumaire. By this time, he had further scores to settle as, when he set out on his second Italian campaign in May 1800, Paris became a centre of intrigue of disgruntled rivals and frustrated aspirants to office; royalist agitation revived in the provinces; and the new régime appeared to hang in the balance. His victory at Marengo in June—shaky though it was, in fact—and Moreau's more decisive victory at Hohenlinden in December restored confidence at home and persuaded the Austrians to negotiate; and, having prepared the ground for the Peace of Lunéville (February 1801), which restored and added to the French gains of Campo Formio, Bonaparte returned once more in triumph to his capital. He lost no time in reasserting and reinforcing his authority. The Tribunate was purged of its more fractious members; a military plot, implicating Moreau and Bernadotte, was nipped in the bud; Madame de Staël, whose salon had become a centre of opposition, was banished from Paris; and the discovery of an " infernal machine ", designed by royalist terrorists to blow up the First Consul on his way to the Opera, was made the pretext for deporting, shooting or guillotining large numbers of his Jacobin opponents. So order was once more restored; but more drastic constitutional measures were required to silence the opposition in the Senate and Legislature. The Peace of Amiens, ending the nine-years war with England in May 1802, afforded the opportunity. Amidst the general jubilation, the Senate proposed at first that the Consulate should be extended for a further ten years; but Napoleon insisted on a plebiscite which, by 3½ million to 8,000 votes, conferred on him the Consulate for life. In addition, a *senatus-consultum* of May 1802 amended the Constitution in such a way as to give him virtually complete dictatorial powers: the Senate, over which he now presided and whose numbers he filled by co-option, was given authority to revise the Constitution at will by means of *senatus-consulta*, to dissolve the Legislature and Tribunate and nominate the subordinate Consuls. Sieyes' national list of " notabilities " was finally scrapped and replaced by a network of electoral colleges, in whose nomination the First Consul was once more the controlling influence. Finally, he was empowered to negotiate treaties without submitting them for approval and was invited to nominate his own successor.

By this provision, Napoleon had taken the first step towards restoring the hereditary monarchy itself. He already possessed, in fact if not in name, all the attributes of an absolute monarch. All that was needed now was to add the trappings of an imperial Crown, an imperial Court and a new imperial aristocracy. External events again provided the opportunity. War broke out with England in 1803 and the royalist leader, Georges Cadoudal, won English support for a plan to kidnap Napoleon and bring him to London. The conspiracy was betrayed to the police by Méhée de la Touche, former Jacobin turned informer. Moreau and Pichegru were both implicated: the former was exiled and the latter strangled in his cell; while the Duc d'Enghien, Condé's grandson, was seized on German territory, smuggled across the border and, after interrogation, shot as an English agent. The excitement stirred up by the affair pointed urgently to the need for a hereditary succession; and, in May 1804, the Senate proclaimed that " the government of the Republic is entrusted to a hereditary emperor ". For the moment, as Napoleon had no son, the heir-designate was his brother Joseph and, after him, Louis. The police were further centralized and strengthened and Fouché, whose intrigues had lost him his office after Marengo, was reinstated and, from now on until 1810, when he was finally dismissed, supplied the Emperor with daily bulletins from the vast network of his agents. Otherwise, the administration remained much as before. The Court, already emerging at the Tuileries under the Consulate, was given greater formality, substance and decorum; and a new imperial nobility was founded by conferring the rank of prince on the Bonaparte brothers, hereditary Italian dukedoms on Bernadotte, Talleyrand and Fouché and further dignities and titles on eighteen Marshals of the Empire, six Grand Imperial dignitaries and a host of other faithful servants. Even Sieyes, that grand old opponent of aristocratic privilege, was soon to appear in the full regalia of a Baron of the Empire. It took time, of course, for the new imperial society and its institutions to assume their full shape; but, meanwhile, the new order received the Pope's blessing and Pius VII, ignoring the protests of *émigré* and royalist dissenters, hurried to Paris and saw the new Emperor crowned at Notre Dame (December 1804).

So the Republic, after teetering for five years on the edge of its grave, was finally buried; and Napoleon, having achieved his ambitions at home, began to devote his attention to other problems. It is, therefore, hardly surprising that his constructive work of legislation in France, which in many respects completed and consolidated that of the revolutionaries, should have belonged to the Consulate rather than to the Empire. The ten years of the Empire were, in fact, singularly barren in legislative achievement and have, in this respect, left little of lasting value to subsequent generations.

Most of the great reforms of the Consulate were carried out in the three years between July 1800 and May 1803. During this period, Napoleon was free to spend most of his time in Paris, surrounded by a small group of ministers and Councillors of State, mainly moderate Republicans or former royalists: of them, Cambacérès, Lebrun, Talleyrand, Gaudin, Portalis, Treilhard and Thibaudeau probably played the most important parts. Yet their role was subsidiary to that of the master, who attended a large part of their meetings, gave their labours unity and direction, and stamped them with the peculiar hallmark of his own love of authority, realism, contempt for privilege and abstract rights, scrupulous attention to detail and respect for an orderly social hierarchy.

The revolutionary period in France had been bedevilled by weak and haphazard financial and banking policy. Under Feuillants, Girondins and Thermidorians inflation ran riot, the metal coinage had disappeared, and a succession of governments had been held to ransom by speculators, financiers and contractors. For a short period, the great Committee of Public Safety had, by means of political and economic Terror, driven speculation underground and given temporary stability to the country's finances. The Directory, too, had belatedly, after years of chaotic inflation, taken measures to restore the currency and centralize taxation; but their measures remained uncompleted. The *coup d'état* of Brumaire and Bonaparte's promise of strong government had restored the confidence of the bankers and it was with the active co-operation of Perregaux, one of their number, that the Bank of France was founded in February 1800. Its original share capital of 30 million francs was increased to 45 millions three years later, when the Bank was given the monopoly of issuing banknotes. But fiduciary issues were kept under tight control, and metal once more became the general currency. It was a measure of the sound financial policy of the period—and of Napoleon's own prejudices against paper-money—that between 1799 and 1814 some 75 million francs in gold and silver returned into circulation.

Most impressive of all the legislative measures carried out by the First Consul and his Council of State was the Civil Code, completed in 1804 and re-named the Code Napoleon in 1807. It was by no means an original piece of work, though Napoleon prided himself more on this single achievement than on all his forty battles. The work of codifying the numerous laws and decrees of the Revolution had been begun by the Convention in 1792; a draft code of 779 articles appeared a year later; and this had expanded to 1,104 articles under the Directory in 1796. Five drafts had, in fact, been discussed before Napoleon and his collaborators began their work in 1800. It was a vast undertaking, yet one already long overdue. Before the Revolution, the monarchy had achieved little in the way of legal unity: some 360 local codes were in force and the country had been broadly divided between the Roman law prevailing in the south and the customary law of the north. While the Revolution had eased the problem by sweeping away feudal privilege and inheritance and withdrawing property-relations from the operation of the Canon Law, the great questions still remained—should the new Code be solidly based on abstract natural law, ignoring the traditions of the past; or should it aim, while taking full account of all changes effected in the relations of properties and persons since 1789, at striking an agreed balance between the rival claims of Roman and customary law?

The Convention had been strongly influenced by the rational arguments of the Enlightenment and recognized such absolute rights as the equality of persons, civil marriage, divorce, adoption, the inheritance of illegitimate children, and the equal division of property among heirs; it had been hostile to the authoritarianism of Roman law and favoured the greater liberalism of customary law. The Code of 1804 strikes a balance between the two: it preserves the legal egalitarian principles of 1789, but they are tempered by a new and sharper insistence on the rights of property and on the authority of parent and husband. For, unlike his predecessors, Napoleon saw much virtue in Roman law: it appealed to his own authoritarian nature; and, besides, its operation might help to overcome much of the moral laxity of post-Thermidorian society: had he not had experience enough of this in the case of his own wife Joséphine? Accordingly, those clauses of the Code dealing with marriage, paternity, divorce and adoption are both those which are most strongly influenced by Roman law and those in the drafting of which Napoleon himself intervened most vigorously. So divorce becomes severely restricted; property, up to a quarter of the whole, may be bequeathed outside the family; illegitimate children may only exceptionally be given recognition; the paternal authority over children, as practised under the Old Régime, is restored; and in the articles dealing with " the Respective Rights and Duties of Husband and Wife " we find such gems as the following : " A husband owes protection to his wife, a wife obedience to her husband "; " married women are incapable of making contracts "; and " a wife may sue for divorce only in the case in which the husband introduces a permanent mistress into the family household ". But this is, of course, only a part of the picture. While rejecting the democratic principles of 1793, the Code adopted in their entirety the new property-rights and rights of citizenship bequeathed by the revolutionaries of 1789; the destruction of feudalism and feudal privilege are endorsed, as are liberty of conscience and employment, while perhaps the most important of all the articles of the Code is that which insists on the equal division of estates among sons. Provisions such as these have profoundly influenced the social development of not only France but some thirty other countries in every continent outside Australasia.

Something of the same blend of authority and equality appears in Napoleon's institution of the Legion of Honour in May 1802. This, far more than the Civil Code, was his own personal invention and met with vigorous disapproval in the Tribunate and Legislature, and even in the Council of State. The Convention had abolished the old distinctive insignia and decorations of the monarchy, such as the Order of St. Louis, as being contrary to equality; yet " civic crowns " had, on occasion, been bestowed on individuals for meritorious service to the nation. It was with both types of distinction in mind that Napoleon devised his Legion. There were to be fifteen " cohorts ", each composed of 250 members of varying rank according to service and selected by a Grand Council presided over by the First Consul. His intention was two-fold : to

create a new order of merit open to all who qualified by personal service, both soldiers and civilians, and regardless of
social origin; and to offset Sieyes' national list of "notabilities" (then still in being) with an institution strictly under his
own direction. The liberal opposition, concerned to limit
Napoleon's autocratic pretensions, could hardly fail to see
the implications. But their objections, as in other matters,
proved unavailing; and the Legion still survives as another
monument to its creator's zeal.

The educational reforms of the Consulate (this time completed under the Empire) also reflect Napoleon's social attitudes and his contempt for women. As we should expect, he
saw the purpose of education as to equip young people for
service to the State—the boys as doctors, civil servants and
officers, or simply as craftsmen, labourers and common soldiers; and the girls as dutiful and obedient housewives and
mothers. The poor should only benefit from the meanest
modicum of instruction, and therefore the primary school—or
école communale, to which the Convention had devoted considerable attention—could safely be left to the municipalities,
and be supplemented by the numerous church schools to which
the Concordat of 1801 opened the door. The Convention
had created about a hundred Central, or public secondary,
schools. These were reorganized under a law of May 1802
and placed under the general control of a Director of Public
Instruction; thereafter, the Church was allowed to invade
the field. But Napoleon's distinctive creation was the *lycée,* a
selective secondary school for the training of leaders and
administrators, with a strictly secular curriculum and with
its direction reserved to the State alone. There were to be
forty-five *lycées* at first with 6,400 places, financed by State
scholarships, of which 2,400 were reserved for the sons of
officers and civil servants and the rest for the most able
pupils of the ordinary secondary schools. They made a poor
start, partly because the military discipline introduced into
them displeased many middle-class parents; but, by 1813, the
education provided was probably the best and the most ad-

vanced in Europe and 6,000 students recruited from them were, at this time, enrolled in French universities. As for the education of girls, it was of relatively minor importance and the greater part of it could be left to the religious orders and thus save public expense. Writing from his headquarters at Finkenstein in Germany during the 1807 campaign, the Emperor urged his Minister of the Interior to see that the girls in the new high school at Ecouen should receive a solid grounding in religion. "What we ask of education (he wrote) is not that girls should think, but that they should believe"; and he added that " care must be taken not to let them see any Latin, or other foreign languages ".

Like any "enlightened despot", Napoleon took an active and continuous interest in the direction of France's economy. His authoritarian views naturally led him to favour State direction rather than to countenance the free-trade theories of Adam Smith or the French "economists" of the 1770's and eighties. But his conception of State intervention was far closer to the mercantilism of Colbert, Louis XIV's great minister of the seventeenth century, than it was to the controlled economy practised by Robespierre and the Committee of Public Safety in the Year II of the Revolution. The Jacobins were naturally concerned to harness the economy to the needs of war, to equip their armies and to feed the civilian population; but they also had the more far-reaching aim of raising the whole status and dignity of human beings. Napoleon's aims were more conservative and more pedestrian : the State must intervene to protect agriculture and to ensure a favourable trade balance and an adequate supply of metal and soldiers for the army; whereas the material conditions of the people, provided they did not lead to public disorder or interfere with recruiting, were of relatively minor concern. Imports must be restricted—English in particular; and even before he launched his Continental System in 1806, Napoleon adopted his predecessors' policy of excluding English goods from France. His passion for regulation actually led him, in defiance of the whole trend of revolutionary legislation, to toy with the idea of resurrecting the trade guilds of the Old Régime: under his direction, the Paris prefect of police in fact sanctioned the revival of the guilds of bakers and butchers in the city; yet he hesitated to go further. In labour relations, he followed the practice that the Constituents had inherited from the Bourbons: workers had been forbidden to organize in trade unions by the Le Chapelier law of 1791; a law of April 1803 repeated the ban; and, in December of the same year, workers were, in addition, compelled to carry a pass-book stamped by their employer. The same spirit pervades the Civil Code of 1804 wherever it touches on labour-employer relations: the guarantee of livelihood promised to the poor in 1793 is abandoned and, in matters of litigation, the employer's word alone is accepted. Yet, inclined as he was by temperament and interest to look, in economic matters, to the past rather than to the future, Napoleon's political realism, in this field as in others, did not desert him. Haunted by memories of the food riots of the Revolution (the danger of a recurrence was particularly great in 1801), he recognized that public order and stability, and for that matter the supply of soldiers for his armies, would depend in no small degree on satisfying the working people's basic needs. Doctrine must therefore, here as elsewhere, yield to the pressing needs of State; hence, in all but years of abundance, strict limits were placed on the export of corn; and, in 1812, the Emperor actually followed the example of the Convention in imposing a *maximum*, or a ceiling, on the price of bread and flour. It was for these and other reasons that Napoleon retained the support and confidence of the French peasants and urban *menu peuple* far longer than that of the bourgeoisie that had called him to power. Had it not been for his firm hold on the army, the liberal opposition, new rich and disgruntled officers and ministers (prominent among them the eternal intriguers, Fouché and Talleyrand) would have been more successful in their frequent efforts to overthrow him. But the loyalty of the common people, for whom the brand of political liberty offered by the opposition had little meaning or attraction, re-

mained remarkably constant and only broke under the weight
of conscription and hardship in the lean years of 1813 and
1814.

It was considerations of State again that prompted Napoleon to re-establish the Catholic Church in France by signing a
Concordat with the Pope in 1801. After its various tribulations in the early years of revolution, as described in earlier
chapters, the Church became finally disestablished by a law of
September 1795. The policy of the Directory had been alternately one of toleration or indifference and of bitter persecution, particularly of non-juring priests suspected or convicted
of treasonable activities. During the period, a variety of cults
had sprung up and, at the time of the Brumaire *coup d'état*,
religious practices were variously observed, and with comparative immunity from persecution, by Catholics (both juring and
non-juring), Protestants, Decadists and Theophilanthropists.
This had produced what the Radical historian Aulard has
called " a rich and varied flowering of religious life"; but it
was not a state of affairs that could commend itself either to
Catholics or *émigrés* or to a ruler of Napoleon's authoritarian
and orderly disposition. He himself was a Voltairean sceptic,
little inclined to mystical experience or beliefs of any kind : it
is doubtful, for example, if he could have shared Robespierre's belief in the immortality of the soul. But, like many
free-thinkers and deists of the time, he was convinced that
organized religion might be good for others, if not for himself—and particularly so for women. Besides, religion would
help to preserve social peace. " In religion," he once wrote,
" I do not see the mystery of the Incarnation, but the mystery
of the social order"; and again : " Society is impossible without inequality, inequality intolerable without a code of morality, and a code of morality unacceptable without religion."
Religion might also be a valuable political weapon. His ex-
periences in Italy and Egypt had warned him of the danger of
allowing " philosophical " preconceptions to dictate policies
that might ruffle the religious susceptibilities of those whom
he proposed to govern. In Egypt, he had strictly forbidden

his army to offend Moslem religious practices; and in his dealings with the Papacy in 1797 he had refused to follow the anti-clerical instructions of the Directory. It was as much to gain Jewish support as to give expression to his own "enlightened" views that he had destroyed the ghettoes in Rome and Venice; and he said on one occasion (and it was not necessarily a cynical observation) that "if I were governing Jews, I should restore the Temple of Solomon". Nevertheless, before deciding to re-establish the Catholic Church in France, he had carefully to balance the political advantages against the opposition that he would undoubtedly provoke. On the one hand, a dozen years of revolution and many more years of "enlightened" thinking had eradicated from men's minds and actions a great deal of the former influence of the Church. The Republican bourgeoisie, for example, had generally discarded religion and did not consider it a necessary concomitant of civil virtue; and, for those that did, such new cults as that of the Theophilanthropists might serve the purpose equally well. Anti-clericalism, too, was strongly entrenched in the army, as became only too evident when the Concordat was finally agreed upon. On the other hand, the mass of the French population, the peasantry, had never become fully reconciled to the abandonment of their old forms of worship, and it was a reasonable calculation that their restoration would remove the main grievances that still kept civil war smouldering in the Vendée and Brittany. Moreover, even in intellectual circles, the old scepticism had lost its former attraction and had given way to a romantic religious revival. Again, France had since 1795 expanded far beyond her pre-revolutionary borders and latent rebellion might be nipped in the bud and Catholic opinion be appeased among the subject populations of Belgium, Switzerland, the Rhineland and Italy. Not only that, but an accommodation with the Pope might help to bring about a general peace on France's terms and remove the apprehensions of many *émigrés*, more catholic than royalist, whom the First Consul was anxious to attract back to France and reconcile with his régime. But, of course, before any settlement could be reached, the Pope must accept two important conditions: "this religion (to quote Napoleon's own words) must be in the hands of the government" and there could be no question of restoring the sequestrated properties of the Church to their old owners.

A new Pope, Pius VII, had been elected shortly before Marengo; and on the eve of leaving Italy in June 1800, Napoleon had already made overtures at Rome. Agreement was reached only after a full year of bargaining in the course of which 1,279 documents and ten separate drafts were exchanged between the principals. The main points at issue were the appointment and payment of bishops, the future of Church property confiscated during the Revolution, the status of the Catholic Church among the religious community at large, and the relations between Church and State. The Pope at first insisted that all refractory bishops should retain their sees and that no recognition should be given to those appointed since the Civil Constitution of 1790; he refused to recognize the rights of the purchasers of Church properties; he wanted the clergy to be paid from endowments; and he demanded that Roman Catholicism should be defined as the sole *religion d'état* (established Church) and that there should be the minimum of interference by the State in the affairs of the Church. For his part, Napoleon argued that all bishops, both refractory and Constitutional, should relinquish their sees and contend for reappointment; that purchasers of Church properties must be guaranteed possession; that the clergy should be paid as State servants; and that the Catholic faith should not be accepted as the "dominant faith"—which implied a restriction of the rights of other believers—but as the "religion of the great majority of the citizens". This was, in fact, the final formula agreed upon. It was also agreed that the government should remove all obstacles to the free exercise of the Catholic religion. The question of reappointment of bishops was settled to Napoleon's satisfaction while saving the Pope the embarrassment of an abject surrender: they should, in fact, resign *en bloc* and be reinstated by the Pope (who issued two separate Bulls—one for jurors and one for non-jurors—for the purpose) after nomination by the First Consul. Moreover, Napoleon won his point that bishops and clergy (the latter to be appointed by the bishops) should be paid salaries by the State, while all clergy should take an oath of allegiance to the government—but not to the Constitution as in 1790. Finally, an elegant formula was found to make it easier for the Pope to accept the surrender by the Church of the lands of which it had been dispossessed: this was crucial as even Napoleon could not have persuaded the numerous purchasers of Church properties, enriched by the Revolution, to accept the settlement on any other terms.

The Concordat appeared, then, to be a compromise; yet on all essential points the First Consul had won his case. Even so, he needed all his prestige, reinforced by the Peace of Amiens recently signed with England, to overcome the bitter opposition within the Tribunate and the Council of State and among the generals. The most serious objection was that Roman Catholicism had, in spite of the agreed formula, become once more the sole and official State religion. To meet it, it was decided, without any Papal sanction whatsoever, to tack on to the Concordat two sets of Organic Laws, one of which was a charter of Protestant liberties, while the other placed the Gallican Church more firmly than ever under the control of the secular power.

Quite apart from the Organic Laws, the partnership of Pope and Emperor did not prove an easy one. Relations became particularly strained over Napoleon's later claim to extend his dominion over the whole of Italy, including the Papal states. In 1809, Rome was annexed to France, and the Pope was arrested in the Vatican and only allowed to return after five years' captivity, first at Savona and later at Fontainebleau. Yet these quarrels were over temporal matters and the Concordat was never revoked, as it well served the purposes of both parties: the Pope had brought back to the fold the most prized of all the Christian Churches, while Napoleon had secured the allegiance of those of his subjects who put the authority of priest before that of emperor. It was an arrangement that outlived a long succession of governments and constitutions; and Church and State in France remained reunited according to the Napoleonic formula for the next hundred years.

Chapter XIII

THE NAPOLEONIC EMPIRE

Up to 1803, Napoleon appeared to his subjects as a peace-maker who, while ensuring France's "natural frontiers", had ended the war with Europe on his own terms and imposed a peace-settlement favourable to France at Lunéville and Amiens. In 1803, war with England broke out again, though it did not become a general war until two years later. From that time on, France had to accustom herself to the Emperor's other image: no longer that of the peace-maker, engaged in giving her new laws and constitutions, but the conqueror and founder of a new Empire, whose dominion extended over the greater part of Europe.

One can argue endlessly as to whether the war with England and the more general conflagration that followed soon after were inevitable or whether, by skilful diplomacy or goodwill, they might have been averted. On the whole, the second alternative appears unrealistic. Once France had embarked on a policy of expanding up to and beyond her "natural frontiers", there could be no absolute limits to her territorial claims on Europe; besides, the existing settlement, above all in Italy, provided a standing invitation to Napoleon to intervene and impose new solutions. Moreover, it was hardly in his character to accept as permanent such delicately balanced agreements as those reached with Austria in 1801 and with England a year later; and as he himself admitted: "In the existing situation, every treaty of peace means no more to me than a brief armistice". Nor must it be forgotten that England, for her part, had colonial ambitions that could be realized only by war with France. But, even excluding such general considerations, the peace signed between France and England at Amiens was far too precarious to prove lasting. To win a breathing-space, Pitt had accepted France's " natural frontiers " which, of course, included her occupation of Belgium. But, a few months later, Napoleon annexed Piedmont, Parma and Elba, was elected President of a newly formed Italian Republic, found new pretexts for continuing to occupy Holland, intervened against the Catholic princes of Germany, and imposed a new constitution on Switzerland. So, within six or eight months of Amiens, the balance of Europe had once more been considerably redressed in France's favour. Moreover, Napoleon showed signs of embarking on a new stage of colonial expansion : he had purchased Louisiana from Spain, sent an expedition (ill-fated as it proved) to San Domingo, and even appeared to be planning a new attack on Egypt and India. In consequence, England, though bound by her Amiens agreement to surrender Malta, clung on to it and, encouraged by Russian support, made it the subject of an ultimatum to the French. So, ostensibly, it was not Napoleon but the old " perfidious Albion " that tore up the treaty and provoked the war that broke out again in May 1803.

Inevitably, as the other Continental powers were not yet engaged, the war had to be fought at sea; and here England enjoyed considerable advantages. The French navy had never recovered from the havoc wrought by the Revolution. The old aristocratic officers had been cashiered, eliminated by mutiny, or had emigrated in their hundreds; and the revolutionary Assemblies, despite their efforts to fill the gaps, had failed to find a Carnot to ensure efficiency and modern tactics, or provide competent new admirals to command their ships. The weakness of the French in naval warfare had been illustrated by their failures to support an Irish rebellion and, more recently, in the disaster attending Napoleon's own expedition to Egypt; since then, their ships had rotted in port. The one outstanding French admiral, Latouche-Tréville, who had given brilliant support to the " patriots " of Naples in December 1792, died in the summer of 1804, soon after serious operations in the present phase of war began. At its outbreak, England possessed 55 ships of the line, while the French had 42, of which only 13 were ready for active service. In consequence, the English quickly took command of the seas: they blockaded the French ports and reoccupied the Caribbean islands of Santa Lucia and Tobago and Dutch Guiana. Napoleon could hope to redress the balance only by striking at London itself which, once the Channel was crossed, would be weakly defended; and, at the end of 1803, he began to prepare for an invasion of Britain by assembling a flotilla of several hundred barges and a large army—the "Army of England"—at Boulogne; these, he intended, should be pushed across the Channel with the aid of his fleet. "Let us be masters of the Straits for six hours," he wrote to Latouche-Tréville, "and we shall be masters of the world." After Tréville's death, the project was temporarily shelved, but Spain's entry into the war as France's ally at the end of 1804 encouraged him to revive it. Villeneuve, the new commander at Toulon, was ordered to elude Nelson's Mediterranean fleet, sail for Martinique escorted by a Spanish squadron, and there to join up with other French squadrons under Ganteaume from Brest and Rochefort. The plan was then to decoy the English fleet into the Caribbean, force it to disperse, and return as a combined force to the Channel where, in temporary command of the seas, they should escort the invasion-barges to England.

The plan, though it started well, miscarried. Villeneuve set out from Toulon on 30 March 1805, successfully evaded Nelson, and reached Martinique on 14 May; while, Nelson, uncertain whether Villeneuve had sailed east or west, did not reach the West Indies until 4 June. But Ganteaume had failed to break the British blockade at Brest; and Villeneuve, having waited the agreed forty days for him and alarmed at Nelson's approach, sailed to Ferrol, as instructed, in the north of Spain. Even if the plan had now been faithfully followed, there would have been considerable—maybe, insuperable—problems involved in its execution. For how was Villeneuve to coordinate his movements with those of Ganteaume? The whole British fleet lay between them; and there was the further problem of finding a suitable wind, for any wind bringing

Villeneuve off Brest would be a difficult one for Ganteaume trying to leave it. To make matters worse, Nelson had managed to warn the Admiralty of Villeneuve's intentions; and a detachment of the main Channel fleet was waiting to intercept him. It forced him into harbour south of his target, first at Vigo and then at Corunna. Here further calamities awaited him. As he sailed north a day out from Corunna, he sighted what he believed to be a British fleet, though it turned out later to be a French fleet under his colleague, Admiral Allemand. So, to avoid an encounter (with the hazards of a north-easterly wind that had blown up), the cautious Villeneuve turned south and, on 20 August, anchored in Cadiz. This sealed the fate of the whole expedition; and the fault was Napoleon's rather than Villeneuve's. When, on 20 October, Villeneuve sailed out from Cadiz on the Emperor's orders, it was no longer to attempt to join forces with Ganteaume at Brest, but to give naval support to the French in the Mediterranean; and Nelson's great victory at Trafalgar on the morrow, which effectively crippled the combined French and Spanish fleets, played no part whatsoever in determining Napoleon to abandon his plan of invasion. This had been decided two months before; and, on 24 August, he had given orders to Berthier, his Chief of Staff, to break camp and for his "Army of England"—now renamed the Grand Army— to be put to better use by marching into central Europe. The second phase of the war had begun.

The third coalition against France, which took shape between April and August 1805, was by no means a foregone conclusion. Although Napoleon himself claimed to regard it as inevitable, it certainly did not arise from any present intentions of Prussia, Austria and Russia—who all eventually joined with England to form it—to settle old scores with France, to challenge her "natural frontiers", or to upset the balance reached at the Peace of Lunéville. England was in no position to take the initiative on the Continent; her future partners were at present inclined to treat her war with France as a private affair between maritime rivals; besides, Russia had never fully accepted her retention of Malta. Prussia had withdrawn from the first coalition in 1795 in order to acquire her share in the partition of Poland, and had taken no part in the second; and her cautious and vacillating ruler, Frederick William III, preferred to keep his powder dry and was easily tempted by Napoleon's repeated offer of the bait of Hanover. Austria was financially exhausted and, though she had lost Belgium and her Italian provinces at Campo Formio and Lunéville, showed no inclination to renew the contest—provided that she was left free to consolidate her Habsburg dominions and maintain her influence in southern Germany; moreover, she was suspicious of Russia's undoubted design to renew her claims on Turkey and Poland. Russia, in fact, was the only one of the future partners whose present ambitions brought her into collision with the French. The young Tsar, Alexander, unlike the French Emperor, was a man of restless rather than of a consistent ambition; but his closest advisers at this time inclined him towards an English alliance, to aim at restoring a united Poland under Russian suzerainty, to mediate between France and England and to act as a brake on the growing influence of France in central Europe. Such policies, of course, were hardly compatible with the alliance that Napoleon was anxious to offer him. But, quite apart from Alexander's ambitions, Napoleon's own aggressive measures and complete unconcern for any European balance were calculated to alarm not only Russia but, eventually, Austria and Prussia as well. After the renewal of war with England, he had seized Hanover, planted French garrisons in Naples, and renewed his threats to Egypt—all seen by Russia as endangering her interests in Turkey and Germany. In consequence, Alexander began, in September 1804, to negotiate with Pitt; and an alliance, aimed at stripping France of Belgium and the Rhineland, took shape in the Anglo-Russian Convention of April 1805. Meanwhile, Austria had clashed with France over the rival claims of princes and Habsburg Emperor in southern Germany; and France, to whom Bavaria appealed for help, soon after signed alliances with Bavaria, Würtemberg and

Baden. So Austria was driven to seek an agreement with Russia; but it remained precautionary rather than active until Napoleon broke the Treaty of Lunéville and further upset the balance in Italy. In March 1805, he accepted the Crown of the newly created hereditary Kingdom of Italy and granted Genoa's request to be annexed to France. Thus the Emperor of the French (a title already sufficiently offensive to the Holy Roman Emperor in Vienna) appeared only too evidently to be coveting the Imperial Crown of Charlemagne. Austria joined the Anglo-Russian coalition in August and invaded Bavaria in September. Prussia, for the moment, remained neutral.

The Grand Army that left Boulogne on 26 August was probably the best that Napoleon ever put in the field : it was certainly the finest fighting force in Europe. Yet it was ill-paid, ill-shod, it carried no baggage-trains and was dangerously short of ammunition; all of which illustrated both the Emperor's parsimony and improvising methods and his faith in speedy victory. The Austrian general, Mack, having invaded Bavaria with 60,000 men, fell back on the Danube where he hoped to link up with the Russians under Kutusov, who was covering Vienna. But Napoleon's speed was such that, by the end of September, he had brought 190,000 troops across the Rhine and, on 20 October, he surrounded Mack at Ulm and compelled him to surrender with 50,000 men. The Russians withdrew and Napoleon occupied Vienna, where he opened peace negotiations. But the Austrians were in no hurry to sign, as their Russian allies had 90,000 men in the field and the Tsar had, unknown to the French Emperor, persuaded the Prussians at Potsdam to commit themselves to an armed mediation. Alexander, who had taken command of the Austro-Russian forces, fancied himself as a commander and was easily persuaded by an incompetent Chief of Staff that Napoleon was in a weak position and could be defeated. Infatuated with the prospect, he let himself be lured to the village of Austerlitz in Moravia, where Napoleon, in the most decisive of his victories, cut his army in two and inflicted a loss of 27,000 men (2 December 1805). The allies, moreover, were demoralized and Francis II signed the Peace of Pressburg (27 December), by which he lost Venetia, the Tyrol and Vorarlberg and his last foothold in Germany by recognizing Bavaria, Baden, and Würtemberg as independent kingdoms. The Prussians, meanwhile, signed an alliance with France and agreed to surrender Neuchâtel and Anspach in return for the long-coveted Hanover.

Prussia, however, soon found herself faced with the uncomfortable choice of either becoming Napoleon's humble vassal or of fighting him single-handed. In February 1806, Frederick William was forced to surrender the Duchy of Cleves and close his ports to England; in July, the formation of the Confederation of the Rhine under Napoleon's protection robbed him of all hopes of playing the leading role in Germany; and, finally, it was whispered that Napoleon, to appease England, was proposing to restore Hanover. In August, Prussia mobilized and, two months later, sent the French an ultimatum to withdraw their troops across the Rhine. Even under these conditions, the suddenness and magnitude of Napoleon's victory were unexpected: the Prussians could, like the French, put 130,000 men in the field and they still basked in Frederick the Great's reflected glory. But, slow-moving and commanded by aged officers, who had learned nothing from the Revolutionary wars, they were crushed in a three-weeks campaign by the double defeat of Jena and Auerstädt and Napoleon's swift pursuit and occupation of Berlin. Frederick William took refuge in Königsberg, while Napoleon, by promising the Poles their national restoration, enlisted a Polish contingent of 30,000, ordered further levies from France, and prepared to meet the Russians.

The French army, fighting for the first time under the unfamiliar conditions of northern Europe, snatched only a bare and bloody victory from its first encounter with the enemy at Eylau (February 1807), but caught the Russian general Bennigsen off his guard at Friedland (June) and inflicted a loss of 25,000 men. Alexander, unexpectedly, sued for an armistice—owing less to French military success than to growing difficulties with his English and Prussian allies. Even more surprisingly—fascinated, it has been said, by Napoleon's personality—he not only made peace but signed an alliance with the Emperor at Tilsit in July 1807, by which the two leaders virtually divided the whole of continental Europe into two spheres of influence—the western to Napoleon and the eastern to Alexander, who should have a free hand with Sweden and Turkey. Meanwhile, Prussia should be stripped of her western and Polish provinces and England should be brought to heel and compelled to acknowledge the long-disputed " freedom of the seas ".

So the campaign of 1805-7 had brought Napoleon dazzling successes; and, though he did not yet know it, he now stood at the pinnacle of his fame and fortune. But it had also brought him new problems : how should he digest his conquests and how should he use them to administer the knock-out blow to England? The answer to the first was to lie in his organization of the Grand Empire, and to the second in the economic blockade of England, termed the Continental System.

As we have seen, Napoleon had, since 1799, followed the mercantilist and restrictive policy of his predecessors in excluding English goods from France and her " natural frontiers " : this accorded with his own mercantilist predilections and with the protectionist interests of the French textile industry which, since 1793, had finally got rid of the " Free-Trade " treaty signed with England in 1786. Since the renewal of war, the system had been extended along the coast-line to Hanover. But neither the original system nor its extension had been primarily intended as a weapon of economic warfare that, by crippling England's trade, should bring her to her knees. The Baltic and Adriatic—let alone the Atlantic—were still open to her shipping, and Napoleon made no consistent efforts to interfere with neutrals carrying British goods, as the Directory had done in 1798. The conquests of 1806-7 changed the picture : now the opportunity arose, provided the Spaniards, Portuguese, Russians and Austrians would co-operate, to seal the Continent off from British ships and commerce. " I wish,"

said Napoleon, "to conquer the sea by the power of the land."
As a first step, he issued the Berlin Decree of November 1806,
which declared the British Isles to be "in a state of blockade",
prohibited all commerce with them, and ordered all goods
coming to and from Britain and her colonies to be seized.
After Tilsit, both Austria and Russia agreed to adhere to the
System. In retaliation, the English took steps both to protect
themselves against the French and to reassert their own
monopoly against the growing encroachment of neutral
nations: by the Orders in Council of November-December
1807, all neutrals trading with the Continent were ordered to
take out a licence and to pay duty on their cargoes in a
British port: failing this, their ships would be seized as
lawful prize. Napoleon replied, in turn, by extending the
operation of his Continental System: his further Decrees at
Fontainebleau and Milan (October-December 1807) threatened all neutral shipping obeying the Orders in Council with
seizure in port or on the high seas as British property. Thus,
on the French side but not on the English, the blockade, from
having been a largely protectionist device for restricting imports from a rival trading nation, had now become a weapon
of economic warfare. The aim was no longer primarily to
protect the industries of France and conserve her bullion—
though this aim was by no means abandoned—but to force
Britain to surrender by choking her commerce and draining her
of her gold.

As long as England retained mastery of the seas, such a
project was bound to be fraught with difficulties and hazards,
for at no time could Napoleon envisage the possibility of
literally starving England into surrender by cutting her off
from her colonies and her food and raw materials from
overseas. But a third of her direct exports and three-quarters
of her re-exports normally went to Europe; if, therefore, the
Continent could be closed to her shipping her trade and
economic life were bound to suffer. At first, the prospects
seemed unfavourable, as, in 1807, England forced her way
once more into the Baltic by shelling Copenhagen and seizing

the Danish fleet. But this proved to be only a partial victory and, during 1808, British trade with Europe (even through the intermediary of neutral vessels) slumped heavily; and not only with Europe, as the Americans, provoked by the Orders in Council, placed an embargo on British goods—and though the embargo was raised a year later, England's seizure of neutral vessels led to war with the United States in 1812. The set-back to her European trade in 1808 led England to relax the operation of the Orders and to distribute licences wholesale to neutral vessels trading with the Continent: no fewer than 44,346 licences were issued between 1807 and 1812 —almost 26,000 of them in 1809 and 1810 alone.[1] This bursting of the barriers proved temporarily successful; but from the spring of 1810 to the failure of Napoleon's Russian campaign at the end of 1812 the Continental System, which was then most vigorously enforced, severely affected British trade and industry and forced up the price of bread. The most dangerous moment of all for Britain came in 1811, when she was hit by an economic crisis and a bad harvest that left in their wake mass unemployment, wage-cuts, Luddite riots and a severe food shortage. The cutting off of all supplies from the Continent might then have proved fatal to her survival, but Napoleon failed to follow up his advantage. Hidebound by his mercantilist preconceptions, he had never considered it a necessary part of his plan to attempt to deprive Britain of supplies of food. In 1810, over 80 per cent of her wheat-imports had come from France and her allies; and, in 1811, it was the despatch of Continental grain that gave her the necessary breathing-space to recover from her crisis.

The year 1811, however, was exceptional, and at no other time could the System, impressive as was its operation, have proved fatal to its victim. For one thing, Britain, by keeping open her channels of communication, found new markets to replace the old: in Buenos Aires in 1806; in Brazil in 1808; in the Near East, following a trade agreement with Turkey, in 1809; and once more in the Baltic in 1810. Meanwhile,

[1] G. Lefebvre, *Napoléon* (Paris, 1953), p. 344.

Napoleon's allies, finding their trade stagnating and their ports declining, began to slip from his control: in 1809, Turkey, Portugal, Spain and the Spanish colonies; Russia a year later; and even Holland, under the Emperor's brother Louis, remained open to British manufactures until 1810. Moreover, not only Napoleon's vassals and allies but the French themselves began to react with increasing vigour against the commercial restrictions that the System imposed on them: this was particularly the case after the Fontainebleau Decree of October 1810, which set up special courts to try cases of contraband and ordered the public burning of smuggled English goods. It was partly in response to this pressure and partly to meet his own financial and military needs that Napoleon, like the English before him, began to sell licences for exports to the enemy: launched in March 1809, the system was regularized by Decrees issued at St. Cloud and Trianon in 1810. So, though France herself suffered an economic crisis in 1811, her trading interests were partially appeased; but not those of her allies, as Napoleon issued licences only to Frenchmen—and, exceptionally, to Americans—and France's interests were continually stressed at the expense of her neighbours'. In fact, it may be doubted if, in the long run, the System and England's counter-blockade proved as harmful to the English as to the French. In England, their net result was probably to slow down temporarily the rate of industrial expansion and to divert investment into other fields;[2] but, in Europe, they aroused untold resentment against the French and contributed substantially, as we shall see, to the chain of events that led through Portugal, Spain and Russia to the downfall of the Empire.

Meanwhile, the Grand Empire, with its network of annexed territories, satellites and vassal principalities, had taken shape. Since 1802, Europe's frontiers had, under the impact of French arms and diplomacy, undergone frequent and drastic

---

[2] For a full discussion, see F. Crouzet, *L'Economie britannique et le blocus continental* (2 vols., Paris, 1958).

revision. These changes variously reflected the transition from Republic to Empire in France, Napoleon's dynastic ambitions, and the needs of war or of the Continental System. In so far as they followed any master-plan, they were inspired by memories of the universal monarchy of Rome or Charlemagne rather than by any recent precedent. Least of all did they betray, despite his protestations at St. Helena, any deep-felt desire of the Emperor to satisfy the national aspirations of the European peoples. Yet he was by no means averse to exploiting such feelings when it seemed opportune, as in his dealings with Italy and Poland. In Italy, the creation of the Cisalpine Republic, based on Lombardy, had roused the hopes of the "patriots" of 1796, even though Venice was ceded temporarily to Austria and Piedmont was annexed and refused her independence. National hopes revived again when the Cisalpine was given the name of Italian Republic in 1802; but all this was changed with the coronation of the Emperor in France. In 1805, there emerged a Kingdom of Italy, ruled in Napoleon's name by his stepson, Eugène de Beauharnais; by 1810 its territories had been extended along the Adriatic to include Venetia (wrested from Austria in 1806), the Marches, Ancona and Trentino. Meanwhile, the French Empire had swallowed Genoa in 1805; Parma, Piacenza and Tuscany (the short-lived Kingdom of Etruria) in 1808; and, in 1809, the Papal states and the Illyrian provinces across the Adriatic— including Carinthia, Croatia and Dalmatia. In 1806, the Kingdom of Naples (the one-time Parthenopean Republic) had been given to Joseph Bonaparte and, in 1808, when Joseph was translated to Spain, to Murat as husband of the Emperor's sister, Caroline. All of these territories appeared to be destined for eventual absorption by the French Empire when, in 1811, the Emperor's son by his second wife, Marie Louise of Austria, was given the title of King of Rome. At that time, apart from tiny vassal enclaves like Lucca and Piombino, Italy was divided into four main parts—the long stretch of French Imperial territory reaching along the Mediterranean coast beyond Rome; the satellite Kingdoms of Italy in the north-east and Naples in the south; and the remaining anti-French bastions of Sicily and Sardinia, held by the English fleet.

To the north of Italy, the Helvetic Republic had, as fashions changed, become the Swiss Confederation. Flanked by Berthier's principality of Neuchâtel and the annexed cantons of Valais and Geneva, its nineteen cantons were subservient to France and dependent on her protection. Further north still, lay the Rhenish provinces and Belgium which had, since 1795, been enclosed within the "natural frontiers". North of Belgium, the Batavian Republic had, in 1804 as the Kingdom of Holland, been conferred on Napoleon's eldest brother, Louis; but Louis had proved over-tender for his subjects' interests and Holland was annexed to France when he lost his throne in 1810.

Unlike Italy and the Low Countries, the frontiers and political system of Germany beyond the Rhine had not been touched by Napoleon's earlier conquests. The campaign of 1805-7, however, led to drastic changes. The first step was the emergence in July 1806 of the Confederation of the Rhine, formed at first by sixteen and later by eighteen German princes, who placed themselves under French protection. Among the signatories were the rulers of Baden, Bavaria and Würtemberg, who had added to their possessions at the expense of Austria; they were later joined by Saxony; and eventually the Confederation stretched from the Duchy of Mecklenburg in the north to the Tyrol in the south. Most of its members, the old hereditary rulers, were nominally independent; but a few, owing their promotion to Napoleon, also owed him a more direct allegiance. Thus the Grand Duchy of Berg, taken from Prussia in 1806, was entrusted at first to Murat and, after his transfer to Naples in 1808, to the Emperor's infant nephew, Louis; and between 1807 and 1810, the Kingdom of Westphalia had been pieced together from parts of Hanover, Brunswick, Hesse-Cassel, and the Rhenish provinces ceded by Prussia after Tilsit, and handed over to the youngest Bonaparte brother, Jerome. The French Empire itself had, by 1811, been extended beyond the Dutch frontier by adding the Hanseatic ports of Bremen, Lübeck and Hamburg and the Duchy of Oldenburg, so that its northern coast-line now reached beyond the southern borders of Denmark to the Baltic Sea.

While the new Confederation served as a counter-weight to the truncated Kingdom of Prussia in the north and Austria in the south and east, Prussian Poland was formed into the Grand Duchy of Warsaw in 1807 and placed under the rule of the King of Saxony. This served the purpose of creating a buffer against Russia—all the more effective as the Poles could be lured by the carrot of independence; it also provided the Emperor with a new mistress, the lovely Countess Marie Walewska. Thus, on the eve of the Russian campaign of 1812, the Grand Empire and its satellites appeared as a congeries of interlocking states. The French Empire itself, its inner kernel, stretched from Hamburg in the north to Rome in the south; divided into 130 departments, it spread over nearly half a million square miles and enclosed a population of 44 millions. Beyond it, to the east and south, lay a complex of satellite and vassal states, some ruled by the Bonaparte clan, others by client-princes, nominally independent but incapable, even had they wished, of asserting their independence. Two states fitted into this pattern in theory rather than in practice—Sweden, where Bernadotte, elected Crown Prince through French influence in 1810, was already planning a betrayal; and Spain, where Joseph, sent to fill a vacant throne in 1808, soon found himself to be a ruler without a kingdom.[8] And outside the whole system lay a group of Continental powers—Austria, Denmark and Prussia—who were nominally equal and independent, but whose alliance, owing to French military preponderance, might, as occasion required, be purchased, cajoled or demanded. Prussia, in fact, in 1812, lost her shaky independence and became another vassal state.

In time, Napoleon dreamed of imposing a greater measure of political uniformity on his conquests; but, as they were

[8] See Chapter XIV.

the product of wars and must serve the purposes of future wars, they were subject to continuous expedients and shifts of policy. Yet, with all their internal variations, they bore the mark of both their creator's orderly and authoritarian mind and of the changing constitutional pattern of France herself. It was hardly conceivable that Napoleon, having assumed dictatorial powers in France, should leave the earlier representative institutions of the "sister republics" and of their successors unchanged. From 1800, there had been a growing tendency for electors' rights to be restricted, for democrats to be pushed aside, for "notables" and aristocrats to take over the main positions of authority, for the executive to be strengthened and the administration to become more fully centralized. In the Italian Republic of 1802, the popular vote was eclipsed in a system of hand-picked electoral colleges; and when the Republic became a Kingdom in 1805, the Legislature was scrapped altogether. In Imperial France, the Tribunate was abolished in 1807, the Legislature was rarely summoned and the Council of State, once it had completed its work on the Civil Code, was confined to its judicial functions. This set the tone for the new constitutions of the Grand Empire, and in those drafted in 1807 and 1808 for the Kingdoms of Westphalia and Naples the Emperor first revealed his evident ultimate intention of dispensing with the elective principle altogether. Whatever freedoms the Emperor might tolerate— religious toleration and internal free trade were among them— they certainly did not include freedom of political expression and the effective right of vote. "It is ridiculous," he wrote to Jerome, "that you should quote against me the opinions of the people of Westphalia. If you listen to popular opinion, you will achieve nothing. If the people refuses its own happiness, the people is guilty of anarchy and deserves to be punished."

Inevitably, in an Empire thus constructed, the people's "happiness" included the all-too-frequent visitations of the customs official, recruiting-sergeant and tax-collector. Such considerations played a large part in the Emperor's calculations.

But though denying the right of democracy or of popular election, as he denied that of national self-determination, Napoleon was nonetheless concerned to carry through drastic political and social reforms in the countries under his domination—both because he found it expedient to woo the peasants and middle classes and because it suited him, as the heir of the Revolution, to transport to Europe such of the principles of 1789 as were not incompatible with his autocracy and military needs. Sending Jerome his new constitution for the Kingdom of Westphalia in November 1807, he writes: "What German opinion impatiently demands is that men of no rank, but of marked ability, shall have an equal claim upon your favour and your employment; and that every trace of serfdom, or of a feudal hierarchy between the sovereign and the lowest class of his subjects, shall be done away with. The benefits of the Code Napoleon, public trial, and the introduction of juries will be the leading features of your government. . . What people will want to return under the arbitrary Prussian rule, once it has tasted the benefits of a wise and liberal administration?" Westphalia was intended as a model for the German Confederation, not least because of the effect it might have on neighbouring Prussia and its former subject provinces; but the recipe prescribed for Jerome was, with modifications, that applied in each one of the annexed or vassal states. Like any "enlightened despot", Napoleon was concerned to centralize and modernize his government, to strengthen his authority (or that of his viceroy) against any "intermediate body" between the sovereign and his people. We therefore find high on the list of his reforms in each of his dominions the building of roads and canals, single customs areas, unified systems of justice and weights and measures, economy in government expenditure, the institution of national armies, written constitutions, the secularization of Church property and dissolution of monasteries. We also find such social reforms, reminiscent of Joseph II, as religious toleration, civil rights for Jews and—almost universally—the abolition of serfdom where it still persisted. Reforms of a different order included the Concordat, which did admirable service in winning supporters and neutralizing opponents in Catholic Belgium, Naples and southern and western Germany. But, far more drastically than any "enlightened despot" before him, he tore up the institutions of the Old Régime by the roots in parts of Europe where they were most deeply embedded and introduced equality before the law, civil marriage and secular education, abolished privileges, corporate bodies, tithe and feudal dues, and applied the new rights of inheritance and property enshrined in the Civil Code. The Civil Code, in fact, above all else, was to be the simple touchstone, the universal panacea He recommends it to Jerome as being the means of introduc ing into Germany the jury system and "legal procedure in open court"; and to Joseph, King of Naples, he writes: "You must establish the Civil Code. . . . It will fortify your power, since by it all entails are cancelled, and there will be no longer any great estates apart from those you create yourself." Thus, at the whim of the ruler, a transfer of both property and status should take place: from the old exclusive owners of inherited estates and privileges to new social groups, enriched by trade or the purchase of land and entitled to their full share of honours, according to their service or social standing, in the new Napoleonic State. But there was to be no question of reviving the old practices of 1793; and neither small peasants nor urban *sans-culottes* would have more than casual pickings from the re-distribution of property and wealth.

While this was the general pattern, the changes brought about tended to be more far-reaching in those areas already incorporated under the Directory and Consulate, or where the emergence of an educated middle class favoured their development. Such was the case with Belgium, the Rhineland, Geneva and the Piedmontese and Ligurian provinces of Italy. Here the Napoleonic system had been almost uniformly applied; and there had been time for new classes to develop which, though suffering from heavy taxes, the lack of political freedom and the restrictions of the Continental System, had benefited nevertheless from economic development, greater opportunities for advancement and the abolition of tithe and feudal obligations on the land; and of whom some, at least, had been appeased by the reconciliation with Rome. Whatever their secret grievances, such people, in fact, never showed any open inclination to shake off the Napoleonic yoke. In the Kingdom of Italy, the régime also had time to become solidly established: the old landed aristocracy proved hard to win, but the Milanese bourgeoisie and officials, many of them enrolled in Masonic lodges, were among the Empire's most loyal supporters. In the rest of Italy—in Rome and the south —the case was somewhat different. In Rome, trade had suffered and religious feelings had been ruffled by the Pope's departure; and here, strangely enough, the French found favour only with the liberal aristocracy. From Naples even Caroline, the Emperor's sister, could write that "all Europe lies crushed under the yoke of France". The Neapolitan nobility certainly refused to co-operate and the small peasants and townspeople, being too poor to gain much benefit from Napoleonic reforms, remained sullen or, when stirred by the priests, actively hostile. Even middle-class "patriots", after 1806, joined disgruntled nobles in forming anti-French secret societies like the *Carbonari* and *Federati*. Yet Murat's administration was enlightened—and remarkably independent—and reform, though it began late, took firm roots: so much so that when the Bourbon King Ferdinand returned in 1815, he did not think it advisable either to restore feudalism or to repeal the Napoleonic Code.

Holland, like Italy, had undergone a number of constitutional changes since its occupation by the French in 1795; but, unlike much of Italy, it had a powerfully entrenched middle class, it had no serfdom, few feudal relics, its people were mainly Protestant, and under the Batavian Republic it had been forged into a unified state. Consequently, the Napoleonic administration had fewer changes to make here than elsewhere. Even so, the guilds, though nominally abolished in 1796, still survived in Amsterdam ten years later; it was not until 1809 that the fiscal discrimination against Jews was finally removed;

and the Civil Code was fully applied only after Holland's incorporation within the French Empire in 1810. Yet remnants of the Old Régime lingered on : to appease the owners of land, land-reform was never completed as in France and Italy; the tithe remained as a secular rent and manorial dues were not redeemed.

The German and Polish provinces were brought into the Napoleonic system only after 1805. In consequence, reforms were here more hurried or more piece-meal; and, on the whole, they showed a greater tendency to make concessions to the old ruling groups and interests : this corresponded both to immediate needs and to the Emperor's growing tenderness for aristocracy. The first Napoleonic province to be established across the Rhine was the Grand Duchy of Berg, with fewer than a million inhabitants and formed, between 1806 and 1808, of a medley of petty principalities and bishoprics. Murat, its first ruler, centralized the administration, unified its customs, and introduced conscription and a land tax—measures consolidated by the commissioners who succeeded him in 1808. But the Civil Code was introduced only in 1811 and a constitution (vesting authority in hand-picked " notables ") in 1812; the estates of the Church were hardly touched; the Concordat was not applied; serfdom, feudal dues and services were abolished; but feudal rents were subject to redemption, and the Emperor intervened on the side of the landlords when the peasants refused to pay. In the event, no one was fully satisfied and the assimilation was incomplete. In contrast, Jerome's " model " Kingdom of Westphalia was submitted from the start to the clean sweep of Napoleonic reform. A constitution was proclaimed in 1807; a centralized and unified administration quickly emerged; the Civil Code and French judicial system were introduced; Church lands were put up for auction; serfdom, privilege and guilds were abolished; though, here again, feudal rents and *corvée* were made subject to redemption or enforced against the resistance of the peasants. Yet assimilation was rapid and, on the whole, successful and here, as in northern Italy, the Napoleonic régime found ready support among the liberal aristocracy and professional bourgeoisie. This, however, was not the case with the northwestern corner of Germany, annexed in December 1810 and placed under a military government, whose main concern was to stamp out smuggling from vulnerable coastal areas.

The Grand Duchy of Warsaw, formed from Prussian Poland after Tilsit, presented its own problems. On the one hand, the Poles had, unlike the Germans, acquired a taste for national independence. On the other hand, the middle class was weak; political and social life was dominated by the nobility, among them an active liberal group that had been fed on Rousseau and French ideas and had carried through the liberal Constitution of 1791. To these, the French appeared as liberators from Russian or Prussian tyranny and aggression. This gave Napoleon a decided advantage, as long as he could appear as the champion of Polish nationalism and did not vitally injure the interests of aristocracy. This was done by creating a unified state, while maintaining in being "liberties" denied or abolished elsewhere, and leaving the social system substantially untouched. Under the brief rule of the King of Saxony, Napoleon's nominee, the Grand Duchy was given a strong central government and a judicial system and administration—with departments, communes and prefects—strictly modelled on the French. The Church was placed under the State and its bishops were appointed by the Grand Duke; a new constitution guaranteed equality before the law and freedom of conscience to all citizens; conscription was introduced and the Civil Code applied in 1810. So, for the first time in its history, Poland was given a strong government and a centralized administration and was beginning to build up a corps of professional civil servants. Though the government was authoritarian, the political aspirations of the nobility were appeased by maintaining a diet, that functioned normally and was composed in the main of noble deputies. Serfdom was abolished, but the peasants gained little as the old land-system with its feudal dues, rents and *corvée* continued in being and tithe and the estates of the Church were left intact. Moreover, to allay clerical anxiety, the Jews were deprived of a part of their constitutional liberties by suspending their political rights and their right to purchase land. From this piece-meal operation the main beneficiaries were the lesser nobility; and it was their loyalty, rather than that of the landed magnates or princes of the Church, that assured Napoleon of a Polish contingent when he went to war again with Russia in 1812.

Most of the princes of the Confederation of the Rhine, which by this time sprawled over the greater part of Germany, were nominally independent and Napoleon's allies rather than his vassals. Consequently, the reforms carried out in their territories reflected those imposed within the Grand Empire only in so far as it suited their private whims and fancies, or accorded with their military obligations to the Emperor. Thus, in Mecklenburg and Thuringia, improved methods were found for raising troops, but the old aristocratic society and the old balance between monarchy and aristocracy were left completely undisturbed; and the King of Saxony, though a reformer by necessity in Poland, was not one in his own hereditary dominions. Yet several of the princes, particularly those in the south, had an interest in consolidating and digesting their recent acquisitions, both lay and ecclesiastical; and this led them, if not to imitate Napoleon or follow his suggestions, at least to emulate the methods of the more " enlightened " of the Kings of Prussia or Sweden. King Frederick of Würtemberg, for instance, was an autocrat, who denied his people any representation or civil liberties, and created an all-pervading police state; yet he abolished serfdom, stripped the nobility of its rights of private justice, granted religious freedom and civil rights to Jews, and secularized the lands of the Church, while leaving guilds, feudalism, aristocratic privilege and the old social order virtually untouched. More " enlightened " were the neighbouring rulers of Bavaria and Baden, who adopted Napoleon's Civil Code and introduced constitutions guaranteeing civil liberties and equality before the law. Yet, with the single exception of the tiny state of

Anhalt-Köthen (29,000 subjects), the French system was nowhere completely followed and the privileges of the old aristocratic society, its system of land-tenure and its freedom to dispose at will of peasant-labour were, in substance, left untouched. Even the most " enlightened " of the independent German princes had learned from Joseph II's sad experience that the old compact between monarchy and aristocracy must at all costs be maintained.

The Revolution had, of course, taught otherwise; and within the Grand Empire, riddled as it was with contradictions and with the seeds of its own decline, Napoleon's conquering armies had shaken the structure of the old social order and laid the foundations of the modern bourgeois state. For all his despotism, his arrogant unconcern for popular and national sovereignty, his dynastic ambitions and his increasing devotion to a hierarchic order, the Emperor in his dealings with Europe still saw himself as the heir and soldier of the Revolution. And, hesitantly and imperfectly as it might be, Europe continued to be " revolutionized " under the Empire as it had been under the Consulate and Directory.

Chapter XIV

THE FALL OF NAPOLEON

It is an interesting parlour-game to discuss and to decide on the date or the episode that marks the turning-point in Napoleon's career. When did the astonishing upward course of his successes begin to go into reverse and enter on the gradual descent that ended in Waterloo and St. Helena? Some would say it began in Spain, others Moscow, others again at Leipzig in 1813; or even, if not at Waterloo, in the redoubt of besieged and embattled France in the spring of 1814. Napoleon himself seems to have taken the longer view as he later confessed that it was "the Spanish ulcer" that destroyed him. It is unlikely that the decline of his fortunes from this time was inevitable—and there was certainly no straight and undeviating line of destruction leading from Baylen and Torres Vedras to Waterloo—but it is certain enough that the Peninsular War, beginning in 1808, became a running sore that drained the Grand Army, gave fresh hope and opportunity to his enemies in England, Austria and Russia, and generally stimulated that "awakening of the peoples" to which his ultimate fall and failure have most commonly been ascribed.

It began in Portugal. Portugal was Britain's oldest trading ally (she was almost a colony) and, once the Continental System was launched in 1806, it became imperative for Napoleon to seal off the whole Iberian coast from English ships and commerce. The Portuguese refused to come to terms and, at Tilsit, he decided on their conquest. But to reach Portugal he had to pass through Spain; and the corruption of the Spanish Court under the feeble and incompetent Charles IV appeared to favour his plans. Spain was ruled, in fact, not by Charles but by the Queen's favourite, Godoy, who had maintained an alliance with France since 1804 in the hope of winning Portugal as a reward. But Spanish military support, particularly after Trafalgar, had been weak and uncertain—before Jena, Godoy had even talked of withdrawing it altogether—and it was both to deal with Portugal and to bring further pressure on the Spanish that Napoleon sent an army under Junot to occupy Portugal in October 1807.

Godoy was soon won back by the promise of the southern part of Portugal for himself; but as Junot's army passed through Spain a crisis occurred that suggested alternative solutions. The Spanish Crown Prince Ferdinand, suspecting Godoy of intriguing to usurp the throne after his father's death, appealed to Napoleon for help to overthrow him. Thus, unexpectedly, the fate of the Spanish succession was committed to the Emperor's care. It was a tempting bait and while he considered possible solutions—to install Ferdinand or a Bonaparte prince?—he sent Murat with an army to Madrid. Godoy had made himself detested and, as Murat approached, a military revolt broke out in favour of Ferdinand. Charles abdicated; Godoy was imprisoned; and, as French troops steadily occupied their country, Charles and Ferdinand were summoned to hear Napoleon's verdict at Bayonne. Both father and son were persuaded to renounce their claims and to pledge themselves to abide by the Emperor's decision; and he, contemptuous of Spanish feelings and lured by the prospect of another Napoleonic kingdom, decided against Ferdinand and ordered the reluctant Joseph from Naples to fill the vacant throne. Meanwhile, Murat (who had hoped to win Spain for himself) was sent to Naples, a Spanish constitution on Napoleonic lines was promulgated at Bayonne, and the Spanish royal family was packed off in captivity to Talleyrand's *château* at Valençay.

It was a serious miscalculation. Ferdinand's summons to Bayonne had already touched off a popular insurrection in Madrid, savagely crushed by Murat; but Napoleon, confident of success in Spain as elsewhere and ignorant of Spanish ways and institutions, refused to read the signs. Yet Ferdinand had shown himself to be a popular candidate and to have championed his cause against Godoy might have assured the French of Spanish gratitude and co-operation, whereas the decision to enthrone Joseph had the opposite effect. Even before Joseph reached Madrid in July 1808, his kingdom was in revolt and, after eleven days' stay, he was driven from the capital. The rebellion began almost simultaneous'y in the Asturias in the north and at Seville in the south and gradually spread over the greater part of Spain. Militarily, it took the form of armed attacks by peasant guerrillas, often supported by regular units, on French troops and convoys and the murder of collaborating Spanish liberals and officials. Politically, it became organized in a series of insurgent Juntas, who usurped local authority, declared war on the French, and even sent deputations to England; and a Central Junta emerged at Cadiz. To France's enemies, it naturally appeared as a spontaneous national uprising against the invading French; and, in London, Sheridan hailed it as a first example of an oppressed nation turning the principles of the Revolution against the French themselves. Yet this was a distortion : the Spanish peasants, far from being won over to the French revolutionary principles, had, as they had already demonstrated in 1793, been more thoroughly immunized against them than any other people in Europe. In fact, the leaders of the Juntas were not middle-class revolutionaries, inspired by the Enlightenment or the principles of 1789, but most commonly priests and noblemen, outraged by the French threat to secularize the properties of the Church or to upset traditional social relations in the village; and as the peasants were deeply devoted to their faith and to the old traditions, as they were to the old Bourbon dynasty, such persons were able to turn the movement to their own advantage and to resist reform. In this sense, it was yet another " Church and King" movement on the Vendée pattern. But it was more than that. For one thing, it was also a patriotic movement, concerned to defend Country as well as Church and King; though Southey was right to stress that " the patriotic fire flamed higher for this holy oil of superstition ". Again there were other elements besides priests and nobles among its leaders, particularly at the national level. In fact, both the Central Junta and the revolutionary Cortes convened in 1810 were dominated by the liberal-patriotic bourgeoisie of Cadiz, that wanted to destroy the *señorios* and the Inquisition as well as to end foreign rule; and, in 1812, the Cortes actually devised a limited monarchical constitution that, in many respects, recalled the French Constitution of 1791.

Whatever its ultimate significance, the rebellion certainly had immediate and dramatic consequences. The Spanish regular army was easily routed by the French; but two French divisions, ordered to occupy Cadiz, were trapped by a Spanish force of 30,000, supported by guerrillas, and forced to capitulate at Baylen (July 1808). The news had an electrifying effect on Europe and Napoleon was compelled to summon a large part of the Grand Army from Germany; at the end of the year, he assumed personal command in Spain and almost succeeded in trapping and destroying Sir John Moore's escaping English contingent at Corunna. But events elsewhere in Europe called him away, and he never found time to return. And, meanwhile, the " Spanish ulcer " had created a new problem by providing the English, at long last, with a foothold on the Continent. For the Portuguese had followed the Spanish example and revolted against the French. To support their old allies, the English exploited their naval supremacy to send an expeditionary force of 13,000 men under Arthur Wellesley, later Duke of Wellington. Junot, cut off from French supplies and reinforcements, was defeated and agreed, by the Convention of Cintra (August 1808), to withdraw his army and his Portuguese allies to France. While Junot thus saved his army for another campaign, the English were able to occupy Lisbon and send arms to the Spanish guerrillas; and the road to Madrid lay momentarily open. It was closed again, however, by Napoleon a few months later; and the British government hesitated for long to engage more than a token force in the Peninsula : it was discouraged by the near-disaster to Moore's army at Corunna and by the losses incurred by its other expeditionary force to Walcheren in Holland. Consequently, Wellington, who was sent out again to Portugal in April 1809, had at all costs to husband his resources, avoid pitched battles and devise a defensive strategy. Using Portugal as his base, he maintained communications with the guerrillas, reorganized the Portuguese army, and made only occasional sallies into Spain. In 1810, Masséna was sent out to Spain with 140,000 troops and ordered, as a first task, to drive the English into the sea. Through jealousy, Soult, who held the south of Spain, failed to give Masséna support; and the French army was unable to pierce Wellington's lines at Torres Vedras and was driven from Portugal. Thereafter, as French attention centred more and more on Russia and Germany, Wellington took the offensive, carried the war into Spain and, after successive victories at Salamanca (1812) and Vittoria (1813), cleared the Peninsula of the invaders.

Yet it is doubtful if Spanish resistance and Wellington's defensive genius could have achieved this result without the repercussions that the Peninsular War had on the rest of Europe; and on Austria, in the first place. The humiliating Treaty of Pressburg, forced on her after Austerlitz, had led to something like a patriotic revival. The cession of the Tyrol, in particular, had been deeply resented and, while the Archduke Charles and Stadion, the new liberal Chancellor, did what they could against the Emperor Francis' resistance to build and modernize the army, a flood of patriotic literature called for a war of revenge. Yet, as long as the Grand Army remained in Germany and the Tsar remained Napoleon's ally, the risk was far too great. But news of the French defeat at Baylen and the withdrawal of troops to Spain changed the picture and assured the war-party of new allies: even the cautious Metternich, Austrian ambassador to France, wrote, prodded by Talleyrand, that the opportunity should not be lost. The French Emperor, in fact, faced formidable problems: the Spanish revolt continued, the English were in Portugal, the Russians could not be relied upon; and, in

Paris, on his return, he found new royalist and Jacobin plots and treason in high places: Fouché and Talleyrand were once more conspiring to overthrow him. Only another victory could restore confidence and save the day. Talleyrand was disgraced and 140,000 new recruits were called to the colours: in all, an army of 300,000 was scratched together, though one half was composed of foreign levies and it was a poor substitute for the army of 1805. The Austrians, on the other hand, were better armed and better led than at Ulm and Austerlitz; and it was only Napoleon's speed and the masterly disposal of his forces in the field that saved him from disaster. A rapid thrust brought him to Vienna, but the bridges were cut and the bulk of the Austrian army was camped on the northern bank of the Danube; in attempting to reach them he was forced back at Essling for a loss of 20,000 men. It was his first major defeat and the news of it stirred up a peasant rebellion in the Tyrol against his Bavarian allies. Led by Andreas Hofer, the insurgents fought for months with courage and ferocity for Holy Church and Austria in the manner of the Spanish and Vendean guerrillas; and similar movements followed in the centre of Italy. But Napoleon held Vienna and was able to bring up reinforcements from the Italian front. On 5 July 1809, with an army of 190,000, he crossed the Danube to meet the Austrians at Wagram. Both sides suffered losses of 20,000 men; but the Austrians, though by no means crushed as at Austerlitz, were beaten in the field and sued for an armistice. By the Peace of Schönbrunn, which followed in October, Austria surrendered the Illyrian provinces to the French, Salzburg to the Bavarians and Cracow and Lublin to the Grand Duchy of Warsaw. A new alliance was sealed between the two Emperors and, to mark his new-found respect for legitimacy, Napoleon discarded Joséphine (who had failed to bear him a son) and married Francis' 18-year-old daughter, the Archduchess Marie Louise. Meanwhile, the Pope had been removed from the Vatican and Rome had been annexed. In Paris, the opposition had been silenced and a new army under

Masséna was being assembled to deal with Spain. On the face of it, the crisis was over and the Empire stood more firmly established than ever.

But the realities were different. The Austrian marriage proved one further source of irritation to the Tsar. At first, there had been talk of marriage with Alexander's sister, Catherine; but the proposal had been badly received at the Russian Court and, anticipating a refusal, Napoleon had, on Metternich's suggestion, transferred his suit to the Austrian Archduchess. While this saved Alexander further embarrassment, the manner in which it was done brought into the open a rift that had been growing between the Tsar and Emperor almost as soon as the ink had dried on their Tilsit and Erfurt agreements. The Russian nobility had never accepted the alliance with Napoleon with good grace: they feared and despised him as the upstart creature of the Revolution; and the Continental System, to which Alexander had committed them at Tilsit, faced them with economic ruin, as it ended their profitable trade in timber with the English. Alexander himself had hoped to gain substantial advantages from the alliance —provided there was no serious attempt made to "revolutionize" the Poles and that he could count on Napoleon's benevolent neutrality—if not on his help—in dealing with the Turks and taking Constantinople. But, already by the time of Erfurt, it had become clear that Napoleon, in pursuit of his own Mediterranean ambitions, would not consent to the partition of Turkey on Russia's terms. Again, to Alexander, with his eyes on Poland, the Grand Duchy of Warsaw was tolerable only as a temporary expedient and he hoped, at least, to gain Galicia as compensation. But, with Austria's defeat in 1809, the Western Galician provinces were ceded not to Russia but to the Grand Duchy; and Napoleon, having concluded his marriage arrangements with Austria, refused to ratify an agreement not to revive an independent Poland. To add to Alexander's irritation, Bernadotte was adopted by the Swedes, his traditional enemies, as Crown Prince with French support—a danger, be it said, that proved to be more apparent than real. Finally, both rulers displayed their mutual disregard by breaking agreements reached at Erfurt: Napoleon by annexing the German Duchy of Oldenburg (whose ruler was the Tsar's own brother-in-law) and Alexander by his ukase of 31 December 1810, which imposed high tariffs on Imperial imports and opened Russian ports to neutral ships, and thereby to English trade. Thus the Continental System was fatally breached and war appeared inevitable.

For a while, it seemed that Alexander would take the initiative. In the spring of 1811, he massed troops on the Polish border and made successive attempts to find allies among the Austrians, Swedes, Prussians and Poles. But Metternich, the new Austrian Chancellor, cautious since his experience of 1809, refused an offer of the Danubian provinces; Bernadotte was negotiating with the French for the acquisition of Norway from Denmark; Frederick William had no spirit to challenge Napoleon; and the Poles, anxious for their independence, had higher hopes of Napoleon than of Alexander. So an offensive strategy was given up for one of caution and attrition: Wellington was to be the model rather than Napoleon.

Napoleon, meanwhile, was warned of Russia's intentions by the Poles and made his own preparations, both by diplomacy and mobilization. Prussia was the first to submit: the "patriot" counsellors were dismissed and a contingent of 20,000 men was promised. Austria appeared to go one better by promising 30,000 troops, but Metternich played a double game and kept his back-door open for negotiations with France's enemies. In all, by calling on both his own and his vassals' resources, Napoleon was able to muster over 600,000 men in Poland. But, by his delays, he allowed his opponents to secure a double diplomatic victory: a peace-treaty with the Turks and, in return for the promise of Norway, Bernadotte's pledge of military support. Even so, the Russians were inferior in numbers: at the beginning of the campaign, their generals,

Barclay de Tolly and Bagration, had a combined strength of 160,000 men compared with the 450,000 under Napoleon's command that crossed the Niemen on 25 June 1812.

In retrospect, Napoleon's bid to conquer Russia by a frontal assault seems to have been an act of unspeakable folly; besides, if he had not the lessons of later "conquerors" to learn from, he had at least that of Charles XII of Sweden who, a bare 100 years earlier, had come to grief in the attempt. In fact, he later admitted to Las Cases at St. Helena that this had been the greatest mistake of his career. But fifteen years of almost continuous victories in the field had given him a sense of invincibility and an arrogant contempt for his opponents; moreover, if it was a gamble (was not the campaign of 1809?), the stakes were high : this time "the final battle" (as he said), the submission of the one remaining Continental rival, the restoration of the Continental System, the surrender of England—and then, maybe, the East. He appears to have had no doubts about the outcome : as ever, he counted on a short war and (incredible as it must seem) the troops were issued with a four-days bread ration and the following convoys carried a three-weeks supply of flour. Again, ignorant of the enemy and of the Russian plains, he hoped to repeat the pattern of his former victories by enclosing his opponents in a great enveloping movement and forcing them to fight a single conclusive battle. Had he succeeded in persuading the Russians to engage he would no doubt have won—even with his vast unwieldy army, which was made up in large part from the half-trained contingents of unwilling allies and of which no more than one-third was composed of seasoned French troops. But the Russians, through no great foresight or superior strategy, were compelled by sheer necessity to retreat and, in retreating, to "scorch" their earth and leave behind them abandoned villages, charred homesteads, ploughed-up fields and long stretches of empty wasteland. So it went on through Vilna and Vitebsk, and at Smolensk (a little over half-way to Moscow), through exhaustion and desertion, only 160,000 of the invading force remained. At Borodino, on the Moskva,

Napoleon at last compelled the new Russian commander, Kutusov, to fight a battle; but, though inflicting heavy casualties, he failed to break his army which retreated behind Moscow. On 14 September, the French army of 100,000 entered the city to find its streets deserted; and, the same night, it was fired by order of its governor. "All the houses of the nobility," wrote an English eyewitness, "all the warehouses of the merchants, all the shops etc. were fired; and . . . the conflagration raged and rendered Moscow one flaming pile." For a month the Emperor made vain attempts to negotiate peace with the Tsar, 300 miles away at St. Petersburg; but, either from political calculation or distaste, he failed to do the one thing that might have turned the scales against his opponents by liberating the Russian peasants from serfdom.

But, by this time, it may well have been too late; for, when, a month later, the great homeward trek began, peasant vengeance was added to the rigours of the winter to make the retreat a living hell. The first snow fell before the army reached Smolensk; from then on, across the Beresina to Vilna, thousands died from exposure in temperatures of 28-35° of frost; thousands more were murdered by the peasants or picked off by the Cossacks. A straggling remnant of 30,000 re-crossed the Niemen in December—a mere twentieth of those who had crossed it in June. The Grand Army no longer existed.

Yet, surprisingly, Napoleon had not lost his confidence. Leaving the army to Murat, he returned to Paris, where further conspiracies had been brewing during his absence, prepared to raise fresh troops, and even called on the Prussians and Austrians to furnish new contingents. And all was by no means lost. In France, once the conspirators had been removed, the Emperor's position was temporarily secure; the Russian army was exhausted and Kutusov, left with 40,000 men, showed no inclination to cross the borders; Prussia feared Russia's intentions in Poland and was torn, as ever, between the conflicting policies of a timid King and a patriotic war-party; and Metternich refused to commit himself: he was as much bothered by Russian ambitions as by the French and he had no desire to take part in a German crusade led by Prussian " patriots ". So Napoleon might have saved a substantial part of his Empire, if he had been willing to cut his losses in Spain or Germany or to accept Metternich's offer of a return to the terms of Lunéville. Yet he feared that an Empire built on war could survive only by further victories and that a negotiated peace would spell its doom. Negotiations would serve to gain time—and he carried them on with his usual feverish activity—but, in the last resort, it was the military gamble that would decide the issue. So by scraping the barrel for new recruits—by calling up National Guards and the conscripts of both 1813 and 1814—he had, by April 1813, mustered another force of 150,000 men to fight in Germany.

Napoleon's determination in itself compelled his opponents to concert their forces. But a new element had crept into the calculation: the protesting voices of the European peoples themselves. The Napoleonic system, whatever its benefits in times of peace, could not fail to appear as an increasingly heavy burden in times of war. A constant feature of that system was to make the occupied and vassal countries pay for the upkeep of French troops as well as their own. Westphalia's two million inhabitants contributed 26 million francs in taxes, of which 10 millions went to sustain a French garrison of 12,500 men. In 1807, Joseph of Naples spent 44 millions on the army and was refunded six. Of a national expenditure of 127 millions in 1809, the Kingdom of Italy paid 30 millions to France and spent 42 millions to maintain troops in France's interest. In the Grand Duchy of Berg taxes more than doubled between 1808 and 1813; in Venetia they trebled. The Italian army rose from 49,000 men in 1810 to 91,000 in 1812.[1] In addition, there were the hardships caused by the Continental System, the quartering of troops, the pillaging and devastation of the countryside as armies

[1] G. Lefebvre, *Napoléon*, p. 505.

passed through on the way to battle. Spain naturally suffered most; but Germany had to harbour the Grand Army of over 700,000 men in the summer of 1811; and, on the eve of the Russian campaign, it was Prussia that bore the heaviest burden. Westphalia suffered less than Prussia, but it was Jerome who raised the alarm in a letter of December 1811:

> There is profound unrest . . . The example of Spain is being recommended and, if war breaks out, every country between the Rhine and the Oder will be the scene of an active insurrection. The underlying cause of these disorders is not only resentment at foreign domination: its deeper causes lie in the ruination of all classes, the crushing burden of taxation, war-levies, the upkeep and quartering of troops, and endless other vexations.

Jerome seems to have been an alarmist, as no such general insurrection followed, even after Moscow, either in the vassal states or in the territories annexed by France. Yet he stresses what is evident elsewhere as well—that it was the burden of taxes and of military occupation rather than the humiliation of serving a foreign master that caused resentment and indignation. This is not to deny that outraged nationalism played a part. In Spain and the north of Italy, as we have seen, the French occupation injured national feelings that already existed or which the Revolution, with its message of popular and national sovereignty, had newly awakened. In Poland the position was different, as here the French—until 1812, at least—appeared as liberators from the yoke of Russia, Austria or Prussia. In Germany the position was different again, as Germany, unlike Poland and Spain, had for centuries been divided into a patchwork of minor and major states and had no clearly defined national boundaries. Here, too, it was not the rural classes—whether landlords or peasants—that formed the mainstay of the national movement, but a combination of liberal country gentry and professional bourgeois (mainly the latter)—the same classes that, after 1815, would fight a more sustained and consistent battle for both national and constitutional rights. But, at this stage, the movement was weak and scattered, and lacked precise objectives—all the more so because it had no contact or sympathy with the peasants and urban masses and because a large part—perhaps the larger part —of the professional classes, far from being hostile to Napoleon, were among his warmest supporters. In fact, the notion dear to many German historians of the past that the Napoleonic system was destroyed by an all-German " war of liberation", or *Befreiungskrieg,* is a myth. Admittedly, there was a sense of German patriotism abroad. It started with the cultural revolution at the turn of the century, when writers like Herder, Tieck, Arndt, Brentano and the Schlegels evoked the legendary glories of the old German Reich, equated Gothic with Germanic and extolled the virtues of the pious and simple German *Volk*. This notion of *Volkstum* was given a sharper, and a political, edge by the philosopher Fichte who, in his lectures in Berlin after the catastrophe of Jena, appealed to the German "Nation" to unite against the despotism of the French. At first, the patriots looked to Austria : it was natural that they should, as Prussia was of fairly recent vintage; but it was also a sign of their confusion and immaturity, as the Habsburg Empire was itself a congeries of dependent, mainly non-Germanic, nations to which Austria's rulers had no intention of giving their freedom. But, after 1807, when two reformers, Stein and Hardenberg, were appointed ministers to Frederick William, Prussia became the white hope of the patriots instead. Stein, in fact, believed in borrowing, though in moderation, from the French principles of 1789; he abolished serfdom and made it possible for the more prosperous peasants to purchase land; he also wanted to summon a national assembly and form a National Guard; and, stirred by the news from Spain, he even supported a call for an all-German rising against Napoleon. But Napoleon got wind of his intentions and he and the Junkers combined to drive him from office; so that most of his plans came to nothing. After this, the Junkers (whose aims were entirely Prussian) were in control and, although the army was reformed and secretly enlarged, there was no further talk of social reform; and

Prussia made no attempt to break with Napoleon until his failure at Moscow was known to have been complete. Yet the patriots' hopes were raised again by Napoleon's further military preparations and by the Tsar's determination to pose as the defender of the rights of nations. Stein was called in by Alexander as an adviser; General Yorck, the Prussian commander, disobeyed the King's orders and joined the Russians who had crossed the East Prussian border; the King was persuaded to agree to arm the civilian population (though with aristocratic officers) in a newly-formed Landwehr, or militia; and, in February 1813, Prussia signed a treaty of alliance with Russia and declared war on France. The Confederation of the Rhine was declared dissolved; Hamburg revolted and was occupied by Russia; and Saxony and Mecklenburg withdrew from the French alliance. England, meanwhile, offered subsidies. But Metternich, preferring to mediate between the two opposing camps while building his army, bided his time. The Austrian rulers had no more sympathy than the Prussian for the "national" aims of the German patriots; and long before the Austrians joined the coalition six months later, the idea of mobilizing for any national "war of liberation" had been killed stone dead.[2]

As Austria hesitated, Napoleon counted on striking quickly in order to dispose of his two other opponents. He had the advantage of numbers: 150,000 against his enemy's 100,000; but he was weak in cavalry, his new recruits were raw and untrained, and his generals had lost much of their fire and cunning. Planning to capture Leipzig, he won two skirmishes at Lützen and Bautzen, and the King of Saxony returned to the fold; but, for lack of cavalry, he could not exploit his successes and, ignorant of the allies' weakness, he agreed to the armistice of Pleiswitz (June 1813). Thereby he had time to call up reinforcements (including cavalry); but the greater advantage lay with his enemies: the Prussian Landwehr was

[2] But see H. A. L. Fisher, *Studies in Napoleonic Statesmanship: Germany* (Oxford, 1908): "The War of Liberation was a movement of peoples rather than a coalition of princes" (p. 384).

now ready for action; Bernadotte brought in 23,000 Swedes; while Austria, having exhausted her negotiations with Napoleon, joined the allies and put 127,000 troops at their disposal. When hostilities resumed in August, Napoleon had some 450,000 men in the field—a force only slightly inferior to the combined strength of his opponents—but he was handicapped by the wavering loyalties of his allies and the weak performance of his lieutenants. Consequently, he could not follow up the advantage of a brilliant victory at Dresden; and, with his forces depleted and deserted by the Bavarians and Saxons, he was decisively defeated at Leipzig (October 1813). He retreated with his remaining 60,000 men across the Rhine, and the battle for France—the first for fifteen years—began.

The Emperor's military genius had not deserted him and the campaign that he fought in France with vastly inferior forces in the spring of 1814 was among the most brilliantly conducted of his whole career. But the political situation had profoundly changed. Germany, Spain and most of Italy were lost and the Grand Empire lay in ruins. Yet, as long as his opponents failed to agree on common war-aims, there was still room to manœuvre and to strike a bargain with the highest bidder : with Metternich, for example, who, fearful of Russian ambitions, insisted on offering the Emperor a peace-settlement based on the "natural frontiers"—the so-called Frankfurt proposals. But, while Napoleon temporized, Holland had risen in revolt and recalled the Stadholder; Castlereagh, the English Foreign Secretary, arrived at allied headquarters at Basel to urge that neither the Low Countries nor the Rhineland should be left in France's possession; and, in February, the allies formally withdrew the Frankfurt offer and demanded that France withdraw behind the frontiers of 1792. A month later, Castlereagh, who held the purse-strings, persuaded his reluctant allies to go even further : at Chaumont, on 9 March, the four powers bound themselves to a twenty-year alliance to defeat Napoleon and re-settle Europe; each partner would, if need be, put an army of 150,000 into the field. Then, and only then, did England pay over her promised subsidy of £5 million. And this was not all: England was only awaiting a favourable response from Napoleon's enemies in Paris to pledge her allies not only to overthrow the Emperor but to enthrone the Bourbon pretender, Louis XVIII, in his place. So, at last, after twenty years, the aims of Burke and the counter-revolution were realized and Europe stood united to crush revolutionary France.

Even so, the project might never have been realized if France herself had stood firm and united to resist the invader. After all, in 1793, the position had appeared as grave. Napoleon was aware of it and talked of arming the people, of mobilizing the National Guard and of reviving the old cry of *la patrie en danger*. But how could he? For a dozen years and more, he had paraded his contempt for " *la vile populace* ", he had shut himself off from the people within his Imperial Court or military headquarters, he had governed by decree or through his Ministry of Police, and discouraged every manifestation of popular initiative. So his requisitioning and despatch of representatives " on mission " to the departments appeared only hollow imitations of the Committee of Public Safety. Besides, his recent defeats and frantic search for recruits (more than a million men in 1812 and 1813 alone) had lost him at last the loyalty and respect of his subjects. Even the Imperial officials were hostile or apathetic and were looking round for new masters to serve. The Legislature, as always in moments of crisis, imposed conditions: the restoration of political liberties and a peace based on France's old frontiers; and was dismissed after a ten-day session. The nation at large, too, wanted peace and showed its indifference or hostility by passively resisting the government's attempts to mobilize it for war: taxes remained unpaid, requisitioning orders went unheeded, and conscripts (particularly those of the 1801-1808 classes, consisting of older and married men) were slow to come forward: in fact, only 120,000 men—less than one-eighth of those nominally conscripted—saw service in 1814. Most serious of all: the civilian population, cowed and dispirited, offered no resistance to the advancing allied troops—

until the marauding activities of the Cossacks and Prussians in the eastern departments goaded the peasants to retaliate. Meanwhile, royalist agents were active everywhere: Bordeaux surrendered without a fight to the English and welcomed the Duke of Angoulême; and once Napoleon had been beaten in the field (and this was after only two months of campaigning) and Paris lay open, the Senate and Legislature, prodded by the allies and the ever-busy Talleyrand, declared Napoleon to be deposed and invited Louis XVIII, who promised a liberal Charter, to fill the throne. The final blow was the refusal of Napoleon's marshals to serve him any longer. After this, he accepted the inevitable and abdicated on 6 April; and, on the 11th, the allies, by the Treaty of Fontainebleau, granted him as a haven the island of Elba in full sovereignty, with the Duchy of Parma for Marie Louise and a substantial pension for himself and his family. He sailed on the 20th and took possession of his new domain a fortnight later.

After Napoleon's departure, the allies signed a Peace Treaty in Paris: France was reduced to her frontiers of 1792—that is, she lost not only Italy and Germany but Belgium and the left bank of the Rhine; but she was not disarmed or occupied or made to pay an indemnity (even Italy's looted art treasures remained in her possession); and the new legitimist France, with the versatile Talleyrand as her Foreign Minister, was to be accepted as an equal partner at the congresses now to be held to negotiate a general settlement of Europe. After this, the allies adjourned their discussions and met again at Vienna. But here the old disputes broke out again over Poland, the Rhineland, Saxony and Italy; and, at one stage, the congress split up into two contending factions. But unity was reimposed from a familiar quarter; for, in March 1815, came the news that Napoleon had left his island-kingdom and landed in the south of France.

In Elba, he had kept in touch with events in Vienna and in France. The French had accepted the Bourbons without enthusiasm only to end the war; and Louis XVIII would be tolerated as long as he left untouched the basic Revolution settlement in land and property. The bourgeoisie and new nobility, who had deposed Napoleon and called in Louis, had also welcomed the Charter, which promised to restore their voting rights and constitutional liberties. But the return in mass of an *émigré* nobility inevitably created problems : the government was tempted to find them posts and estates and there were soon rumours that the sequestrated properties of the Church and aristocracy would be restored to their former owners. The army, too, was disaffected, largely because it was an object of suspicion to the new régime and its officers had been retired, ignominiously it seemed, on half-pay. It was, no doubt, factors such as these that account for the enthusiastic welcome that attended Napoleon's triumphal progress to the capital, where he arrived on 20 March. Louis XVIII had already fled and the last episode in Napoleon's public life—that of the Hundred Days—had begun.

But, however enthusiastic the reception, there could be no question of returning to the autocracy of the past : either he must appeal to the old Jacobin and revolutionary traditions of 1793 or he must come to terms with the liberals by outbidding the liberties of Louis XVIII's Charter. He chose the latter course, took two former liberal opponents, Carnot and Benjamin Constant, into partnership, and with Constant's help issued an " Additional Act to the Constitutions of the Empire ". It satisfied no one, as it estranged the " patriots " by its appeal to aristocracy and ruffled the liberal " notables " by restoring manhood suffrage; and it soon became evident to all that Napoleon was only awaiting a more favourable turn of events to dismiss the Chamber and rule as before.

So, once more, everything depended on the gamble of a rapid victory beyond the frontiers. On hearing of his return from Elba, the congress powers had patched up their quarrels, declared Napoleon an outlaw, and renewed their pledges to secure his overthrow. While they mobilized their resources, he prepared to strike a swift blow. Of a total mobilization of 700,000 men, he could put 120,000 immediately into the field and with these he arrived at the Belgian frontier on 14 June, before Wellington and Blücher, the allied commanders, were aware of his intentions. The allies had larger forces—a mixed army of 96,000 under Wellington and 124,000 Prussians under Blücher—but they were scattered over a wide front, and Napoleon counted on the element of speed and surprise to win him an initial victory. He almost succeeded; yet it is doubtful if it could have affected the final issue. Napoleon defeated Blücher's Prussians at Quatre Bras on the road to Brussels; but, owing to a confusion of orders—and, maybe, to a loss of skill by the supreme commander—the expected enveloping movement failed to materialize and Blücher's army survived to fight another day. Consequently, when Napoleon's force of 74,000 faced Wellington's 67,000 two days later at Waterloo, he was defeated both because he was outgeneralled by Wellington (whose skill he learned to appreciate too late) and because Blücher appeared on the scene with his Prussians at a crucial stage of the battle.

It was the gambler's last throw. With incredible optimism, Napoleon returned to Paris, still believing that he might impose his will on the Chamber, arouse the people to make fresh sacrifices and conjure up another army in the place of the old. The only hope—no doubt a slender one—would have been to make a direct appeal to the people: the old revolutionary Faubourg St. Antoine still acclaimed him and the army might have responded. But the Chamber, stirred by Fouché, refused to co-operate and, concerned for his dynasty, he chose to abdicate in favour of his son. The Chamber, however, preferred to set up a provisional government and, when Louis XVIII re-entered Paris escorted by the Prussians on 8 July, it submitted. This time, the allies were determined on sterner measures. By the second Treaty of Paris (20 November 1815), France's frontiers were pushed back to those of 1790 (hereby she lost the Sarre and Savoy), and she was subjected to a military occupation of three-to-five years and made to pay an indemnity of 700 million francs. Napoleon, meanwhile, had surrendered to the British at Rochefort, hoping to receive asylum in England, if not in the United States. But his captors were too scared by his past performance and the glamour of his name to allow themselves to be magnanimous. He was packed off to St. Helena, an island 5,000 miles away in mid-Atlantic, and he died there in 1821.

From his exile in St. Helena grew the Napoleonic Legend. It eclipsed the image of the upstart despot and the dreamer of world empire behind that of the champion of 1789, the victim of the spite of kings rather than of the anger of the peoples. The image, though not entirely false, was a one-sided one; and it owed its origin and its persistence as much to the actions of his conquerors as to the Emperor's own fertile imagination. For by insisting, in their settlement of Europe, on enveloping Napoleon and the Revolution in a single act of vengeance and oblivion, they inevitably presented them to the peoples as common objects of hatred or of veneration.

Chapter XV

PERSPECTIVES

The coalition powers, having adjourned to Vienna after the first Treaty of Paris (May 1814), had, within a year, completed their labours and, even before Napoleon's defeat at Waterloo, had agreed upon the principal lines of the territorial re-settlement of Europe. The main provisions of the Treaty of Vienna (June 1815) were to join the former Austrian Nether-lands (Belgium) and the Duchy of Luxembourg to Holland to form a single buffer state (the Kingdom of the Netherlands) against France in the north; to give Prussia the Rhineland and a part of Saxony; to create in Germany a Confederation of thirty-nine states under the presidency of Austria; to restore Lombardy to Austria and to give her Venetia (as Napoleon had done at Campo Formio) and the overlordship of Parma, Mod-ena and Tuscany : while the Spanish Bourbons were restored to Naples and Sicily and the Pope to Rome and his Papal states. Meanwhile, the Grand Duchy of Warsaw was entrusted to Russia; Norway was transferred from Denmark to Sweden and Finland from Sweden to Russia; and Great Britain enlarged her colonial possessions by gaining Cape Colony and Ceylon from Holland, Mauritius, Tobago and St. Lucia from France and Malta from the Knights of St. John. The settlement was supplemented by the second Treaty of Paris (November 1815) which, as we have seen, punished France for her part in the Hundred Days by pushing back her frontiers to those of 1790; in fact, she narrowly missed having to surrender Alsace and Lorraine as well.

In this settlement the objects of the peace-makers were evi-dent : to punish and restrain the aggressors; to reward the victors, often by satisfying or balancing claims voiced since 1780; to destroy Napoleon's Grand Empire and restore the old pre-revolutionary dynasties—the Hohenzollerns, Habsburgs, Bourbons and German secular princes—to their ancestral domains; and to re-establish something like the old balance of power. In all this, in spite of the posturings of Alexander and the loud denunciations of Napoleon's contempt for national rights, no consideration whatsoever was given to the national aspirations of the European peoples: the Poles were re-divided among Prussians, Austrians and Russians; the Norwegians were handed over to the Swedes, the Belgians to the Dutch, the Venetians to the Austrians; and Italy resumed its old chess-board pattern of foreign-dominated states. Not only that but, haunted by their fears of revolution, the powers pledged themselves to a twenty-year agreement termed the "Concert of Europe", whose purposes were both to settle disputes without recourse to war (in itself an admirable innovation) and to maintain by force their political settlement against all efforts by Bonapartist pretenders, liberals, democrats or nationalists to upset it. While all five major powers bound themselves, on Castlereagh's initiative, to this agreement, the absolute monarchs of Russia, Prussia, and Austria, prompted by the Tsar, wanted to go further. Eighteenth-century rulers, reared on the teachings of the Enlightenment, had eschewed the old crusading slogans and ideological battle-cries; but the fear of revolution and the revival of religion had changed all this and provided new opportunities; so the Tsar and his associates formed a Christian union or "Holy Alliance", whose object was to wage an ideological crusade against the rationalist and sceptical ideas of the Enlightenment and Revolution. Eventually, all European rulers signed this undertaking except an oddly-assorted trio: the Prince Regent of England (advised by Castlereagh that it was "a piece of sublime mysticism and nonsense"), Pope Pius VII and the infidel Sultan of Turkey.

Thus, ostensibly, the victor powers appeared determined to restore the old order and restrain, by violence if need be, the political forces released on Europe by the Revolution. This was not their whole intention and a great part of their settlement was sensible and just and not vindictive; but in so far as it deliberately attempted to obliterate the memory and the effects of the last quarter-century of history, their work was doomed to failure. This, as in all their previous efforts to hold back the Revolution, arose partly from their own dissensions. From the start, Castlereagh had made it clear that Britain, while pledged to maintain the frontiers agreed at Paris and Vienna and to prevent a Bonapartist restoration, would not support armed intervention in any state's internal affairs. His successor, Canning, carried the discrimination further; and, after 1822, Britain not only refused to suppress but actively encouraged national and liberal movements in Greece, Spain, Belgium and Latin America; even Russia was not averse to doing so where it suited her imperial interests as in Greece and Serbia; and, by 1830, the Congress System, with Metternich as its only consistent upholder, lay in ruins. But even more decisive in obstructing the restoration of old Europe than the divisions among the powers were the new forces released and the changes that had come about as the result of twenty-five years of war and revolution. These changes were by no means entirely confined to France and her satellites of the Napoleonic era: it is no exaggeration to say that every state in Europe west of Russia and Turkey and south of Scandinavia had already felt their impact; and it was a process of change that, far from being reversed or arrested by the victory of France's enemies, would continue to disrupt the old order and to shape the future.

Society itself had, in the first place, been thoroughly uprooted: the old aristocratic society described in our first chapter had either been disrupted or transformed beyond the point of no return. This was, of course, particularly true of France herself, where, from 1789 onwards, the old aristocracy had been stripped of its rights of jurisdiction, its monopoly of high office in army, Church and State, its feudal dues and services (eventually without compensation), its titles and privileges and its rights to dispose freely of common lands and to bequeath its estates undivided to elder sons. Part of the

aristocracy had lost much more : the *noblesse de robe* had for-
feited its old hereditary offices, and the properties of *émigré*
nobles as of all the dignitaries of the Church—bishops, canons,
abbots and cathedral chapters—had been confiscated and were
only exceptionally restored. Admittedly, the aristocracy had
not disappeared. The majority, though shorn of their titles
and privileges, had retained their lands even at the height of
the Jacobin Terror. Napoleon had used undistributed
"national properties" to endow his new Imperial nobility,
partly composed of the "notables" of the Revolution and
partly of old aristocrats reconciled to his new régime. These
titles and bequests were recognized by Louis XVIII in 1814;
and, since then, the Restoration monarchs, while respecting the
rights of the purchasers of Church and noble lands, had
created new titles and found new estates to reward their
followers returned from emigration. Thus the aristocracy had
been enlarged, owned substantial properties and, moreover,
wielded considerable power in the Chambers and the minis-
tries. But it was a new aristocracy, closely associated with
trade and finance and with the bourgeois holders of large
estates, and sharply separated from the old *noblesse* by the
land-settlement of 1789 and the operation of the Code Napoleon.

The status of the peasantry, too, had been radically changed :
of the former serfs, in the first place; though they, in France,
had been few in number. Far more important than the abolition of serfdom had been the removal from the soil of the
burden of tithe and seigneurial obligations; and some peasants (though a minority) had been able to benefit from the
sale of *biens nationaux*, particularly after the law of June
1793 had made it possible, for a short while, for villagers to
band together to bid for smaller lots. The poor and landless
peasants had also succeeded, by their resistance to enclosure
and the appropriation of common lands, in retaining some of
the collective rights and protection of the old rural community :
remnants of these survive to the present day. In short, the
transfer of land between classes had been on a relatively

modest scale; and it was the bourgeoisie rather than the peasantry that had reaped the main reward; the losers were the Church rather than the nobility and those least favoured were the poorest peasants.[1] Yet the peasantry as a whole had gained a new social status and a measure of economic security that account more than any other factor for the persistent conservatism of much of rural France during the nineteenth century.

A similar process, though more recent and less complete, had followed beyond France's own traditional borders. We have already seen that the assimilation of France's new laws and institutions, and the consequent social changes, were most rapid and most thorough in the territories that she directly absorbed within her Empire or that lay closest to her frontiers. Thus, the overthrow of feudal survivals and aristocratic privilege was almost as complete as in France herself in Belgium, the Rhenish provinces, parts of Switzerland, Savoy, Lombardy and Piedmont. In Venice, even before its absorption into Napoleon's Kingdom of Italy, the destruction of the old civic oligarchy had been the work of Austria—in much the same way as the first blows to aristocratic, patrician and ecclesiastical immunities in Tuscany and Lombardy had been dealt, even before 1789, by "enlightened" Austrian reformers like Joseph II and Leopold. But this, as in Naples (where the reforms of the Bourbon Charles III had also preceded the Revolution), had been only a beginning; and it was Napoleon's Civil Code and the energetic rule of his viceroys and vassals that finally uprooted feudal tenures (and serfdom, where it still persisted) throughout most of the Italian peninsula. Sicily, under the English, saw similar reforms, and even the reactionary Ferdinand I, though he withdrew the liberal constitution and restored the Holy Office at Palermo, slowed down but did not reverse this process. But, although the old immunities and privileges of the aristocracy were thus diminished or withdrawn, the effects on the peasantry were not generally the same as in France. For one thing, the re-distribution of pro-

[1] For a summary see N. Hampson, *A Social History of the French Revolution* (1963), pp. 251-4.

perty that followed the sequestration of Church estates was less widespread: though middle-class and even aristocratic purchasers prospered, little or nothing was done to help the poorer peasants to acquire land: they might even be the losers through the forfeiture of traditional common rights. In Lombardy and Piedmont, it is true, the abolition of feudal dues and tithe benefited all rural proprietors and made for a degree of general peasant prosperity; but, in the south—in Calabria, Naples and Sicily—the problem was one of large estates and an impoverished and landless peasantry rather than of feudal tenures, tithe and servile obligations; and for this the revolution exported from France after 1795 offered no solution. Consequently, the basic land-problems remained and, through the tribulations and shattered hopes of the Risorgimento, have survived to the present day.

Patrician and aristocratic society had been disrupted in Holland and parts of Germany in much the same way as in the north of Italy. King William of the United Netherlands was persuaded to retain the substance of French reforms in order to appease his new Belgian subjects; and Prussia's newly restored, or acquired, provinces in the west (the Rhineland, Berg and parts of Westphalia) similarly inherited the social results of the Civil Code and the abolition of feudal dues, tithe and serfdom. Metternich had higher hopes of the southern German states, now restored to Austria's sphere of influence; but, here again, such reforms as their rulers had carried out as Napoleon's allies were largely left untouched. Even traditionalist Prussia, in her eagerness to shake off the Napoleonic yoke, had found it expedient to borrow from the French—to abolish personal servitude and allow a minority of middle-class officers to hold commissions in her armies: though hardly a social revolution, it was nevertheless a beginning. The Habsburg Empire, though resolutely hostile to experiment, had inherited what remained of Joseph's land-reform in Austria, Bohemia and Hungary, and more of Napoleon's in northern Italy and Illyria; yet the hard core of labour service survived till 1848. In Sweden, Bernadotte, the sole usurper to be allowed to keep his throne, had helped to weaken aristocratic privilege by opening public office to men of humble birth. In Spain, the pro-French liberals of Madrid and Catalonia and the anti-French liberals of Cadiz had competed for middle-class favour by abolishing tithe and breaking up the *señorios*; but this was one of the few countries of Europe in which the clock had firmly been put back by the monarch restored in 1814. In Poland, alone of the countries occupied by Napoleon's armies, though serfdom had been abolished, the land-system and relations between landlords and peasants had otherwise been left untouched; and Alexander, for all his liberal talk, refrained from doing more.

It is evident that the uprooting of feudal survivals, the removal of impediments to trade and industry and the freeing of the soil from seigneurial dues, tolls and jurisdiction would, in themselves, promote and stimulate the growth of bourgeois society. In France, as we have seen, it was the middle classes (including the wealthier peasants) that reaped the greatest benefits from the Revolution; and Napoleon, though denying them political liberty and spreading the rewards less widely, did nothing to change this pattern. Essentially the same can be said of the French-occupied countries other than Poland: the sale of sequestrated properties, the sweeping away of old feudal enclaves and immunities, the opening of careers to men of talent, the creation of a new class of civil servants, the liberation of the internal market from restrictive tolls and guilds—not to mention the prohibition of workers' associations—all helped to promote the growth and raise the social status of the bourgeoisie. In such ways, too, particularly where labour had been released from the land, the ground would be cleared for the development of industrial capitalism. Yet it was not revolutionary or Napoleonic France but England, her most inveterate and persistent opponent, that reaped the lion's share of industrial and commercial expansion and emerged from the twenty-years contest with the balance tipped even more firmly in her favour than when it started. The war

imposed a heavy tax-burden on the English: between 1793
and 1815 they paid £52 million in subsidies to their allies
alone; and as we have noted, England's industrial expansion
was slowed down by the Continental System. But she found
new markets, gained new colonies and, once the war and the
painful post-war readjustments were over, she managed in a
remarkably short time to lord it over all comers as the unchallenged "workshop of the world". Meanwhile, civil war
and revolution had wrought havoc among France's manufactures; and, even under Napoleon, her production in many
fields stagnated, she lost further colonies to England, and the
commerce of her great Atlantic ports sank to a trickle of their
former volume. And this, although she was able, under Napoleon's Empire, to exploit the resources and dominate the
markets of a large part of the Continent; to compel her vassals
and allies to pay the greater share of the cost of her wars; and
to use the Continental System to promote her own national
advantage at the expense of her neighbours—even those she
had enclosed within her own frontiers. The explanation for
this phenomenon lies partly in the dislocation caused by
revolution (though not after 1799), in the greater social stability afforded to her peasants, and the blockade imposed by
Britain on her coast-line. But perhaps even more important:
England alone had, in the 1780's, been involved in an Industrial Revolution that not only "revolutionized" her technical
processes but had begun to transform her society by calling
whole new productive classes—industrial manufacturers and
factory workers—into being. For France, and her neighbours,
the clean sweep of revolutionary and Napoleonic reform had
cleared the way for a similar social transformation, and technical innovation had made progress, after 1800, in the textiles
of Lyons and Normandy and in the mines of Belgium and the
Sarre. But this was only a beginning; and, to create the new
industrial society, in which *sans-culottes* would give way to
proletarians and workshop masters to industrial manufacturers, it needed an industrial as well as a political revolution.
The Revolution of 1789 had hastened this process in some

ways while delaying it in others. The remedies would be found in the years of peace that followed—mainly after 1830.[2]

In another field of human activity, the impact of the Revolution had been more immediate and more direct. We have seen that, a mere three years after its outbreak, a new type of army had begun to appear in France—a national mass-army composed of both civilian volunteers (later conscripts) and regulars, staffed by mainly middle-class officers, equipped with the latest weapons and trained in the principles of mobile and offensive warfare. It took time, of course, via the *amalgame* and *levée en masse* of 1793 and Jourdan's conscription-law of 1798, for it to attain the perfection of Napoleon's Grand Army of 1805; and it needed the organizing skill of Carnot and Napoleon's practical genius in the field, both drawing on the teachings of Bourcet, Guibert and Du Teil, to complete the transformation. But it was only the new conditions created by the Revolution that made it possible to put their innovations to the best advantage; France's enemies recognized this and some were not slow to learn the lesson. England, whose social problems were very different from those of the Continent, confined herself to modernizing her weapons and putting larger armies into the field: in 1813-14, departing from previous practice, she had made provision for nearly 300,000 men in her regular army and 140,000 sailors in her fleets. Prussia, her complacency badly shaken by the fiasco of Jena, went a great deal further towards imitating the French. Hardenberg noted that the Revolution had given France " unexpected power " and urged that her example be followed by applying (though with caution) " democratic principles " to the reorganization of both army and State. The Junkers were not prepared to go as far as Hardenberg or Stein would have wished; but the army reforms that followed under Gneisenau and Scharnhorst abandoned many of Frederick's old principles by calling the nation to arms in the ranks of the Landwehr and Landsturm, giving commissions to men of non-noble

[2] For the operation of this " dual revolution ", see E. J. Hobsbawm. *The Age of Revolution*, pp. 168-81.

birth, disbanding their foreign mercenaries and dispensing with a large part of their cumbrous baggage-trains. Napoleon's southern German allies went further and created national armies directly modelled on the French. So the army of Frederick the Great, suited to an aristocratic society, ceased to be the pattern for all others to follow; and the army of Napoleon, the product of the Revolution with its appeal to the nation-at-arms, began to take its place.

Other institutions, too, had been profoundly altered. Wherever Napoleon's armies had passed, the French Civil Code had been implanted, the administration had been overhauled, pockets of ecclesiastical and seigneurial justice had been uprooted and a nationwide system of law courts and juries had been introduced. Cheap and efficient government had replaced or amalgamated the myriad of competing and overlapping authorities and jurisdictions surviving from a feudal past. Poland, for the first time in her chequered history, had known efficient administration and a national civil service; the lesson was never fully forgotten. In Germany, from 1803 onwards, Napoleon had abolished the outworn Holy Roman Empire, hacked through the tangled network of petty principalities and Free Cities and reduced their number from 396 to forty. The main casualties were the Free Cities, reduced to four, and the princely bishoprics, whose territories had been distributed wholesale among their secular neighbours: thus ancient Imperial cities and principalities like Liège, Treves, Mainz, Coblenz and Salzburg had been swallowed up by larger units of administration. Of the surviving German states, eighteen had eventually been grouped together in the Confederation of the Rhine and had begun to be welded into a common customs union. Here again, there was no going back to the pre-revolutionary past. Old dynasties were re-enthroned, liberal constitutions were withdrawn, and most of Europe's rulers were incapable of understanding the new forces that were at work; but there was remarkably little re-shuffling of the Grand Empire's geographical boundaries and many of its institutions were left substantially untouched. The Civil Code

remained in a score of European states from Belgium to
Naples and from the Rhineland to the new Kingdom of
Poland, carved out of Napoleon's Grand Duchy of Warsaw.
The Vienna confederates dissolved Napoleon's Confederation
of the Rhine and put in its place a larger Confederation of
thirty-nine German states. It was presided over by Austria and
was by no means intended to foster German national aims;
but, whatever the purposes of its authors, it created the frame-
work for a closer political union and soon began to devise a
single tariff area. Perhaps most significant of all: no serious
attempt was made to re-constitute the old Holy Roman Empire
or to restore the sovereignty of the ecclesiastical principalities.
And Catholic Austria showed no more readiness to return
Salzburg than Protestant Prussia to return Mainz, Treves and
Cologne to the temporal authority of the Church.

Relations between Church and State had, in fact, been profoundly and permanently affected by the years of revolution
and Napoleonic reform. Admittedly, the settlement of 1815
had been attended by a notable religious revival: the Pope
was re-enthroned at St. Peter's amidst general jubilation; the
Index, the Inquisition and the Jesuit Order were reinstated;
ultramontanism was all the rage; the Catholic Church recovered its control over education and, in Spain, Bavaria,
Sardinia and Naples, most of its old authority; and, as we have
seen, rulers of all denominations professed to base their policies on Christian principles. But a great deal of this was short-
lived, as the temporal power of the Church had been undermined and the rule of episcopal princes had become almost a
thing of the past. In France, Charles X might, at his coronation, be anointed with oil in the tradition of his forefathers;
but the Church had been stripped of its estates and, in spite of
a temporary assumption of authority, was henceforth to be
shackled more firmly to the secular power than ever under
Francis I or Louis XIV. Elsewhere, Church estates continued
to be sold and monasteries to be dissolved, and Catholic rulers
were often not averse to using the greater freedom in their
dealings with the Papacy that Napoleon's Concordat had

suggested to them as an example to be followed. The Papal authority was inevitably weakened in western Europe by the addition of large numbers of Catholic subjects to the Protestant rulers of Prussia and the Netherlands. Moreover, of all the princely prelates of the pre-revolutionary days, the Pope alone retained his temporal dominion; and, fifty-five years later, he, too, would have to surrender it as part of the price to be paid for Italian unification under the Catholic King of Sardinia.

Nationalism, too, survived as a legacy of the Revolution. Napoleon, though he suppressed and despised the national spirit, had unwittingly fostered it. Later, at St. Helena, he claimed credit for having deliberately sought to unite the 15 million Italians and 30 million Germans, like the 30 million French and 15 million Spaniards, "each into one nation". The union with France of Piedmont, Parma, Tuscany and Rome, he told Las Cases, were "only temporary measures, intended to guarantee the national education of the Italians". It was a useful propaganda-point, as by this time it had become evident to all that the victor powers, having loudly denounced Napoleon's own imperialist methods, were showing no concern whatsoever for the national aspirations of the peoples they had liberated. In reality, as we have seen, Napoleon himself crushed national movements in Spain and Italy; and he told Louis in 1810 that one of his major ambitions in Germany was to "side-track (*dépayser*) the German spirit". Yet, quite apart from the revolutionary principles that the French armies carried around Europe, his administrative reforms, the Civil Code, the destruction of feudalism, the rationalization of government, the institution of uniform weights and measures and removal of internal customs could hardly fail to have something of the same unifying effects on the occupied countries as the reforms of the Constituent Assembly and Convention had had on France herself. Not only this; but he had deliberately exploited the national spirit in his dealings with Poles and Italians: the Kingdom of Italy, for example, though by no means satisfying the wider aspirations of Italian patriots, had been created partly with the intention of raising their hopes for the future. Inevitably, the dashing of these hopes had alienated many, whose sympathy for the French had turned, in the course of time, to resentment and hostility and even to the organization of anti-French secret societies. In Germany, this national resentment, while it never burst into open rebellion, had become more sharply focused by identifying itself with the national policies of Prussia or Austria. 1815, of course, instead of finding solutions (except in Spain), exacerbated the problem and drove the German, Italian and Polish nationalists—not to mention the Belgian, the Greek and the Latin American—to seek more desperate remedies in the coming decades.

Another result of the 1815 settlement was to bring nationalism and liberalism together. Though both stemmed, in large measure, from the years of revolution, their partnership had not generally been close in Napoleon's Europe. Patriots, if we include nationalism of the Spanish as well as the German and Italian kind, were inclined, after 1808, to be hostile rather than sympathetic to the French. Liberals, on the other hand, being composed of middle-class "notables" rather than of petty craftsmen, nobles or peasants, were more often the allies than the opponents of France. In France herself, liberal political ideals had been proclaimed and fostered by Constituents, Girondins and Thermidorians, whereas, for differing reasons, they had been discouraged or proscribed by the Jacobin Convention and Napoleon. But, though muzzled or held in check in France under the Consulate and Empire, in Europe liberals had naturally gravitated towards the French, who brought reforms, rather than towards their own rulers who opposed or obstructed them. There were, of course, notable exceptions: the Italian Jacobins who, after 1805, formed secret societies to oppose the French, included liberals as well as revolutionary democrats in their number; in Spain, anti-French liberals predominated in the Central Junta at Cadiz and in the Cortes that adopted the Constitution of 1812; and, in Germany, there were liberals among the patriots who looked to Prussia both to lead a German crusade against Napoleon and to reform her own feudal institutions. Yet it is probably true to say that, in Italy and Germany, no less than in Holland, Switzerland and Poland, liberals generally welcomed Napoleon's reforms and tended to pin their hopes on the survival rather than on the collapse of his Empire. The 1815 settlement, by its very nature, tended to end this divorce between patriots and liberals. In Spain, peasant nationalism died a natural death with the ending of the French occupation and the restoration of Church and dynasty; and, in 1820, the liberals of both the Napoleonic and the anti-Napoleonic camp, reunited by the departure of the French, joined forces to re-proclaim the Constitution of 1812. In Germany and Italy, the Congress settlement offered no greater hopes for liberals than it did for nationalists; both suffered equally from the policies of the three eastern and central powers. Austria, in particular, remained until 1848 the target of their common animosities; for Austria now occupied the northern Italian states, dominated the German Confederation, and invoked more persistently than any of her partners the provisions of the European "Concert" in order to intervene against German, Italian, Spanish and Belgian patriots and liberals.

Democracy, another product of the Revolution, had a somewhat different history. Though inherent in Rousseau's concept of the "sovereignty of the people", it was not, like liberalism, an inevitable outcome of the victory of the Third Estate. Like their fellows in other countries, the French middle classes of 1789 had wished to end royal "despotism", destroy aristocratic privilege and to extend the franchise to all men of property; but, although proclaiming the common Rights of Man, they had no intention of sharing political authority with the "lower orders" or "Fourth Estate". This partnership and the equal voting rights that went with it had, as we have seen, come about through circumstances outside their own control; for it had proved impossible to deal adequately with privilege and despotism without the active support of the common people of town and countryside. Yet this democratic stage of the Revolution had been short-lived: the Constitution of 1793, after being put into cold storage by the Jacobins, was repealed by their successors; male adult suffrage was withdrawn and the popular movement destroyed. After that, there was no further suggestion, either under the Directory or Napoleon, of restoring democracy in France; and, in Europe, although there were popular-democratic movements in Italy and at Geneva, the pattern imposed was generally the same as in France. Yet democracy, though receiving such little official encouragement, took root: in the first instance, in a country that, far from being drawn into France's political orbit, became her most implacable opponent. The English radical movement, enriched by the lessons learned from revolutionary France, had been temporarily disorganized by persecution after 1792; but it revived around 1807 and contributed its democratic ideas to the reform movements of the nineteenth century. Here again, the Industrial Revolution played an important part; as it created in England, earlier than elsewhere, a politically literate working class, which eagerly read the writings of the democrats and assured the radical movement of a mass basis in the factories and mines. In other countries, after its defeat in 1795, democracy was slower to revive. To the Congress powers it appeared an even greater menace than nationalism and liberalism, and it was savagely suppressed as long as the Congress System lasted. It reappeared in France in the Revolution of 1830; and its later development there, as in North America and other European countries, was a result as much of industrialization as of the spread of revolutionary ideas.

Apart from these more tangible bequests, the Revolution also left its myths and traditions to the century that followed. In the first place, the tradition of popular revolution itself: the violence, heroism and passionate idealism of the " days " of 1789, 1792 and 1793 were re-enacted by similar crowds, though stirred by new objectives, throughout Europe in 1848 and, in France, in 1871. The Spanish liberals of 1820 and 1836, like the French, German, Belgian, Swiss and Italian liberals of 1847-8, drew their inspiration from the Declaration of the Rights of Man and the Constitution of 1791. Even in England, it seemed natural to attribute the great popular ferment of 1830 and 1831 to the contagious influence of the French. Many of the popular "tribunes" of the later revolutions—Lamartine, Ledru-Rollin, Kossuth, Mazzini, Garibaldi—found ready-to-hand models in the Gironde and the Mountain of 1792; and, everywhere, insurgent nationalism—in Greece, Belgium, Poland, Germany and Italy—inherited, with suitable adaptations, the tricolour of revolutionary France. The egalitarian Republic of the Year II left its own enduring and nostalgic memories: it was proclaimed at city halls by radicals and socialists in Paris, Berlin and Vienna in 1848 and died with the Paris Commune in 1871. The tradition of the nation-at-arms, of revolutionary defence and total war—another legacy of Jacobin France—has had a longer history: invoked in succession by Gambetta, Clemenceau and De Gaulle, it has served as a pattern for belligerents of both sides in two world wars. Babeuf and the Equals, though singularly ineffective in the France of 1796, found emulators in the Italian Carbonari, the Russian Decembrists and the French Blanquists. For socialists "Babouvism" had a more particular message: Babeuf's plan for the communal sharing and ownership of property was, in the 1830's, handed down to the French workingmen's clubs by his disciple, Buonarotti, was translated into English by the Chartist Bronterre O'Brien, and has since been closely studied by Socialist leaders from Marx to Jaurès and Lenin. Bonapartism, on the other hand, has tended to separate itself from the main-stream of the revolutionary tradition and has offered its own remedies to those anxious to temper liberty with "order" and end the "anarchy" of warring parties by grafting authoritarian forms on to parliamentary institutions. It has been a peculiarly French phenomenon, and the cult of the *coup d'état*, the plebiscite, the Man of Destiny and *la grande nation* has played no small part in France's post-revolutionary history—from the revival of the Empire by Louis Napoleon to General Boulanger and the Algerian *coup* of May 1958.

And as the Revolution had its counter-revolution, so the revolutionary tradition has also bred its antithesis. All over Europe, Burke's *Reflections* evoked a response among those whom the Revolution had dispossessed or threatened to dispossess, or who clung to the traditional values as a bulwark against the pervasive contagion of the Rights of Man. Burke was followed by Gentz in Germany and Austria and by Bonald and Joseph de Maistre in France; and so an ideology of counter-revolution grew up, dedicated to the restoration of Throne and Altar and hostile to the whole trend of European thought from Newton and Montesquieu to Voltaire and Rousseau. Counter-revolution appeared to triumph all along the line in 1815 and the stage seemed set for the return to the old boundaries, dynasties, institutions, Church and ways of life. But, as we have seen, Europe had, in the intervening years, changed beyond the possibility of restoration; and even Metternich's system, buttressed by the pledges rather than the performance of the other Congress powers, was impotent to hold back the revolutionary current that broke out again in full flood in 1848. But the defeat of 1848 drove a new wedge between nationalism and liberalism; ultramontanism revived, as in 1815, and in turn bred anti-clericalism and disputes over education that have persisted to the present day. 1871 deepened the conflict in France and provoked a new conservatism, often divorced from religion and fighting the revolutionary tradition on purely secular ground: thus Taine's bitter condemnation of the Revolution of 1789 surpassed Burke's in venom by feeding on the fears engendered by the Paris Commune.

In France, this battle has persisted and one may, therefore, be too readily inclined to trace the whole history of nineteenth-century Europe as a projection of the Revolution. Yet this would be a gross distortion. In Victorian England and Imperial Russia the Revolution had comparatively little influence. In western, central and southern Europe that influence was substantial and continuous up to 1848: until then, revolutionary France, both past and present, served as a powerful international force that attracted the loyalties and inspired the thoughts and activities of patriots, liberals, radicals and socialists in many countries. But after the defeats and disillusionment of 1849 this was no longer so. Though laws and institutions deriving from the French remained and traditions lingered on, new forces had arisen to shape the destinies of nations and lead them along other paths. The older generation of German and Italian liberals and patriots strove hard to emulate the French, but the unified Germany and Italy that emerged in 1870 were not moulded in their image but in that of Bismarck and Cavour, who owed comparatively little to the ideas of 1789. Industrialism in Europe, proceeding along the lines traced by the Industrial Revolution in England, proved in the long run as potent a force for social change as the political revolution originating in France. It was from the former rather than the latter revolution that there emerged an industrial working class and the new dominant social conflict between capital and labour; and modern socialism, as formulated by Marx, derived as much from England's industrial experience as from the teachings of the *philosophes* and the French revolutionaries. Again, Europe's overseas expansion and its eventual domination of the whole non-American world were the outcome of the explosive forces developing within the new industrial society. The challenging principles of 1789 and 1793 were certainly not lost sight of and were, in fact, thereby exported to peoples who had been untouched by the earlier ferments in " revolutionary Europe ". Yet, by and large, they have tended to lose their relevance or to become absorbed or to be submerged by the ideologies of later revolutions. The battle for the Rights of Man went on, but it has been fought out under banners and with slogans very different from those of 1789.

MAPS

PRE-REVOLUTIONARY FRANCE

Boundary of France
Boundaries of provinces

50   0   50   100   150
MILES

CORSICA
on same scale

CHARLES BREEN.

EUROPE in 1792

EUROPE in 1812

||||| Empire of the French.

≡ States under Napoleonic control.

⠿ States allied with Napoleon.

☐ Independent States.

North Sea

Ireland

GREAT BRITAIN

London

EMPIRE OF THE FRENCH

Paris

Atlantic Ocean

PORTUGAL

Lisbon

Madrid

SPAIN

Mediterranean

THE FRENCH EMPIRE in 1812

Boundary of Empire   Boundaries of Departments

CHARLES GREEN.

EUROPE in 1815

⁓⁓⁓⁓⁓ Boundary of the
Germanic Confederation

North
Sea

Ireland

GREAT

BRITAIN

London

NETHERL

Paris

FRANCE

Atlantic Ocean

PORTUGAL

Madrid

Lisbon

SPAIN

Medite

M

CHARLES GREEN.

PARIS in 1789

1. Madeleine
2. Champs Elysées
3. Tuileries Gardens
4. National Assembly
5. Jacobin Club
6. Palais Royal
7. Corn Market
8. Louvre
9. Châtelet
10. Temple
11. Hôtel de Ville
12. Place de Grève
13. Palais de Justice
14. Pont Neuf
15. Pont Royal
16. Cordeliers Club
17. Ile de la Cité
18. Notre Dame
19. Ile St. Louis
20. Bastille
21. Salpêtrière
22. Gobelins
23. Ste. Geneviève
24. Luxembourg
25. Invalides
26. Ecole Militaire
27. Champ de Mars

FURTHER READING

FURTHER READING

In the vast bibliography of Revolutionary and Napoleonic Europe the student is advised to tread warily and to seek constant guidance. Here, to save him linguistic embarrassment, only English and French titles are cited. A useful bibliographical guide to the eighteenth century in Europe is J. S. Bromley and A. Goodwin (eds.), *A Select List of Works on Europe and Europe Overseas 1715-1815* (1956). Detailed *Bibliographies* will also be found in the following general series: W. L. Langer (ed.), *The Rise of Modern Europe*: L. Gershoy, *From Despotism to Revolution, 1763-89* (1944); C. Crane Brinton, *A Decade of Revolution, 1789-99* (1934); and G. Bruun, *Europe and the French Imperium, 1799-1814* (1938). In the *Clio* series: E. Preclin and V. L. Tapié, *Le XVIIIe siècle* (2 vols. 1952); and L. Villat, *La Révolution et l'Empire* (2 vols. 1936). In the *Peuples et Civilisations* series (L. Halphen and P. Sagnac eds.): P. Sagnac, *La Fin de l'ancien régime et la Révolution américaine, 1763-89* (3rd ed., 1952); G. Lefebvre, *La Révolution française* (3rd. ed., 1951; Eng. trans. under title *The French Revolution from its Origins to 1793* (1962)); G. Lefebvre, *Napoléon* (4th ed., 1953).

In addition to the above, the following *general histories* may be recommended: W. F. Reddaway, *A History of Europe from 1715 to 1814* (4th ed., 1951); L. R. Gottschalk, *The Era of the French Revolution, 1715-1815* (1929); R. Mousnier and C.-E. Labrousse, *Le XVIIIe siècle: l'époque des "lumières" (1715-1815)* (3rd ed., 1959). E. J. Hobsbawm, *The Age of Revolution: Europe 1789-1848* (1962) is original and suggestive. Occasional recourse should also be had to vols. *VI-X* of the older *Cambridge Modern History* (1900-1910) and to appropriate chapters in *The New Cambridge Modern History* (1957—), vols. VII-IX (of which only vol. VII has appeared to date).

Wars and diplomacy may be studied in A. Sorel, *L'Europe et la Révolution française* (8 vols., 1895-1904); A. Fugier, *La Révolution française et l'empire napoléonien* (1954); J. H. Rose, *The Revolutionary and Napoleonic Era* (7th ed., 1935); and L. Gershoy, *The French Revolution and Napoleon* (1933). For *warfare*, see A. Vagts, *A History of Militarism* (new ed., 1959); C. Falls, *The Art of War* (1961); R. A. Preston, S. F. Wise and H. O. Werner, *Men in Arms* (1956); and B. H. Liddell Hart, *The Ghost of Napoleon* (1933). For *international law*, see J. L. Brierley, *The Law of Nations* (5th ed., 1955); and R. Pares, *Colonial Blockade and Neutral Rights, 1739-1763* (1934). For *constitutions*, see J. A. Hawgood, *Modern Constitu-*

tions since 1787 (1939); and M. Beloff, *The Age of Absolutism, 1660-1815* (1954). *Economic development* may be studied in A. Birnie, *An Economic History of Europe, 1760-1939* (1962). For *science and technology*, in addition to Mousnier and Labrousse (already cited), see A. Wolf, *A History of Science, Technology and Philosophy in the Eighteenth Century* (rev. ed., 1952); D. McKie, *Antoine Lavoisier* (1952); and A. P. Usher, *A History of Scientific Inventions* (1929).

EUROPE ON THE EVE OF THE FRENCH REVOLUTION

An excellent introduction is provided by the opening chapters of M. S. Anderson, *Europe in the Eighteenth Century, 1713-1783* (1961). A stimulating and provocative account of political movements and ideas is given by R. R. Palmer, *The Age of the Democratic Revolution. A Political History of Europe and America 1760-1800*, vol. I, *The Challenge* (1959). Economics, science, institutions and warfare may be studied in works cited above. For *aristocratic society*, see A. Goodwin, *The European Nobility in the Eighteenth Century* (1953). In the extensive and well-ploughed field of *political ideas and Enlightenment*, the following select few titles may be recommended: P. Hazard, *European Thought in the Eighteenth Century: from Montesquieu to Lessing* (1954); C. L. Becker, *The Heavenly City of the Eighteenth Century Philosophers* (1932); Kingsley Martin, *French Liberal Thought in the Eighteenth Century* (2nd ed., 1954); A. Cobban, *In Search of Humanity* (1960) and *Rousseau in the Modern State* (1934); and P. Gay, *Voltaire's Politics: the Poet as Realist* (1959). For the influence of *America on European thought*, see H. N. Fairchild, *The Noble Savage* (1928); M. Kraus, " America and the Utopian Ideal in the Eighteenth Century ", *Mississippi Valley Historical Review*, vol. XXII (1936); and L. Gottschalk, " The Place of the American Revolution in the Causal Pattern of the French Revolution," *Publications of the American Friends of Lafayette*, No. 2 (1948). For *enlightened despotism*, see F. Hartung, *Enlightened Despotism* (Hist. Assoc. pamphlet, 1957).

The problems of individual European countries up to 1789 may be studied in the following brief selection:

FRANCE: Elinor G. Barber, *The Bourgeoisie in Eighteenth-Century France* (1955); D. Dakin, *Turgot and the Ancien Régime in France* (1939); F. L. Ford, *Robe and Sword. The Regrouping of the French Aristocracy after Louis XV* (1953); F. Funck-Brentano, *The Old Régime in France* (1929); C.-E. Labrousse, *Esquisse du mouvement des prix et des revenus en France au XVIIIe siècle* (2 vols., 1933), and *La Crise de l'économie française à la fin de l'ancien régime et au début de la Révolution* (1944); E. Levasseur, *Histoire des classes ouvrières et de l'industrie en France avant 1789* (2nd ed., 2 vols., 1901); J. Lough, *An Introduction to Eighteenth-Century France* (1960); D. Mornet, *Les Origines intellectuelles de la Révolution française, 1715-1787* (1933); R. R. Palmer, *Catholics and Unbelievers in Eighteenth-Century France* (1939); H. Sée, *La France économique et sociale au XVIIIe siècle* (4th ed., 1946. Eng. trans. under title *Economic and Social Conditions in France in the Eighteenth Century*, 1927); and, above all else, read: A. de Tocqueville, *The Old Régime and the French Revolution* (Anchor Books, 1955); and Arthur Young's *Travels in France, 1787-1789* (ed. C. Maxwell, 1929).

ENGLAND: T. S. Ashton, *An Economic History of England: the Eighteenth Century* (1955); H. Butterfield, *George III, Lord North and the People* (1949); M. D. George, *England in Transition* (1953); L. S. Namier, *The Structure of Politics at the Accession of George III* (2nd ed., 1957); R. Pares, *King George III and the Politicians* (1953); J. Steven Watson, *The Reign of George III, 1760-1815* (1960); C. R. Ritcheson, *British Politics and the American Revolution* (1954); S. Maccoby, *English Radicalism, 1762-1785* (1955).

BELGIUM (AUSTRIAN NETHERLANDS): T. K. Gorman, *America and Belgium: a Study of the Influence of the United States on the Belgian Revolution of 1789-90* (1925); P. Harsin, *La Révolution liégeoise de 1789* (1953); Suzanne Tassier, *Les Démocrates belges de 1789: essai sur le Vonckisme et la révolution brabançonne* (1930).

HABSBURG EMPIRE (other than Belgium): F. Fejtö, *Un Habsbourg révolutionnaire, Joseph II* (1953); K. J. Kerner, *Bohemia in the Eighteenth Century* (1932); H. Marczali, *Hungary in the Eighteenth Century* (1910); P. F. Sugar, "The Influence of the Enlightenment and the French Revolution in Eighteenth-Century Hungary", *Journal of Central European Affairs*, XVII (1958), 331-55; E. Wangermann, *From Joseph II to the Jacobin Trials* (1959).

SPAIN: R. Herr, *The Eighteenth-Century Revolution in Spain* (1958).

ITALY: L. Salvatorelli, *A Concise History of Italy* (1940).

GERMANY AND PRUSSIA: W. H. Bruford, *Germany in the Eighteenth Century* (1939); W. L. Dorn, "The Prussian Bureaucracy in the Eighteenth Century", *Political Science Quarterly*, 1931-2; P. Gaxotte, *Frederick II* (1941); H. Rosenberg, *Bureaucracy, Aristocracy and Autocracy: The Prussian Experience, 1660-1815* (1958).

SWEDEN: R. N. Bain, "The Hats and Caps and Gustavus III", *Cambridge Modern History*, vol. VI (1900); R. Svanström and C. V. Palmstierna, *A Short History of Sweden* (1934).

UNITED PROVINCES: A. Cobban, *Ambassadors and Secret Agents: The Diplomacy of the First Earl of Malmesbury at The Hague* (1954); F. Edler, *The Dutch Republic and the American Revolution* (1911); B. H. M. Vlekke, *The Evolution of the Dutch Nation* (1954).

SWITZERLAND: E. Chapuisat, *La Prise d'armes de 1782 à Genève* (1932).

POLAND: R. N. Bain, *The Last King of Poland and his Contemporaries* (1909); B. Lesnodarski, "Les facteurs intellectuels de la formation de la société polonaise moderne au siècle des lumières", in *La Pologne au Xe congrès international des sciences historiques à Rome* (Warsaw, 1955), pp. 167-261; R. H. Lord, *The Second Partition of Poland* (1915).

RUSSIA: P. Putman (ed.), *Seven Britons in Imperial Russia, 1698-1812* (1952); B. H. Sumner, *Peter the Great and the Emergence of Russia* (1950); G. Scott Thomson, *Catherine the Great and the Expansion of Russia* (1947); R. Portal, *L'Oural au XVIIIe siècle* (1951.)

OTTOMAN EMPIRE: H. A. R. Gibb and R. Bowen, *Islamic Society and the West*, vol. I, *Islamic Society in the Eighteenth Century* (1950-57).

FRENCH REVOLUTION:

The printed source-material on the Revolution is enormous; here only a small part will be indicated. Young's *Travels in France* have already been mentioned. There are useful extracts from revolutionary newspapers in G. Walter (ed.), *La Révolution française vue par ses journaux* (1948). Speeches may be studied in H. Morse Stephens (ed.), *The Principal Speeches of the Statesmen and Orators of the French Revolution, 1789-1795* (2 vols., 1892). Four volumes of the definitive edition of Robespierre's speeches, writings and correspondence, ed. by M. Bouloiseau, G. Lefebvre, and A. Souboul, are now completed. The most comprehensive collection of documents in English translation is that by J. H. Stewart, *A Documentary Survey of The French Revolution* (1951). Of particular interest to the student of the Paris sections and popular movement is that by W. Markov and A. Soboul (eds.), *Die Sansculotten von Paris: Dokumente zur Geschichte der Volksbewegung 1793-1795* (1957)—with texts in both French and German. J. M. Thompson's *French Revolution Documents 1789-94* (in French) has a useful selection of laws and decrees; and L. G. Wickham Legg's more old-fashioned *Select Documents Illustrative of the History of the French Revolution. The Constituent Assembly* (2 vols., 1905) pays some attention to the revolutionary press.

Successive generations of Frenchmen have had their say on the causes, history and meaning of the French Revolution: the views of the different schools have been summarized and discussed by P. Geyl in *Encounters in History* (1963), pp. 115-87; and in two Historical Association pamphlets—one by A. Cobban, *Historians and the Causes of the French Revolution* (rev. ed., 1958); the other by G. Rudé, *Interpretations of the French Revolution* (1961). Of the older histories, those by Thiers (1823-7), Mignet (1824), Carlyle (1837), L. Blanc (1847-62), Taine (1876)—and even those of Michelet (1847-53), Acton (1895-99), Aulard (1901) and Jaurès (1901)—though of great literary and historiographical interest—may be ignored by the general student; but Tocqueville's comparative study of the Ancien Régime and the Revolution (1856), already cited, has a greater modern relevance and is indispensable reading. Of later French historians, the best general studies are by A. Mathiez, *La Révolution française* (3 vols., 1922-7; Eng. trans., 1927); G. Lefebvre, *La Révolution française* (1951; Eng. trans. *up to 1793 only*, 1962) (cited above); and A. Soboul, *Précis d'Histoire de La Révolution française* (1962). A more limited, pseudo-Marxist, interpretation is by D. Guérin, *La Lutte de classes sous la première République: bourgeois et " bras nus "* (1793-1797) (2 vols. 1946). Of other general accounts, in addition to those by Brinton and Gottschalk (already cited), the following are recommended: G. Salvemini, *The French Revolution 1788-1792* (Eng. trans., 1953); J. M. Thompson, *The French Revolution* (1943); A. Goodwin, *The French Revolution, 1787-1794* (1953); and Norman Hampson, *A Social History of the French Revolution* (1963).

Concerning the internal history of the main stages of the Revolution, the twilight-zone linking the " aristocratic revolt " of 1787-88 with the revolutionary outbreak of 1789 is admirably treated in its political aspects by J. Egret, *La Pré-Révolution française 1787-1788* (1962). The " aristocratic revolt " is also treated by H. Carré in *La Fin des parlements, 1788-1790* (1912); by P. Renouvin in *Les Assemblées provinciales de 1787* (1921); and by A. Goodwin in " Calonne, the Assembly of Notables and the Origins of the Révolte Nobiliaire ", *English Historical Review* (1946), 203-34, 329-77; but its social aspects have still been largely neglected. The best work on the outbreak of the Revolution is G. Lefebvre's *Quatre-Vingt-Neuf* (1939; Eng. trans. *The Coming of the French Revolution*, 1947). The Introduction to Labrousse's *Crise de l'économie française* (cited above) should also be read; as should G. Lefebvre's masterly study of the peasant-movements of 1789, *La Grande peur de 1789* (1932). Some value may also be found in F. Braesch's tendentious *1789: l'année cruciale* (1941).

The work of the Constituent Assembly is well summarized in P. Sagnac, *La Législation civile de la Révolution française* (1898); and the laws and decrees of the whole revolutionary period are presented in L. Cahen and R. Guyot, *L'Œuvre législative de la Révolution* (1913). The ideas underlying the legislation of 1789-91 are discussed by E. Thompson in *Popular Sovereignty and the French Constituent Assembly 1789-1791* (1952); and political movements of the period are treated by A. Mathiez in *Les Grandes journées de la Constituante 1789-91* (1913) and *Le Club des Cordeliers pendant la crise de Varennes et le massacre du Champ de Mars* (1910). The events of 1792 are related by Mathiez in *Le Dix aout* (1931) and by P. Carron in *Les Massacres de septembre* (1935). For the struggle between Gironde and Mountain in 1792-3, see the contrasting views of Mathiez in *Girondins et Montagnards* (1930) and M. J. Sydenham in *The Girondins* (1961). For the work and composition of the great Committee of Public Safety, see R. R. Palmer, *Twelve who Ruled* (1941); and, for an important part of its duties in 1794, A. Ording, *Le Bureau de police du Comité de Salut public* (Oslo, 1935). The most up-to-date and comprehensive treatment of the Year II, and particularly of the relations between the Revolutionary Government and the popular movement and Paris sections, is A. Soboul's *Les Sans-Culottes parisiens en l'an II: mouvement populaire et gouvernement révolutionnaire, 2 juin 1793—9 Thermidor an II* (1958). The role of the Paris Commune in the events leading up to Thermidor is discussed by P. Sainte-Claire Deville in *La Commune de l'an II* (1946). For the operation of the Terror in the provinces, see above all R. C. Cobb, *Les Armées révolutionnaires: instrument de la Terreur dans les départements avril 1793—floréal an II* (2 vols., 1961-3).

The post-Thermidorian period has been far more sketchily treated by historians. For the year following Robespierre's fall, students are referred to A. Mathiez, *La Réaction thermidorienne* (1929); G. Lefebvre, *Les Thermidoriens* (4th ed., 1960); and to K. D. Tönnesson's study of the popular movements of Germinal-Prairial, *La Défaite des sans-culottes: mouvement populaire et réaction bourgeoise en l'an III* (Oslo, 1959). For the Directory, see G. Lefebvre, *Le Directoire* (1946); A. Vandal, *L'Avènement de Bonaparte* (2 vols., 1907-8); and D. Thomson, *The Babeuf Plot: the Making of a Republican Legend* (1947).

Coming to special aspects. Institutions (other than military) may be studied in J. Godechot, *Histoire des institutions de la France sous la Révolution et l'Empire* (1951); reference should also be made to

M. Marion's *Dictionnaire des institutions de la France aux XVIIe et XVIIIe siècles* (1923). Godechot, again, has made the first comprehensive study of the *counter-revolution* in *La Contre-Révolution: doctrine et action 1789-1804* (1961). Financial aspects are treated in J. Bouchary, *Les Manieurs d'argent à Paris à la fin du XVIIIe siècle* (3 vols., 1939-43); M. Marion, *Histoire financière de la France depuis 1715* (1914); S. G. Harris, *The Assignats* (1930); R. G. Hawtrey, "The Collapse of the French Assignats", in *Econ. Journal*, XXVII (1918), 300-14; and M. Marion, *La Vente des biens nationaux* (1908). Relations between Church and State are treated by J. McManners in *French Ecclesiastical Society under the Ancien Régime: a Study of Angers in the Eighteenth Century* (1960); A. Latreille in *L'Eglise catholique et la Révolution française* (2 vols., 1946-50); J. Leflon in *La Crise révolutionnaire, 1789-1846* (1949); A. Aulard in *Christianity and the French Revolution* (Eng. trans., 1927); and in the following works by A. Mathiez: *Les Origines des cultes révolutionnaires 1789-1792* (1910); *Rome et le clergé français sous la Constituante* (1907); *La Révolution et l'Eglise* (1910); *La Question religieuse sous la Révolution* (1930); and *La Théophilanthropie et le culte décadaire, 1796-1802* (1904).

The social study of the Revolution was launched by Jaurès in his *Histoire socialiste de la Révolution française* (4 vols., 1901); but it made a slow start and is still, relatively speaking, in its infancy. The great pioneering works, since Jaurès, have been G. Lefebvre's great work on the peasant-question, *Les Paysans du Nord pendant la Révolution française* (2 vols. 1924; new ed., 1957), his *Questions agraires au temps de la Terreur* (1932); and Mathiez' *La Vie chère et le mouvement social sous la Terreur* (1927). For other essays in social analysis—in addition to those by Soboul, Cobb and Tönnesson, already cited—see C. Crane Brinton's *The Jacobins* (1930); D. Greer's *The Incidence of the Terror during the French Revolution* (1935) and *The Incidence of the Emigration during the French Revolution* (1951); N. Hampson's *La Marine de l'an II* (1959); and G. Rudé's *The Crowd in the French Revolution* (1959). Other social studies, on agriculture, food supplies, sales of *biens nationaux*, relations between classes, population, operation of the Maximum laws etc., have appeared in the *Annales historiques de la Révolution française* and in local journals. See also A. Cobban, *The Social Interpretation of the French Revolution* (1964).

Among a mass of biographical literature, the following may be recommended: J. M. Thompson, *Robespierre* (2 vols., 1939); M. Reinhard, *Carnot* (2 vols., 1950-2); L. R. Gottschalk, *Marat* (1927); O. J. G. Welch, *Mirabeau* (1951); L. Madelin, *Fouché* (2 vols., 1900); G. Walter, *Hébert* (1939); R. Barthou, *Danton* (1932); and L. Gershoy, *Bertrand Barère, a Reluctant Terrorist* (1962).

REVOLUTIONARY EUROPE

For the foreign policy of Revolutionary France and its international relations, see in addition to the general histories and works by Sorel, Fugier, Rose and Gershoy (cited on p. 315 above), P. Rain, *La Diplomatie française de Mirabeau à Bonaparte* (1950); and R. Guyot, *Le Directoire et la paix de l'Europe* (1911). For the outbreak of war in 1792, see J. H. Clapham, *The Causes of the War of 1792* (1899); and, more particularly, G. Michon, *Robespierre et la guerre révolutionnaire, 1791-1792* (1937). On foreign agents in Paris, see A. Mathiez, *La Révolution et les étrangers* (1918). For the French Army, see Lefebvre's *Napoléon* and works by Vagts, Liddell Hart, etc., already cited. For the "natural frontiers", see G. Zeller, "La Monarchie d'ancien régime et les frontières naturelles", *Revue d'histoire moderne*, VII (1933), 305-33. For European constitutions of 1791-1813, see H. B. Hill, "The Constitutions of Continental Europe, 1789-1813", *Journal of Modern History*, VIII (1936), 82-94; and J. Godechot, *La Grande Nation* (see below). For European plebiscites, see Sarah Wambaugh, *A Monograph on Plebiscites* (1920).

For the spread of French revolutionary ideas in Europe in 1789-93, see G. Lefebvre, *The French Revolution from its Origins to 1793* (already cited), Part III. The most comprehensive accounts of the "revolutionizing" of Europe up to 1799 are those by J. Godechot, *La Grande nation: expansion révolutionnaire de la France dans le monde de 1789 à 1799* (2 vols., 1956); and *Les Révolutions* (1770-1799) (1963). Students should also look out for the appearance of the second volume of R. R. Palmer's *The Age of the Democratic Revolution*, which will deal with similar problems.

For the impact of the Revolution on the different countries of Europe, the following may be consulted:

ENGLAND: A. Cobban (ed.), *The Debate on the French Revolution* (2nd ed., 1950); P. A. Brown, *The French Revolution in English History* (1918); G. S. Veitch, *The Genesis of Parliamentary Reform* (1913); J. Deschamps, *Les Iles britanniques et la Révolution française* (1949); H. W. Meikle, *Scotland and the French Revolution* (1912); R. Birley, *The English Jacobins* (1924); J. Holland Rose, *William Pitt and the Great War* (1911); E. Burke, *Reflections on the Revolution in France* (Everyman ed., 1910); T. Paine, *The Complete Writings* (ed. P. Foner, 2 vols., 1945).

IRELAND: R. B. MacDowell, *Irish Public Opinion, 1750-1800* (1944);

H. McAnally, *The Irish Militia 1793-1816* (1949); R. Jacob, *Rise of the United Irishmen, 1791-1794* (1937); R. Hayes, *Ireland and Irishmen in the French Revolution* (1932); H. L. Calkin, " La propagation en Irlande des idées de la Révolution française ", *Ann. hist. de la Rév. franç.*, 1955, pp. 143-60.

BELGIUM: In addition to the works of Gorman, Harsin and Tassier cited above, see H. Pirenne, *Histoire de Belgique,* vol. 5 (1921); and S. Tassier, *Histoire de Belgique sous l'occupation française en 1792 et 1793* (1934).

HABSBURG EMPIRE (other than Belgium): In addition to the works of Kerner, Marczali, Sugar, and Wangermann (cited above), see P. Bödy, " The Hungarian Jacobin Conspiracy of 1794-5 ", *Journal of Central European Affairs*, XXII (1962), 3-26; and K. Benda, " Les Jacobins hongrois ", *Ann. hist. de la Rév. franç.*, 1959, pp. 38-60.

SPAIN: See Herr (cited above).

ITALY: P. Hazard, *La Révolution française et les lettres italiennes* (1910); Agatha Ramm, *The Risorgimento* (Hist. Assoc. pamphlet, 1962); G. B. Maclellan, *Venice and Bonaparte* (1931); M. Reinhard, *Avec Bonaparte en Italie* (1946); P. Gaffarel, *Bonaparte et les républiques italiennes, 1796-9* (1895).

GERMANY: G. P. Gooch, *Germany and the French Revolution* (1920); J. Droz, *L'Allemagne et la Révolution française* (1949); P. Sagnac, *Le Rhin français pendant la Révolution et l'Empire* (1917).

SWEDEN: R. Petiet, *Gustave IV Adolphe et la Révolution française* (1914).

UNITED PROVINCES (Holland, Batavian Republic): L. Legrand, *La Révolution française en Hollande* (1894); R. R. Palmer, " Much in little: the Dutch Revolution of 1795 ", *Journal of Modern History*, XXVI (1954), 15-35.

SWITZERLAND (Helvetic Republic): E. Chapuisat, *La Suisse et la Révolution française* (1945).

POLAND: See works of Bain, Lesnodarski and Lord, cited above.

RUSSIA: C. de Larivière, *Cathérine II et la Révolution française* (1895).

OTTOMAN EMPIRE: B. Lewis, "The Impact of the French Revolution on Turkey", *Journal of World History*, 1953-4.

The thesis of a "Western" or "Atlantic" Revolution, as propounded by Godechot and Palmer, is discussed by various experts in P. Amann ed., *The Eighteenth-Century Revolution: French or Western?* (Boston 1963).

NAPOLEONIC ERA

Of the vast store-house of Napoleonic literature, here only a small sample is offered to the reader. The most scholarly and comprehensive treatment of the whole Napoleonic period in all its aspects is G. Lefebvre's *Napoléon* in the *Peuples et Civilisations* series, cited on p. 315, it also has an extensive bibliography of material published up to 1952. Among other useful general accounts are Bruun's *Europe and the French Imperium, 1799-1814* (already cited); L. Madelin's *Le Consulat et l'Empire* (2 vols., 1933); and F. M. H. Markham's excellent short survey, *Napoleon and the Awakening of Europe* (1954). H. A. L. Fisher's more old-fashioned *Napoleon* (1912) still has value. Memoirs and biographies of Napoleon are legion, both factual and fanciful, many of them worthless; the following are recommended to the English reader: J. H. Rose's *The Life of Napoleon I* (11th ed., 1934); and J. M. Thompson's *Napoleon Bonaparte: his Rise and Fall* (1952). Opinions on Napoleon are discussed by P. Geyl in *Napoleon For and Against* (Eng. trans., 1949); by P. Farmer in *France reviews its Revolutionary Past* (1944); and by J. Savant in *Napoleon in his Time* (Eng. trans., 1958); and his role in history in D. Dowd's brief sketch, *Napoleon: was he the Heir of the Revolution?* (1957). For a selection of Napoleon's correspondence, see J. M. Thompson (ed.), *Letters of Napoleon* (1934).

For the consolidation of Napoleon's authority in France, see F. Porteil, *Napoléon Ier et l'organisation autoritaire de la France* (1956); J. Thiry's *Le Coup d'état du 18 brumaire* (1947), *L'Aube du Consulat* (1948), and *Le Sénat de Napoléon* (1931); J. Bourdon, *La Constitution de l'an VIII* (1942); E. d'Hauterive, *Napoléon et sa police* (1943); and A. Aulard, *L'Etat de France en l'an VIII et IX* (1897). For the reforms made under the Consulate, see, in addition to Lefebvre and Madelin (cited above), M. Leroy, *L'Esprit de la législation napoléonienne* (1898); P. Belle, *Portalis et les travaux préparatoires du Code civil* (1949); and C. Durand, *Le Fonctionnement du conseil d'état napoléonien* (1949). For Napoleon and the Catholic Church, see, in addition to the works of Latreille and Leflon (cited earlier), H. H. Walsh, *The Concordat of 1801* (1934); G. L. M. J.

Constant, *L'Eglise de France sous le Consulat et l'Empire* (1928); and C. Latreille, *L'Opposition religieuse au Concordat* (1910). For the political organization of Imperial France (including the annexed territories), see G. Lefebvre's *Napoléon*, pp. 342-376; and for French economic life, see A. Chabert, *Essai sur le mouvement des revenus et de l'activité économique en France de 1798 à 1820* (1949); and J. Vidalenc, "La Vie économique des départements méditerranéens pendant l'Empire", in *Revue d'histoire moderne et contemporaine*, 1 (1954), 165-98.

Of the numerous works on the Napoleonic army, warfare and military campaigns, the following are recommended: Lefebvre's *Napoléon* and studies by Vagts and Liddell Hart (already cited); S. Wilkinson, *The Rise of General Bonaparte* (1930); J. Colin, *Education militaire de Napoléon* (1900); T. A. Dodge, *Napoleon: a History of the Art of War* (2 vols., 1904-7); C. Oman, *History of the Peninsular War* (7 vols., 1902-30); E. Tarlé, *Napoleon's Invasion of Russia in 1812* (Eng. trans. 1942); H. Houssaye, *1814* (1888, in French); and A. F. Becke, *Napoleon and Waterloo* (1914). The standard work on the war at sea is A. T. Mahan's *The Influence of Sea Power upon the French Revolution and Empire, 1793-1812* (2 vols., 1893); see also J. H. Rose, "Napoleon and Sea Power", in *Camb. Hist. Journal*, 1 (1924), 138-57.

Diplomacy and foreign policy may be studied in the works of Sorel, Fugier and Rose (already cited); and in R. B. Mowat, *The Diplomacy of Napoleon* (1924); H. C. Deutsch, *The Genesis of Napoleonic Imperialism* (1938); V. J. Puryear, *Napoleon and the Dardanelles* (1951); H. Butterfield, *The Peace Tactics of Napoleon, 1806-1808* (1929); E. Dard, *Napoleon and Talleyrand* (Eng. trans., 1937); A. Vandal, *Napoléon et Alexandre Ier* (3 vols., 1891-6); H. Heath, *Napoleon and the Origins of the War of 1812* (1929); F. A. Updyke, *The Diplomacy of the War of 1812* (1955); and E. Driaud, *Napoléon et l'Europe* (5 vols. 1910-27).

For the Continental System and England's counter-blockade, see F. E. Melvin, *Napoleon's Navigation System* (1919); E. F. Hekscher, *The Continental System: an Economic Interpretation* (1922); W. F. Galpin, *The Grain Supply of England during the Napoleonic Period* (1925); E. Tarlé, *Le Blocus continental et le royaume d'Italie* (2nd ed., 1931); F. Crouzet, *L'Economie britannique et le blocus continental* (2 vols., 1958); and Lefebvre's *Napoléon*, pp. 342-76. For the political organization of the Grand Empire and the "revolutionizing" of Europe in 1802-13, see especially Lefebvre's *Napoléon*, pp. 427-79; students are also referred to H. A. L. Fisher's *Napoleonic Statesmanship in Germany* (1903); A. Hardman, *Napoléon et la Pologne, 1806-1807* (1909); A. Fugier, *Napoléon et l'Espagne* (1930) and

Napoléon et l'Italie (1947); J. Rath, *The Fall of the Napoleonic Kingdom of Italy* (1941); and R. M. Johnston, *The Napoleonic Empire in Southern Italy and the Rise of the Secret Societies.* (2 vols., 1904).

Among numerous accounts of the fall of Napoleon and the growth of "nationalism", the following are suggested: those by Lefebvre, Fugier, Rath, Johnston, and Markham (already cited); F. D. Scott, *Bernadotte and the Fall of Napoleon* (1936); G. S. Ford, *Stein and the Era of Reform in Prussia 1807-1815* (1922); J. d'Ursel, *La Défection de la Prusse* (1907) and *La Défection de l'Autriche* (1912); W. C. Langsam, *The Napoleonic Wars and German Nationalism in Austria* (1930); F. Ponteil, *La Chute de Napoléon Ier et la crise de 1814-15* (1943); and the early chapters of R. W. Seton-Watson, *Britain in Europe, 1789-1914* (1937). There is an interesting account of the Spanish rebellion of 1808-14 in K. Marx and F. Engels, *Revolution in Spain* (1939).

The standard work in English on Napoleon's last years at St. Helena is Lord Rosebery's *Napoleon: the Last Phase* (1900). See also O. Aubry, *St. Helena* (1937); and P. Gonnard, *The Exile of St. Helena: the last Phase in Fact and Fiction* (Eng. trans., 1909).

AFTERMATH

For the post-war settlement of Europe, students are referred to D. Thomson, *Europe since Napoleon* (1957), part II: "Europe in 1815"; and to two works by C. K. Webster: *The Foreign Policy of Castlereagh, 1812-1815: Britain and the Reconstruction of Europe* (1931); and *The Congress of Vienna, 1814-1815* (1919). For post-war European society, intellectual movements and perspectives, see F. B. Artz, *Reaction and Revolution, 1814-1832* (1934); and E. J. Hobsbawm, *The Age of Revolution* (cited on p. 315). For Church and State, see E. E. Y. Hales, *Revolution and Papacy, 1769-1846* (1960). For the legacy of French Revolutionary ideas, see E. L. Woodward, *French Revolutions* (1934); and Lord Elton, *The Revolutionary Idea in France, 1789-1871* (1952). For liberal and national movements, see Thomson and Artz (cited above); R. Hinton Thomas, *Liberalism, Nationalism and the German Intellectuals, 1822-47* (1952); F. Ponteil, *L'Eveil des nationalités et le mouvement libéral, 1815-1848* (1960); and A. Colquhoun, *The Risorgimento* (1958).

GLOSSARY

GLOSSARY

Aides. Excise duties on wines and spirits under the Old Régime in France.

Amalgame. The merger between regulars and volunteers carried out within the French army in 1793.

Anobli. A recently ennobled commoner of the Old Régime.

Armée révolutionnaire. A citizen army of *sans-culottes* (see below), raised in various centres in the autumn of 1793 and primarily intended to ensure the grain-supply of Paris and other cities.

Assignat. Revolutionary paper-money, at first issued to finance the sale of Church lands, but in general use after the summer of 1791.

Ateliers de charité. Public workshops set up in 1789 to give work to the unemployed.

Aufklärung. The German for "Enlightenment".

Autel de la patrie. A civic altar, dedicated to the Nation, erected in the centre of the Champ de Mars in the west of Paris.

Bailliage, sénéchaussée. A local centre of royal jurisdiction, presided over by a *bailli* or a *sénéchal*, of which the first operated in the northern and the second in the southern part of France.

Banalités. A feudal monopoly entitling the local *seigneur* (lord of the manor) to compel his tenants to bring their corn, flour and grapes to his mill, bakehouse and winepress.

Barrières. The customs posts surrounding the City of Paris, erected by the Farmers General shortly before the Revolution.

Biens nationaux. Confiscated properties of Church, aristocracy or "suspects", nationalized and sold by auction during the Revolution.

Bourgeois, Bourgeoisie. A generic term more or less synonymous with urban middle classes—bankers, stockbrokers, merchants, large manufacturers, and professional men of every kind.

Brissotins. Followers of Jacques-Pierre Brissot at the time of the Legislative Assembly.

Brumaire. The "foggy" month (23 October to 20 November) of the Revolutionary Calendar. The term is applied, in particular, to Bonaparte's *coup d'état* of 18th-19th Brumaire of the Year VII (9-10 November 1799).

Cahiers de doléances. The lists of grievances drawn up separately by the three "orders" in towns, villages and guilds in preparation for the Estates General of 1789.

Capitation. A tax levied on individual incomes, originally paid by all classes; but, during the eighteenth century, the clergy were legally exempted and the nobility were often so in practice.

Cens. A feudal money-rent.

Champart. A feudal rent in kind.

Chouans. Counter-revolutionary peasant guerrillas operating in Brittany and Normandy after 1793.

Comité des Trente. The Committee of Thirty, attended by Duport, Talleyrand, Mirabeau, Sieyes and others and often credited with an exaggerated responsibility for the events of 1789.

Comités révolutionnaires, or "revolutionary" committees. The local committees attached to the Sections (see below) and responsible for police and internal security.

Committee of General Security. One of the two main government committees of the Year II, specifically charged with responsibility for police and internal security.

Committee of Public Safety. The more important of the two leading government committees of the Year II. Generally responsible for the conduct of both internal and external affairs, its powers overlapped with those of the Committee of General Security in police and judicial matters.

Complot de l'étranger. The "foreign plot" which Pitt and his agents in France were alleged, and widely believed, to be hatching against the Republic in 1793-4.

Cordeliers Club. The more "plebeian"; and generally the more radical, of the two major Clubs of the Revolution in Paris. The best-known of its leaders were (at various times) Marat, Danton, Hébert and Ronsin.

Corvée. The peasant's obligation to do unpaid labour on the roads, or make payment in lieu.

Districts. Name given to the 60 electoral units into which Paris was divided in April 1789. After May-June 1790, they were superseded by the Sections (see below).

Don gratuit. The "voluntary gift" made by the Assembly of the French clergy to the Crown in lieu of paying the usual taxes.

Dvoryanstvo. Russian Court nobility.

Emigrés. Nobles and others who emigrated from France, from July 1789 onwards, during the Revolution.

Enragés. The extreme revolutionary party, led by Jacques Roux, Jean Varlet and Théophile Leclerc, who, while condemned by the Jacobins and Cordeliers alike, yet had considerable influence on the Paris *sans-culottes* in 1793.

Faubourgs. Literally "suburbs", originally lying outside the Paris City walls but, since 1785, enclosed within them. More particularly, the term is applied to the great popular "faubourgs" of St.-Antoine and St.-Marcel.

Gabelle. The salt-tax, most unpopular and vexatious of the indirect taxes of the Old Régime in France.

Généralités. Areas roughly corresponding to the old provinces into which France was divided, from Richelieu's time onwards, for taxation purposes. There were 23 *généralités*, each in charge of an *Intendant*, in 1789.

Girondins. (See footnote to page 128.)

Hidalgo. A poor Spanish country gentleman or nobleman.

Hobereau. A poor French country gentleman or nobleman.

Illuminati. Members of a sect dedicated to furthering the ideas of the Enlightenment in various countries.

Intendants. (See *généralités*.)

Junkers. Name given to Prussian (originally all-German) landed gentry.

Laboureurs. The more prosperous type of French peasant proprietor.

Lazzaroni. The poorer classes of the city of Naples.

Lettres de cachet. "Sealed letters" issued in the name of the King and committing offenders to detention without trial.

Levée en masse. Law of 23 August 1793 mobilizing the whole French nation for war. Subsequently used to denote the nation-at-arms in any country.

Liberum veto. The principle of unanimity applied to voting in the Polish Diet in the eighteenth century.

Lit de Justice. Ceremonial meeting of the *Parlement* of Paris (see below), presided over by the King, seated on a *lit* or pile of cushions. On such occasions the *Parlement* had no right to remonstrate before registering edicts.

Livre. In 1789, roughly equivalent to 1s. 8d. There were 20 *sous* to the *livre*.

Lods et ventes. A feudal due levied on the sale of land.

Marc d'argent. A silver mark worth 52 francs. This was the annual amount that had to be paid in direct taxes in order to qualify as a deputy to the National Assembly by a law of December 1789. Following protests, the qualification was changed, in August 1791, to one of "active" citizenship.

Maréchaussée. Rural constabulary of the Old Régime in France.

Menu peuple. The common people: wage-earners and small property-owners. (See also *sans-culottes*.)

Métayers. Share-cropping farmers, generally sharing their produce on a fifty-fifty (or less advantageous) basis with the landowner.

Mountain. Name acquired by the main group of Jacobin deputies led by Robespierre who, after their election to the National Convention in September 1792, sat in the upper seats of the Chamber.

Muscadins. Term applied by the *sans-culottes* to bourgeois citizens and middle-class youth in the period after 9th Thermidor. It suggests foppery and fine clothes.

Noblesse. French aristocracy or nobility, whose core was formed by the original *noblesse d'épée* (nobility of the sword), who derived their traditional privileges from military service to the Crown. More recent additions were the *noblesse de robe* (magisterial nobility), created by the sale of public offices, mainly since Louis XIV's time; and the *noblesse de cloche*, formed by the privileged holders of municipal offices.

Parlements. The most important of the French courts of ordinary royal jurisdiction intended mainly as High Courts of Appeal. Of the 13 *Parlements*, by far the most important was that of Paris, whose jurisdiction extended over a large part of the country and which, particularly under weak or indolent Kings, had acquired the habit of "remonstrating" before consenting to register royal edicts—thus virtually usurping legislative powers.

Partie congrue. The salary paid by tithe-holding abbeys and chapters to French parish priests not holding tithes in their own hands.

"Patriots". Name given to the radical party in England and Holland before the French Revolution and, during the Revolution, to its supporters and advanced reformers in every country (in the latter case, as an alternative to "Jacobins"). Not to be confused with patriots (without quotation marks) as upholders of a national cause.

Pays d'elections. The majority of the French provinces of the Old Régime, in which there were no local assemblies to apportion taxes or to aspire to a limited form of self-government. (See *pays d'états*.)

Pays d'états. Provinces, mainly on the frontiers and recently acquired, which had retained their traditional Estates, whose functions were strictly circumscribed but, on occasion, aroused hopes of a wider measure of self-government.

Prévôt des marchands. The senior magistrate of the royal government of the City of Paris prior to the Revolution.

Privilégiés. The French privileged orders, i.e. the clergy (though, generally, only the higher clergy is intended) and nobility.

Rentiers. People living on fixed or unearned incomes, e.g. pensioners, stock-holders.

Revolutionary Government. Term applied to the strongly centralized government established by Robespierre, Saint-Just and their associates on the Committee of Public Safety after October 1793.

Sans-culottes. An omnibus term (literally, those who wear trousers and not knee-breeches) sometimes applied to all the poorer classes of town and countryside; but, more particularly, to urban craftsmen, small shopkeepers, petty traders, journeymen, labourers and city poor. By extension, attached as a political label to the more militant revolutionaries of 1792-5 regardless of social origins.

Séance royale. The "royal session" summoned by Louis XVI at Versailles on 23 June 1789 to hear his views on the issues dividing the three Estates.

Sections. The 48 units into which Paris became divided for electoral (and general political) purposes, in succession to the 60 Districts (see above), by the municipal law of May-June 1790.

Señorios. Large landed estates held by Spanish grandees.

Sociétés populaires, or "popular" societies. General term applied to the political clubs formed in the various Paris Sections after the summer of 1791. Many were closed down in the spring of 1794, others after Thermidor (see below), and the rest in the early months of 1795.

Sou. (See *livre.*)

Szlachta. The Polish gentry or lesser nobility.

Taille. The principal direct tax paid by all commoners (*roturiers*) in France before the Revolution, usually levied on personal income (*taille personnelle*), more rarely on land (*taille réelle*).

Terror. The term is used here not so much to describe a method as to define a period—the period September 1793 to July 1794, when the Jacobin government imposed its authority by varying means of compulsion—military, judicial and economic.

Thermidor. The month in the Revolutionary Calendar covering parts of July and August. In particular, applied to the two days in Thermidor (9th and 10th) of the Year II, which saw the overthrow of Robespierre and his associates. Hence, *Thermidorians*: i.e. Robespierre's immediate successors.

Third Estate (or *tiers état*). Literally, the representatives of the non-"privileged" of the three Estates summoned to attend the States General. More generally, it is used to denote all social classes other than the aristocracy, upper clergy or privileged magistrates—i.e. *menu peuple* as well as bourgeoisie.

Ukase. A decree of the Russian Tsar.

Unterthanspatent. The Emperor Joseph II's law of 1781, which formally abolished serfdom and relieved the lot of the peasantry within the Habsburg dominions. It was substantially amended both before and after the Emperor's death in 1790.

Vingtième. A tax on income levied on all except the clergy. Nominally a "twentieth" tax, it was more often extended to a tenth—or even, on occasion, to a quarter—of revenue.

Year II. The second year of the French Republic—i.e., from 22 Sept. 1793—21 Sept. 1794. Most often applied to the period of office of the great Committee of Public Safety (28 July 1793—28 July 1794).

INDEX

INDEX

Abbeville, 11, 27

Absolute monarchy, 28-32, 56-7, 108

Ajaccio, 225

Alexander I, Tsar of Russia, 246, 247, 249-50, 269, 270-1, 277, 285, 290; and the war of 1812, 271-3

Alsace, 127, 192, 195, 202, 209, 284

Amar, André, 157, 166, 173

America, Americans, 9, 10, 43, 44, 54, 58, 59, 111, 251, 252; *and see* American Revolution, United States

American Revolution, 13, 44-45, 54, 58-9, 65, 76, 79, 106, 107, 181, 191, 194, 220, 221

Amiens, Treaty of, 204, 228, 242-3

Amsterdam, 10, 25, 34, 45, 60, 190, 212, 259

Andalusia, 11, 14, 23

Antraigues, Comte d', 35

Antwerp, 60

Aragon, 11

Archduke Charles, of Austria, 175, 268

Aristocracy, before the French Revolution, 14-19, 40-42; and the French Revolution, 99-100, 112-13, 121-2, 216-17; in Napoleonic Europe, 257-63; after 1815, 286-90; *and see* " aristocratic revolt," *noblesse d'épée, noblesse de robe,* " feudal reaction "

" Aristocratic revolt," 78-82, 87, 115, 192

Armées révolutionnaires, 140, 146, 149, 153, 222, 331

Armies and warfare, 55-6, 108, 204-8, 292-3; *and see* Battles, Grand Army

Arras, 143

Artois, Comte d', 92, 97, 99, 104, 126-7, 201; as Charles X, 295

Assignats, 112, 129, 136, 139, 145, 165, 172, 331

Ateliers de charité, 102, 114, 124, 331

Augereau, General, 174, 207

August decrees, 100, 103

Austerlitz, *see* Battles

Austria, Austrian Empire, 25, 28, 31-2, 39, 42-3, 46, 48n, 53, 59, 60-3, 69, 104, 121, 125, 126, 127-9, 168, 174, 175, 179, 192, 196, 197, 199, 213, 288, 289; and the French Revolution, 188-9, 199; and war with Revolutionary France, 201-4, 207, 210; and the campaign of 1805, 245-8; and the Continental System, 250; and the war of 1809, 268-9; and the war of 1813, 277-8; and the Hundred Days, 281-3; and the settlement of 1815, 284-7, 294, 297; *and see* Belgium, Hungary, Francis II, Joseph II, Leopold II

Austrian Netherlands, *see* Belgium

Avignon, 117, 209

Babeuf, Gracchus, 162, 172-3, 176, 219, 299

Fontana Press

Fontana Press is the imprint under which Fontana paperbacks of special interest to students are published. Below are some recent titles.

- ☐ The Structures of Everyday Life *Fernand Braudel* £9.95
- ☐ The Wheels of Commerce *Fernand Braudel* £9.95
- ☐ The Perspective of the World *Fernand Braudel* £9.95
- ☐ France 1789–1815: Revolution and Counterrevolution
     D. M. G. Sutherland £5.95
- ☐ Crown and Nobility, 1272–1461 *Anthony Tuck* £4.95
- ☐ Racial Conflict in Contemporary Society
     John Stone £3.50
- ☐ Foucault *J. G. Merquior* £3.50
- ☐ War and Society in Renaissance Europe, 1450–1620
     J. R. Hale £3.95
- ☐ The Age of Manufactures, 1700–1820 *Maxine Berg* £4.95
- ☐ The Conservative Party from Peel to Thatcher
     Robert Blake £3.95
- ☐ The Politics of the Judiciary (third edition)
     J. A. G. Griffith £3.50
- ☐ Musicology *Joseph Kerman* £3.95
- ☐ Ethics and the Limits of Philosophy
     Bernard Williams £3.95

You can buy Fontana Press books at your local bookshop or newsagent. Or you can order them from Fontana Paperbacks, Cash Sales Department, Box 29, Douglas, Isle of Man. Please send a cheque, postal or money order (not currency) worth the purchase price plus 15p per book (maximum postal charge is £3.00 for orders within the UK).

NAME (Block letters) _____

ADDRESS _____

_____

_____

While every effort is made to keep prices low, it is sometimes necessary to increase them at short notice. Fontana Paperbacks reserve the right to show new retail prices on covers which may differ from those previously advertised in the text or elsewhere.